MW00774371

STEWARDS OF MEMORY

STEWARDS of MEMORY

The Past, Present, and Future of Historic Preservation
at George Washington's Mount Vernon

Edited by Carol Borchert Cadou
with Luke J. Pecoraro and Thomas A. Reinhart

University of Virginia Press
CHARLOTTESVILLE AND LONDON

University of Virginia Press
© 2018 by the Rector and Visitors of the University of Virginia
All rights reserved
Printed in the United States of America on acid-free paper

First published 2018

ISBN 978-0-8139-4151-6 (cloth)
ISBN 978-0-8139-4152-3 (paper)
ISBN 978-0-8139-4153-0 (e-book)

9 8 7 6 5 4 3 2 1

Library of Congress Cataloging-in-Publication Data
is available for this title.

Cover art: Early published image of Mount Vernon by George Isham Parkyns, in *Sketches of Select American Scenery* (Philadelphia: John Ormrod, 1799), no. 1. (Mount Vernon Ladies' Association)

**MOUNT
VERNON**

Support provided by the David Bruce Smith Book Fund and the Fred W. Smith National Library for the Study of George Washington at Mount Vernon.

To the Regents and Vice Regents, past and present,
of the Mount Vernon Ladies' Association

Contents

Acknowledgments

The Mount Vernon Ladies' Association of the Union (MVLA), owners of George Washington's estate, have labored for more than 160 years to preserve the private residence of the nation's first president as a place to educate and inspire people from around the globe as they learn about the accomplishments of Washington and those who surrounded him in the early republic. In 2013, Mount Vernon celebrated the 160th anniversary of the association's estate purchase as well as the opening of the Fred W. Smith National Library for the Study of George Washington. I was delighted to partner with Douglas Bradburn, founding director of the National Library, on a symposium that celebrated both events by convening a discussion on the state of preservation efforts at Mount Vernon within the greater context of American historic preservation. Entitled *Unveiling the Past at Mount Vernon: Shining New Light on the Man by Preserving the Place,* the two-day event brought together senior scholars, emerging scholars, undergraduate and graduate students, historic site colleagues, and a range of historians to discuss the state of the field. We recognized the important yet fleeting nature of the symposium's presentations and discussions. Doug immediately suggested a volume of essays to capture the intermingling of thoughts, recollections, and advice offered by senior scholars as well as the new methods of historic preservation offered by the next generation. That germ of an idea grew to a more holistic survey of the state of the field through the lens of Mount Vernon, where American historic preservation began. I am grateful for Doug's enthusiasm and support to embark on this volume through the University of Virginia Press. His foresight was well placed; institutional cutbacks and retirements beyond Mount Vernon have changed the preservation landscape since 2013, and two of the senior preservation scholars in this volume have retired from their long-held posts.

In seeking to craft a collection of essays that would capture the symposium content as well as the state of preservation efforts at Mount Vernon and beyond, we were aided by thoughtful reviewers provided by the University of Virginia Press. Their important comments and suggestions shaped the direction of and contributions to the manuscript. We are grateful for the time and care they offered the project.

The David Bruce Smith Fund provided the financial means necessary for the National Library to publish this work. We are indebted to Mr. Smith's interest in advancing history education through written means and for his continued generosity to Mount Vernon.

There are many contributors to this work who merit recognition and thanks. Douglas Bradburn was key to envisioning and launching the publication, collaborating on an introduction, and leading the project through its early stages. Vice Regents Liz Mauran (Rhode Island), chair of the Preservation Committee, and Andrea Sahin (Massachusetts), chair of the Collections Committee, offered support and enthusiasm along the way, as did many vice regents of the MVLA. I am grateful for all of the authors who drafted essays, in particular Scott E. Casper, Carter L. Hudgins, Carl R. Lounsbury, and George W. McDaniel. Their writings formed the nucleus of the early manuscript and informed the volume's direction. As the project developed, Mount Vernon's director of archaeology, Luke J. Pecoraro, and director of architecture, Thomas A. Reinhart, not only brought expertise and new chapters to the volume but also joined as associate editors. Their passion for preservation, perspective, and willingness to juggle yet another ball amid the many priority projects in their respective divisions was crucial to completing the manuscript.

Illustrations are key to understanding material culture and changes over time. Dawn Bonner, manager of visual resources at Mount Vernon, identified and provided appropriate images to complement the text. In addition to joining project coordinator Elyse Werling in coordinating the submission of the manuscript, executive assistant Tyler Branscome Walinsky organized the volume's illustrations as well as secured permissions as necessary. For the publication of images not owned by the MVLA, we are grateful to the Chicago History Museum, Colonial Williamsburg Foundation, Drayton Hall Preservation Trust, Olana Partnership, and Tulane University's Southeastern Architectural Archive. All have made important contributions to this publication.

A volume owes its success to those individuals who are able to view it in the greater context of the field. I thank Boyd Zenner, editor, architecture and environment, and our talented colleagues at the University of Virginia Press for their advice, corrections, and stewardship from manuscript to bound volume. Boyd's guidance as we thought and rethought the volume's scope and contents was as critical as Morgan Myers's patience.

Most significantly, we thank the MVLA for the preservation of George Washington's Mount Vernon, which made this work possible. Since 1853, the MVLA has taken seriously its position as a steward of national memory and a leader in American historic preservation. Although theories and methods of preservation are ever-changing, Mount Vernon's ladies, staff, and supporters remain as vigilant today as Ann Pamela Cunningham—founder of the MVLA—was in 1874 when she charged her successors to "let no irreverent hand change it; no vandal hands desecrate if [with] the fingers of—progress!" We will all continue to seek innovative yet practical means to preserve George Washington's estate grounds, buildings, objects, and landscapes so that they might educate future generations about him and our nation's founding. Collaboration and dialogue with our preservation colleagues will be crucial to the success of this undertaking, and we gratefully look forward to their future thoughts, advice, and counsel, as well as the next time we convene for a symposium at Mount Vernon.

Carol Borchert Cadou
Charles F. Montgomery Director and CEO
Winterthur Museum, Garden & Library
Winterthur, Delaware

Abbreviations

AMVLA	Archives of the Mount Vernon Ladies' Association
GW	George Washington
MVLA	Mount Vernon Ladies' Association
MVLA AR	Mount Vernon Ladies' Association Annual Report, NLSGW
MVLA, Minutes	*Minutes of the Mount Vernon Ladies' Association of the Union* (Mount Vernon, VA: MVLA), printed annually, available at NLSGW
NLSGW	Fred W. Smith National Library for the Study of George Washington, Mount Vernon, VA
PGWDE	Theodore J. Crackel et al., eds., *The Papers of George Washington, Digital Edition* (Charlottesville: University of Virginia Press, 2008).

A Chronology of Historic Preservation at Mount Vernon in National Context

1799: Two years after serving as the first president of the United States, George Washington dies at age sixty-seven on December 14 at his Mount Vernon plantation from epiglottitis. He leaves behind no direct descendants. Instead, Washington departs his wife of forty years, Martha; a five-farm plantation of nearly 8,000 acres; and 317 enslaved men, women, and children owned by Washington and the estate of Martha's first husband, Daniel Parke Custis. By the terms of Washington's will, the first president grants Martha "the use, profit and benefit of my whole Estate, real and personal, for the term of her natural life." He also directs that at her death, "it is my Will & desire that all the Slaves which I hold in my own right, shall receive their freedom."[1] George Washington is buried at Mount Vernon on December 17, 1799. As news of Washington's death travels, both houses of Congress adjourn, and the young nation mourns the loss of its founding father; from small towns to the cities of New York and Philadelphia, the country's citizens honor Washington through funeral processions and gun salutes.

Portrait of George
Washington by Adolf
Ulrik Wertmüller,
c. 1795. (MVLA;
purchased with funds
provided by the
Connoisseur Society
of Mount Vernon,
2011; photograph by
Edward Owen)

Early published image of Mount Vernon by George Isham Parkyns, in *Sketches of Select American Scenery* (Philadelphia: John Ormrod, 1799), no. 1. (MVLA)

1800: George Washington is remembered and revered with eulogies printed and published throughout the United States. Mount Vernon's image is also widely circulated through print sources. George Isham Parkyn's *Sketches of Select American Scenery* calls the house a "celebrated Domain" that "unites in picturesque beauty, all that can be attractive to an admirer of elegant nature."[2] Visitors flock to Mount Vernon, where the extended Washington family receive those who wish to see where the illustrious general, president, and founding father lived and is buried. George Washington's private residence becomes a pilgrimage site well known to the American public through published images and visitor accounts.

1802: On May 22, Martha Dandridge Custis Washington dies at the age of seventy at Mount Vernon and is buried next to her husband. While George Washington's slaves are free, those enslaved individuals owned by the Custis estate are divided between Martha Washington's grandchildren and removed to their respective plantations. The contents of Mount Vernon's Mansion House and outbuildings are disbursed according to Martha Washington's will as well as sold at public and private sales. Mount Vernon ownership, including the mansion and approximately four thousand acres of surrounding land, transfers to the Washington family. Supreme Court justice Bushrod Washington, George Washington's nephew, inherits Mount Vernon and brings his own belongings and enslaved workers to the plantation. Bushrod Washington owns the property until his death in 1829, making modifications to the mansion (including a porch on the south facade and balustrade to the piazza roof) and erecting a host of structures on the landscape (including porters' lodges at the west gate entrance and a gazebo on the east lawn).

1816: Following the transfer of Pennsylvania's state capital to Lancaster in 1799, Independence Hall (formerly the Pennsylvania State House) is designated state surplus and threatened by redevelopment. The city of Philadelphia purchases the historic landmark to save it from demolition.

1841: John Augustine Washington III, George Washington's great grand-nephew and the current owner of Mount Vernon, leases from his mother, Jane Charlotte Washington, enslaved teenagers Edmund Parker and his sister, Hannah. After escaping from Mount Vernon at the outbreak of the Civil War, Edmund Parker returns to the estate in the 1870s where he is employed to guard George Washington's tomb, a position he holds for thirty-four years. As tomb guard, Parker speaks with thousands of visitors each year. His presence and interpretation of life under slavery educates and informs the visitors' understanding of the plantation during George Washington's ownership.

1853: Ann Pamela Cunningham of South Carolina founds the Mount Vernon Ladies' Association (MVLA) with the intention to purchase Mount Vernon from John A. Washington III in order to preserve George Washington's residence and to prevent its sale to land speculators. The MVLA becomes the nation's first historic preservation organization as well as one of the first national women's organizations. On December 2, 1853, Cunningham publishes an appeal to "the Ladies of the South" in the *Charleston Mercury* to join her in the preservation of George Washington's residence so that "pilgrims to the shrine of pure patriotism" will not find his home "surrounded by blacking smoke and deafening machinery."[3] The appeal is extremely successful as the MVLA launches a major fundraising campaign, garnering donations from every state of the union. Cunningham builds a coalition of prominent women drawn from across the United States; she titles herself regent and names her fellow members vice regents. Prominent men also join Cunningham's cause, most notably former congressman, Massachusetts governor, and Harvard University president Edward Everett. Garnering nationwide support though 129 orations he delivers on George Washington, Everett raises $68,394 toward the purchase of Mount Vernon.

1858: John Augustine Washington III is financially unable to maintain Mount Vernon given the demands of upkeep and the many visitors wishing to see how and where George Washington lived. The now-iconic east front of the mansion is recorded with the piazza supported by makeshift wooden posts. After soliciting the U.S. government and the Commonwealth of Virginia for support, Washington agrees to sell the mansion and 200 acres of surrounding land to the MVLA in return for $200,000. He signs the purchase agreement on April 6, 1858, and accepts a down payment of $18,000.

1860: On George Washington's 128th birthday, February 22, 1860, the MVLA takes possession of the Mount Vernon estate, which includes the mansion, tomb, and two hundred acres. John Augustine Washington III leaves behind a handful of original objects, including Jean Antoine Houdon's famous lifelike sculpture of George Washington. Ann Pamela Cunningham and her secretary, Sarah Tracy, take up residence and are joined by Upton Herbert, who is hired as superintendent and charged with executing the most critically needed repairs. The preservation needs of the estate are superseded by the importance of maintaining George Washington's grounds as neutral territory during the Civil War.

East front of Mount Vernon Mansion House, c. 1858. (MVLA)

Both Union and Confederate forces agree to restrict fighting at Mount Vernon in honor of Washington, and they lay down their arms when touring the general's property. Mount Vernon remains preserved throughout the Civil War despite the intense fighting surrounding it. By 1873, Cunningham and vice regents from north and south—Illinois, North Carolina, West Virginia, New Jersey, the District of Columbia, Rhode Island, Wisconsin, New York, Maine, Delaware, and Georgia—put aside regional differences as they convene to focus on the preservation of the historic site and are photographed with the Houdon bust.

1863: Hancock Manor, the home of John Hancock, is torn down in Boston, Massachusetts. This event galvanizes early historic preservation efforts in the Northeast and begins the impetus for the modern historic preservation movement.

1872: Congress and President Ulysses S. Grant create Yellowstone National Park due to a report by Ferdinand V. Hayden that warns of imminent despoilment through settlement and exploitation of its resources. This is the first federal action to protect resources, natural or historic, for the public good.

1885: Colonel Harrison Howell Dodge begins his lengthy tenure (1885–1937) as Mount Vernon's third resident superintendent and ushers in an era of extensive preservation efforts.

1888: Mary Jeffery Galt reacts to the loss of Powhatan's Chimney—a surviving chimney stack purported to belong to a house built by John Smith at the site of Werowomoco—by founding the Association for the Preservation of Virginia Antiquities (APVA, now Preservation Virginia). Early efforts of the group focus on preserving Jamestown Island, beginning in 1894 the archaeological work that continues today.

1894: At Mount Vernon, Elizabeth A. Rathbone, vice regent from Michigan, raises funds in her home state for the reconstruction of Washington's coach house.

Early photograph of the regent (Ann Pamela Cunningham) and vice regents on Mount Vernon's east lawn, c.1873. (MVLA; photograph by Leet Brothers)

Resident superinten-
dent Harrison Howell
Dodge posing with the
original Mount Vernon
cornerstone, c. 1930.
(MVLA)

The building, which stood at the end of the south lane by April 1776, is known
to have disappeared from the landscape sometime between 1855 and 1858. Excavation uncovers the original foundations, which are repaired; oral tradition
passed down by "old servants" allows Colonel Dodge to reproduce it "practi-
cally." The work costs $270.

1906: President Theodore Roosevelt signs the Antiquities Act of 1906, providing
the president with the power to create national landmarks. This is the first major

effort on behalf of the federal government to preserve buildings and land for the public interest.

1910: The Society for the Preservation of New England Antiquities (SPNEA, now Historic New England) is established. The formation of SPNEA creates another preservation-driven foundation (similar to the APVA) and raises interest and awareness for treating historic sites as nonrenewable resources.

1916: The National Park Service is established; historic and natural sites of significance are acquired by the federal government for public visitation and use. Sites connected with George Washington are among early preservation initiatives, and the first national historical park, Washington's wartime headquarters in Morristown, New Jersey, is designated in March 1933.

1916: Recognizing that candles and kerosene lamps pose a fire hazard to George Washington's wooden mansion, the MVLA considers the proposal of inventor

George Washington's Revolutionary War headquarters at Morristown, New Jersey. (MVLA; photograph by Robert Shenk)

and businessman Thomas Alva Edison to install electricity in the mansion. Concerns for the long-term preservation of the historic building outweigh those of authenticity, and the MVLA approves Edison's plan. He plants a tree in honor of Washington while on the estate.

1923: Henry Ford visits Mount Vernon and is alarmed to discover that George Washington's wood-frame buildings are not adequately protected from fire. Ford donates the MVLA's first fire engine—a built-to-order American-LaFrance Combination Chemical and Hose Car—which arrives on September 21. Ford also encourages the MVLA to establish a fire department, and the MVLA subsequently provides housing and equipment for an onsite employee fire team.

Thomas A. Edison planting a tree at Mount Vernon, 1916. (MVLA)

James Garfield Duvall
behind the wheel of
Mount Vernon's first
fire truck, donated
by Henry Ford, 1923.
(MVLA: photograph by
"M.J.W.")

1926: John D. Rockefeller, Jr., begins funding the restoration of Williamsburg, Virginia. Reverend Dr. W. A. R. Goodwin champions the preservation of the city that served as Virginia's capital from 1699 to 1780. At first acting anonymously, Rockefeller eventually funds the preservation of more than eighty original buildings.

1927: Annual visitation to Mount Vernon exceeds 500,000 for the first time.

1928: After President Calvin Coolidge establishes the George Washington Bicentennial Commission in 1924, construction begins on the Mount Vernon Memorial Highway, the first scenic parkway to be built and maintained by the U.S. government. Later renamed the George Washington Memorial Parkway, the highway is completed in time for the bicentennial of George Washington's birth in 1932.

1931: Charleston, South Carolina, establishes the "Old and Historic Charleston District," the first historic district in the United States. Acting in response to threats to Charleston's rich architectural resources, the city passes a zoning ordinance designating a historic district and establishing a board of architectural review to regulate the design of new development. The board does not obtain jurisdiction over the demolition of historic structures until 1966.

1931–39: Morley Jeffers Williams, an engineer and landscape architect, is hired by the MVLA. He subsequently oversees the removal from the mansion of a post-Washington-era porch on the south side (1932) and a balustrade atop the piazza (1936). He also undertakes the first systematic archaeological excavations at Mount Vernon. The effort toward systematic documentation of the mansion and outbuildings, as well as his archaeological work, are on par with similar projects being carried out at Colonial Williamsburg and by the National Park Service, and form a solid foundation for well-informed restoration to take place on the estate.

1933: Charles Peterson establishes the Historic American Buildings Survey (HABS) within the National Park Service. The program engages architects, draftsmen, and photographers left unemployed by the Great Depression. Teams nationwide compile an irreplaceable record of the country's rapidly disappearing early architectural heritage. The HABS records all manner of structures—from high-style dwellings to vernacular agricultural buildings—and sets a standard for architectural documentation that remains in use.

1935: Congress passes the Historic Sites Act "to preserve for public use historic sites, buildings, and objects of national significance for the inspiration and benefit of the people of the United States." The act is the first assignment of historic preservation as a government responsibility and makes permanent the HABS.[4]

1949: Congress charters the National Trust for Historic Preservation in response to a growing movement to create a national organization to support widespread local preservation efforts. The trust is modeled on the British National Trust and is tasked with the acquisition and maintenance of historic properties.

Morley J. Williams conducting excavation work near the bowling green at Mount Vernon, 1931. (MVLA)

1951–52: The MVLA reconstructs George Washington's greenhouse and slave quarters complex, which burned in 1835. Research brings together documentation from Washington's papers, illustrated insurance policies from the first decade of the nineteenth century, photographs, illustrations, and archaeological evidence to craft the reconstruction. The structure incorporates eighteenth-century materials from a number of demolished structures in the region, most notably bricks salvaged from the original White House.

1955: Frances Payne Bolton, vice regent for Ohio, purchases nearly five hundred acres of Maryland shoreline across the Potomac River from Mount Vernon in order to prevent commercial development within George Washington's view. Along with concerned stakeholders, Bolton's acquisition galvanizes support for land conservation to preserve the viewshed, leading to the formation of Piscataway National Park and continued preservation of Mount Vernon's eastern vista.

1960: The National Park Service initiates a limited register of National Historic Landmarks, the precursor of the National Register of Historic Places. This action places awareness and emphasis on sites of significance with a stringent set of guidelines for eligibility. Mount Vernon is added in October 1966.

Reconstruction of the Mount Vernon greenhouse, March 9, 1951. (MVLA; photograph courtesy of Violetta Landsdale Brown Berry, vice regent for Maine, 1930–68)

U.S. Secretary of the Interior Stewart L. Udall and Frances Payne Bolton, president of the Accokeek Foundation. (MVLA)

1964: Mount Vernon visitation reaches an all-time high of 1.3 million.

1966: Congress passes the National Historic Preservation Act in response to the Federal Aid Highway Act of 1956 and the Urban Renewal Program of the early 1960s, both of which brought about unprecedented loss of historic resources in America's cities, culminating in the demolition of New York's Pennsylvania Station in 1963. The act is signed by President Lyndon Johnson, establishing the Advisory Council on Historic Preservation, state historic preservation officers, and the National Register of Historic Properties.

Matthew Mosca con-
ducting paint analysist
in the New Room, 1981.
(MVLA)

1979–80: Mount Vernon becomes one of the first historic houses to undertake a comprehensive campaign of microscopic paint analysis. Matthew Mosca takes nearly 2,500 paint samples throughout the mansion to determine the eighteenth-century paint finishes of the rooms. The results of this research informs a building-wide restoration campaign in the 1980s.

1983: Howard University architecture students design a memorial to the enslaved individuals buried at Mount Vernon's slave cemetery. A cooperative effort between Black Women United for Action and the MVLA, the memorial raises greater awareness of the impact of plantation slavery at the home of the first president, resulting in ongoing efforts to educate the public about Washington's conflicted relationship with slave ownership.

1984–85: The MVLA asks the Virginia Department of Historic Landmarks to conduct a one-year archaeological survey of the 424-acre estate. The rediscovery of the House for Families, an early Washington-period slave quarter, and blacksmith shop prompts the MVLA to consider a cultural resource program similar to those run at other plantation sites and Colonial Williamsburg.

1987: Mrs. Clifton M. Bockstoce, vice regent for Connecticut, donates funds to establish a permanent archaeology program at Mount Vernon. This action provides permanent operating funds for a research division at Mount Vernon, which had been absent since 1939. The department is expanded in 1994 to include full-time staff dedicated to architectural conservation as well as research.

1991–2007: Mount Vernon embarks on a building campaign to reconstruct the estate's lost eighteenth-century structures based on historical archaeology,

Slave memorial designers at the slave cemetery, left to right: Dr. Harry G. Robinson, David Edge, Glen Rorie, and Adetunji Oyenusi, 1993. (MVLA)

documentary research, and period-accurate building practices. The reconstructions include an exact replica of George Washington's sixteen-sided treading barn (1996), stercorary (George Washington's "Repository for Dung"; 2001), distillery (2007), slave cabin (2007), and blacksmith's shop (2009).

2012: The Department of Historic Preservation and Collections is established, uniting all preservation efforts at Mount Vernon, including the archaeology, architecture, curatorial, horticulture, and livestock collections and programs.

2014: Mount Vernon archaeologists begin the excavation of the plantation's slave cemetery, located in close proximity to George Washington's tomb. They leave the remains of the enslaved undisturbed and use ground-penetrating radar as

Dogue Run Farm's sixteen-sided treading barn replicated in 1996 on the Pioneer Farm Site at Mount Vernon. (MVLA; photograph by Dean Norton)

George Washington's reconstructed distillery at Mount Vernon, 2006. (MVLA: photograph by Russ Flint)

well as topsoil excavations to identify the location, size, and outline of the cemetery's grave shafts. By 2018, they identify the location of seventy graves of the enslaved men, women, and children who lived and worked on the property prior to 1860. This project coincides with broader trends in historical archaeology to better understand the totality of plantation slavery, as well as the opening of the National Museum of African American History and an in-house Mount Vernon exhibit on slavery, *Lives Bound Together: Slavery at George Washington's Mount Vernon.*

2018: One hundred and sixty years after Ann Pamela Cunningham signs the purchase agreement with John Augustine Washington III for Mount Vernon, George Washington's estate is historically preserved and interpreted for national and international audiences, welcoming more than one million visitors

Slave cabin replicated at Mount
Vernon in 2007. (MVLA; photograph by Russ Flint)

annually. The property contains thirty-four original, reconstruction, replica,
and period-appropriate structures. The sixteen original buildings constructed
during the lifetimes of George Washington and his heirs—and which remain
on their original site—include the mansion (1734, 1758, 1775–87), north colonnade (1778), servants' hall (1775), kitchen (1775), spinning house (1767), salt

Plan view of archaeological excavations at the slave cemetery, 2015. (MVLA)

house (1775), gardener's house (1776), storehouse (1775), smokehouse (1775), wash house (1777, 1783), stable (1783), north seed house (1785), south seed house (1785), icehouse (1771, 1776, 1785), old tomb (before 1750), and new tomb (1831, 1835, 1837). Thirteen reconstructed buildings lost to time stand rebuilt on their original site or footprint: the south colonnade (1874), greenhouse (1950), slave

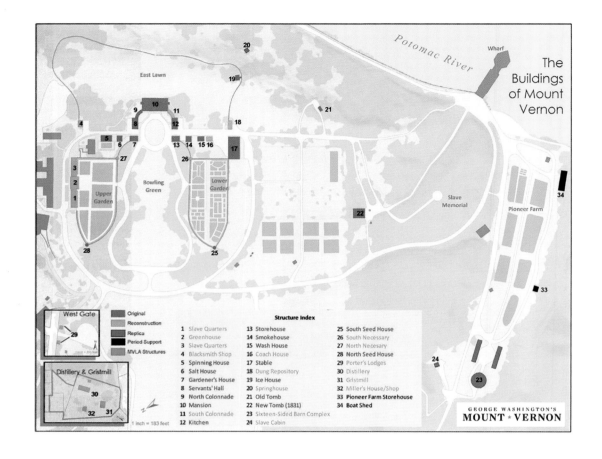

The Buildings of Mount Vernon

East Lawn

Potomac River

Wharf

20

19

10

9

11

21

8

12

18

4

5

6 7

13 14 15 16

17

27

26

3

2

1

Upper
Garden

Bowling
Green

Lower
Garden

28

25

22

Slave
Memorial

Pioneer Farm

34

33

24

23

Structure Index

Original
Reconstruction
Replica
Period Support
MVLA Structures

1 Slave Quarters	13 Storehouse	25 South Seed House
2 Greenhouse	14 Smokehouse	26 South Necessary
3 Slave Quarters	15 Wash House	27 North Necesary
4 Blacksmith Shop	16 Coach House	28 North Seed House
5 Spinning House	17 Stable	29 Porter's Lodges
6 Salt House	18 Dung Repository	30 Distillery
7 Gardener's House	19 Ice House	31 Gristmill
8 Servants' Hall	20 Springhouse	32 Miller's House/Shop
9 North Colonnade	21 Old Tomb	33 Pioneer Farm Storehouse
10 Mansion	22 New Tomb (1831)	34 Boat Shed
11 South Colonnade	23 Sixteen-Sided Barn Complex	
12 Kitchen	24 Slave Cabin	

West Gate

29

Distillery & Gristmill

30

32 31

1 inch = 183 feet

GEORGE WASHINGTON'S
MOUNT ★ VERNON

Map of the thirty-four original, reconstruction, replica, and period support structures at Mount Vernon, 2017. (MVLA; map by Andrew Butts)

quarters (1950), blacksmith shop (2009), north necessary (1941), coach house (1894), stercorary (2001), north porter's lodge (c. 1870), south porter's lodge (c. 1870), gristmill (1932), distillery (2007), and miller's house (1932). Replica buildings—replacing buildings no longer standing but rebuilt on nonoriginal locations—include the springhouse (1860), sixteen-sided treading barn complex (1996), and slave cabin (2007). All serve the continued historic preservation mission of the MVLA to preserve and interpret George Washington's plantation, its structures, collections, landscape features, views, and vistas.

Notes

1. John C. Fitzpatrick, ed., *The Last Will and Testament of George Washington and Schedule of His Property to Which Is Appended the Last Will and Testament of Martha Washington,* rev. ed. (Mount Vernon, VA: MVLA, 1992), 1–2.

2. George Isham Parkyns, *Sketches of Select American Scenery* (Philadelphia: John Ormrod, 1799), no. 1.

3. Ann Pamela Cunningham, "To the Ladies of the South," *Charleston Mercury,* December 2, 1853.

4. Historic Sites Act of 1935, 49 Stat. 666; 16 U.S.C. sections 461–67.

STEWARDS OF MEMORY

Introduction

DOUGLAS BRADBURN AND CAROL BORCHERT CADOU

When the Mount Vernon Ladies' Association took ownership of George Washington's estate in 1860, they launched the American historic preservation movement in Mount Vernon, Virginia. This group of private citizens united to purchase and preserve the famous mansion and tomb from ruin so that future generations could see where and how Washington had lived. Such an effort—to save historic buildings along with their contents and landscapes, preserving them as they had been—was an unfamiliar American impulse. "Progress" was the mantra of the nineteenth century, and the United States believed itself to be a transformational force in the world, with a manifest destiny to convert and improve the world while simultaneously eliminating what it believed were the crude vestiges of the past. With its initiative to preserve both the built and unbuilt environments associated with Washington, the Mount Vernon Ladies' Association (MVLA) launched the preservation movement in a spirit members believed to be sacred to the memory of the country and perhaps even crucial for the preservation of the union.[1] To these women and their followers, historic preservation served to protect not only the material world of the past but the nation's founding principles.

During a time when public roles for women were limited, the MVLA also exemplified a new type of civic identity, demonstrating that Americans could be innovators even as they conserved the past. By forming an association governed by a corporate board of women, dependent wholly on private money to serve preservation ends, the MVLA established a model for a host of similar women's organizations at the end of the nineteenth century. By 1910, there were one hundred American historic house museums, the vast majority privately owned. Many of these museums were staffed by women, and most celebrated a great patriot or great historical event in the United States.[2]

Since the turn of the twentieth century, many types of historic preservation groups—and motives for historic preservation—have emerged. Philanthropists such as Henry Ford and John D. Rockefeller reconstructed entire early American towns and imagined model villages as tools for educating visitors about the country's past. In 1916, President Woodrow Wilson established the National Park Service for the preservation of American wilderness and monuments, and in 1931, Charleston, South Carolina, dedicated the nation's first historic district, appropriately called the "Old and Historic Charleston District." Perhaps most significantly, the U.S. Congress chartered the National Trust for Historic Preservation in 1949 and passed the National Preservation Act in 1966.

Today, a diverse constellation of preservation groups, missions, and motives represents a host of competing priorities as well as conflicting visions of what needs to be preserved and for whom. Modern historic preservation is not a simple process. The knowledgeable advice of a variety of experts and specialists is required: historians, archaeologists, conservationists, teachers, curators, museum educators, fundraisers, community activists, craftsmen, and lawyers all play a role in the creation and dissemination of historical information and the defense of the built environment. Preservation-minded groups and individuals will not always agree, because Americans have never universally agreed about the nature of the past. Additionally, money for preservation is always in short supply, and competition for it is fierce.

The MVLA has pursued its mission for more than 150 years. It pioneered land conservation efforts in the 1950s and 1960s, the archaeological excavation of sites associated with enslaved African Americans in the 1980s, the restoration and reconstruction of long-vanished buildings in the 1990s, and the opening of a museum for the exhibition and interpretation of the collections in 2006 and a presidential library for George Washington in 2013. Taken together, the essays in this volume survey the state of historic preservation today from the vantage point of current preservation activities at Mount Vernon. They offer a window into one institution's continuing efforts to manage the challenges of representing the past fairly and of serving the needs of preservation, history, and cultural memory in the face of limited resources. The chapters represent both the practical and theoretical aspects of preservation work in the twenty-first century. The editors and essayists hope that this distinctive approach will engender discussions on the ways in which these parallel components of historic preservation can shape the future of the field.

In 2017, more than one million people visited Mount Vernon. The American people's affection for the house is longstanding, dating back to shortly after the American Revolution. Washington's Mansion House, which had been expanded piecemeal since the 1740s, was neither the largest nor the most well-appointed nor the best-known estate in colonial Virginia, but after the American Revolution it became the most famous. George Washington's resignation from public life at the conclusion of the war transformed Mount Vernon into a symbol of the new nation's rejection of military rule in favor of a civilian who, like the legendary fifth-century BCE Roman Lucius Quinctius Cincinnatus, left his plow to defend his nation in battle and returned to his farm after the job was done. For the new citizens of the United States, Mount Vernon became integral to one of the first great American myths: the virtuous retirement of Washington "like the heroes of old."[3] George Washington could not have been *Cincinnatus* without Mount Vernon.

A description of the house that was widely circulated in the 1780s refers to Washington's residence as "ancient, but magnificent."[4] One might speculate that for such a new country, the idea of an "ancient" and monumental dwelling added a sense of permanence to what was still an uncertain future. This is perhaps why during the last two decades of the eighteenth century visitors flocked to Mount Vernon, wrote poetry about it, and circulated printed images of the "seat of the illustrious Washington."[5] In the 1780s and 1790s, Mount Vernon mattered to the story of America's revolution as much as Bunker Hill, Trenton, and Yorktown. The site also provided a spiritual journey for some. As one enthusiastic visitor noted in early 1785, "I had feasted my imagination for several days in the near prospect of a visit to Mount Vernon, the seat of Washington. No pilgrim ever approached Mecca with deeper enthusiasm."[6] It was a vision that had very little to do with the reality. Mount Vernon, however symbolic, was a plantation built on slave labor, a system increasingly decried in many parts of the new United States and far from emblematic of the "freedom" associated with American independence.

Mount Vernon assumed a different significance after George Washington's death in December 1799. The "illustrious seat" was transformed into a final resting place of the venerated father of the country. Pilgrims came in droves to hear stories of Washington, feel his presence, and marvel at his increasingly legendary life. John Pintard of New York was received by Martha Washington in 1801, noting that "she conversed without reserve & seeming pleasure on every subject that recalls the memory & virtues of her august consort." Pintard also "visited the Tomb where are deposited the remains of the beloved Father of our country" and wrote, "I cannot pretend to describe my sensibility & emotions as I walked over the grounds & apartments once owned & trod by Washington."[7] Those visitors passing Mount Vernon on the Potomac River witnessed salutes to Washington as the sails of passing ships were lowered, colors displayed at half mast, and guns fired as a mark of respect. Mount Vernon had changed from the home of a living legend to the mausoleum of the nation's patriarch.

It was thus challenging for the Washington family members who inherited the

DOUGLAS BRADBURN AND CAROL BORCHERT CADOU

estate to maintain Mount Vernon as either a working plantation or a national historic site. The family found it onerous to operate a profitable farm, particularly when they were inundated with tourists who openly carried away mementos. As early as 1820, a visitor complained that "in the General's time, all was well managed, particularly the farm and gardens. He, the Cincinnatus of his time, was up early, and always vigilant. Now all is ruin, and ruin personified mourns for him."[8] Another, commenting on the Mansion House, gardens, and grounds, noted that Washington's design could still be seen "but there were general symptoms of decay visible; and I was sorry that so little effort was made to repair the silent ravages of time. Were I the owner of this seat, I would preserve everything as nearly as could be in the style in which Washington left it, but I would not suffer any thing to moulder away neglected and forgotten."[9] To these visitors, the estate bespoke "neglect and apathy."[10] Even so, this notion of preserving "everything as nearly as could be" was an aspiration gaining increasing support as the real "heroes" of the founding generation began to disappear.[11]

By the 1850s, a short five decades after George Washington's death, Mount Vernon was in a severe state of disrepair. One visitor claimed, "By the end of half an hour, we were glad to be off. We felt hurried away by the revulsion of feeling. We came with veneration strongly excited. Disgust took its place; and we left, breathing hard words in reference to the present state of matters at Mount Vernon."[12] In 1853, South Carolinian Louisa Cunningham wrote to her daughter, Ann Pamela, of her journey down the Potomac River and of being on deck as the boat passed Mount Vernon. "It was a lovely moonlight night that we went down the Potomac," she wrote. "I went on deck as the bell tolled and we past Mount Vernon. I was painfully distressed at the ruin and desolation of the home of Washington, and the thought passed through my mind: Why was it that the women of his country did not try to keep it in repair, if the men could not do it? It does seem such a blot on our country!"[13]

Louisa Cunningham's description of Washington's estate and her concern for its future had a profound effect on her daughter. Ann Pamela Cunningham, then thirty-seven years old, wrote a bold letter to the editor of the *Charleston Mercury* newspaper calling for the preservation of Washington's home. She addressed the letter, which was published on December 2, 1853, "To the Ladies of the South," asking,

> Will you, can you, look on passively and behold the home and grave of the matchless patriot, who is so completely identified with your land, sold as a possession to speculators, without such a feeling of indignation firing your souls as will cause you to rush with one heart, one spirit, to the rescue? . . . Can you still stand with closed souls and purses, while the world cries "Shame!" on America?—suffer Mount Vernon, with all its sacred associations, to become—as is spoken of, and is probable—the seat of manufacturers and manufactories? Noise and smoke, the busy hum of men, destroying all sanctity and repose around the tomb of your own world of wonder? Oh, it cannot be possible! What? Such sacrilege, such desecration, while you have hearts to feel the shame, and the power to prevent it? Never! Forbid it, shades of the dead! That pilgrims to the shrine of pure patriotism should find it forgotten, surrounded by blacking smoke and deafening machinery![14]

Although her language was flamboyant, Cunningham's message came through clearly. She articulated the case for the preservation of George Washington's estate in the face of expanding industry and the possibility of purchase by land speculators. The letter elicited an immediate positive response, and its writer duly formed a board of women well positioned to lead fundraising efforts aimed at purchasing Mount Vernon. On March 19, 1856, the Virginia legislature enacted a bill to charter the Mount Vernon Ladies' Association of the Union, providing Cunningham's movement with both legal status and national standing. In June of the same year, Cunningham visited John Augustine Washington III, owner of Mount Vernon, and secured an agreement for the sale of the house. The purchase agreement, which obliged Washington to transfer Mount Vernon to the association for $200,000, was finally signed on April 6, 1858. The sum of $18,000 sealed the contract, with the remainder of the purchase price to be paid in installments, the last payment falling due in 1862.[15]

Since 1860, when the MVLA took possession of Mount Vernon, the preservation mission has focused on retaining as much of George Washington's world as possible and restoring the estate to its eighteenth-century appearance. As Ann Pamela Cunningham so dramatically exhorted her fellow MVLA members in her farewell address of 1874, "Ladies! The Home of Washington is in your charge. . . . The mansion, and the grounds around it, should be religiously guarded from change—should be kept as Washington left them. . . . See to it that you keep it the Home of Washington! Let no irreverent hand change it; no vandal hands desecrate it [with] the fingers of progress!! Those who go to the Home in which he lived and died, wish to see in what he lived and died! Let one spot in this grand country of ours be saved from change!"[16]

While Cunningham is credited with establishing the first national women's organization and launching the historic preservation movement in America, she should also be recognized for developing the concept of "whole place preservation," a phrase used today to describe the marriage between historic preservation and land conservation.[17] Cunningham's vision for Mount Vernon, coupled with the work of her fellow members of the MVLA, established a protocol for addressing historic sites holistically. The objective was to restore all of Mount Vernon "as far as possible, to the condition in which the great proprietor left it."[18] The MVLA sought the preservation not just of George Washington's main house and tomb but of the entire estate, including all structures, gardens, landscapes, vistas, and views. Its aim was to allow visitors to see Mount Vernon as George Washington himself had designed it, and in that way gain insight not only into a great man who left no autobiography but also into the wide range of individuals—enslaved and free, obscure and prominent—who lived and died at Mount Vernon.

Since the nineteenth century, the association has pioneered and embraced a variety of new technological and preservation methodologies. In the 1950s and

1960s, board member Frances Payne Bolton, vice regent for Ohio, organized one of the nation's earliest land trusts and initiated the creation of Piscataway National Park for the express purpose of preserving George Washington's view across the Potomac River.[19] In the 1970s and 1980s, Mount Vernon's preservation specialists turned to microscopic scientific analysis to determine the original interior paint colors of the mansion, fending off critics who suggested the colors were too bold or garish for George Washington and the eighteenth century.

Preservation efforts at Mount Vernon have also been marked by a spirit of collaboration among disciplines and departments. During the first decade of the twenty-first century, archaeology and architecture staff members partnered on the reconstruction of Washington's stercorary and blacksmith's shop at the Mansion House Farm, as well as the reconstruction of the distillery on nearby Dogue Creek Farm. The architecture staff referred to early photographs of a slave dwelling on Washington's land when they reconstructed a cabin that demonstrated the living conditions of enslaved fieldworkers. Following the establishment of Mount Vernon's Department of Historic Preservation and Collections, architecture, archaeology, collections, and curatorial staff jointly conducted a restoration of the mansion's New Room, utilizing the latest paint analysis technologies and laser scanning to research and document this interior space. And most recently, Mount Vernon launched the first application of building information management technology to historic structures, utilizing three-dimensional modeling.[20] All of these efforts have contributed to a broader public understanding of George Washington, his plantation, and the variety of ways in which historic preservation serves as a critical component of history education. The work of Mount Vernon's staff has served to inform American historic preservation efforts far beyond the brick walls of Washington's estate.

When the Fred W. Smith National Library for the Study of George Washington opened in September 2013, it immediately became a place where the historic preservation community could meet and avail itself of Mount Vernon's considerable resources. Lydia M. Brandt, one of the library's inaugural resident fellows, brought the preservation of Mount Vernon's memory in American visual culture to the forefront of discussion. The George Washington Symposium, held in November 2013, created a venue for senior scholars and preservationists to share experiences and insights with emerging scholars as the participants discussed and debated the future of historic preservation in America. The library continues to serve as a venue for discussion and presentation of preservation topics and advances.

In order to assist the reader, a chronology of Mount Vernon's initiatives within the context of American historic preservation is provided in the front matter. The volume proper begins with Carl R. Lounsbury's introductory essay, "New History in Old Buildings: Architectural Research and Public History in the Chesapeake," outlines the dramatic changes that have taken place in the presentation, interpretation, and research of historic sites and their built environment over the last fifty years. He points to the Historic Preservation Act of 1966 as one of the catalysts that moved architectural research and preservation forward. Lounsbury calls on us to recognize the impact that "the new social history" of the 1960s and 1970s has had on the field in the twentieth and twenty-first centuries, and challenges us to continue to search for clues to the past in a variety of records, both written and unwritten to unlock—and thereby preserve—the histories of all people who contributed to and informed early American society. Advances in scholarship and scientific analysis have always transformed the possibilities of historical preservation, leading in the 1970s and 1980s to dramatic reinterpretations of some revered historical houses and spaces. Today's evolving methodologies, changing sensitivities, and new technologies similarly equip the curator, archaeologist, and historian with an extraordinary range of options for rethinking and reinterpreting historic spaces.

Following Lounsbury's model of inquiry, Thomas A. Reinhart and Susan P. Schoelwer take a fresh look at the last room added to the mansion, the New Room. Their essay, "'Distinguished by the Name of the New Room': Reinvestigation and Reinterpretation of George Washington's Grandest Space," illustrates how historic spaces changed over time to meet the evolving needs and interests of their owners and users. The authors demonstrate that careful research and analysis of material culture and eighteenth-century correspondence, vocabulary, and room use can provide new insights into both historic sites and their inhabitants. In doing so, they suggest practical ways in which modern curators and architectural historians can call on language, architecture, objects, and estate inventories to recreate and preserve the past.

Building on Reinhart and Schoelwer's commentary, Luke J. Pecoraro discusses historic archaeology as a tool for unearthing and preserving the multiple histories of a historic site. In his essay, "'We Have Done Very Little Investigation There; There Is a Great Deal Yet to Do': The Archaeology of George Washington's Mount Vernon," he argues for the cultural landscape as a preservation priority at all historic sites, and particularly at Mount Vernon, where the history of the land is inseparable from that of its owner.

Robert L. Fink, Thomas A. Reinhart, and Alyson Steele take the technical discussion of preservation methods into the digital realm in "Mount Vernon's Historic Building Information Management System: Digital Strategies for Preservation in the Twenty-First Century." They describe how historic sites can usefully employ a present-day construction tool—building information modeling (BIM)—to create a better system for understanding and managing historic buildings and landscapes. In time, the documentation and references populating Mount Vernon's HBIM system will allow the stories of the people who built the places of the past to become as clear as the architectural drawings of the structures themselves.

Looking at the nation's historic sites and preservation work holistically, George W. McDaniel encourages the field to think beyond traditional house museum agendas in his essay, "Stepping Up and Saving Places: Case Studies in Whole Place Preservation." As he notes, whole place preservation requires the integrated management of buildings, landscapes, views, and sounds in order to provide visitors with a preserved site that offers a smooth transition from contemporary life to the historical world. McDaniel describes several models of successful whole place preservation, including Monticello, Olana (artist Frederic Church's residence), Petroglyph National Monument, Drayton Hall (the plantation residence of the Drayton family), and Mount Vernon. Citing the leadership roles taken by management staff at these sites, he challenges professionals at all historic properties to broaden their preservation agendas and to create partnerships with a range of constituencies in order to further American historic preservation.

Lydia Mattice Brandt offers Mount Vernon as a case study for understanding the dialogue and relationship between American historic preservation and popular culture in "The Dangers of Preserving while Popular: The Mount Vernon Ladies' Association's Image of Mount Vernon versus Contemporary Architecture." She describes the work done by the MVLA in the service of preserving the mansion as both structure and symbol, and enumerates various attempts made by the public to replicate it. Through such migrations of historic imagery and designs into the modern public realm, she defends the possibility of preserving place, history, and memory.

In "Saving Mount Vernon, in Black and White: Toward an Alternative History of Historic Preservation," Scott E. Casper turns to the role that memory has played in the preservation of Mount Vernon. He details the ways in which nineteenth- and twentieth-century African Americans drew on their memories and knowledge of slave life to interpret Mount Vernon to visitors as well as assist the MVLA with its architectural restoration. He emphasizes that the recollections of formerly enslaved individuals and their descendants, as well as other workers, are a neglected data source in the preservation of historic sites, and urges historic preservation professionals to recognize this material as concrete contributions to historic site preservation.

In the volume's final essay, Carter L. Hudgins provides a retrospective look at America's historic house museums and the people who have cared for them as he sounds a "call to action" to the preservation field. In "Mount Vernon and America's Historic House Museums: Old Roles and New Responsibilities in the Preservation of Place," Hudgins unpacks the challenges faced by sites as they seek to be relevant today and in the future. He proposes a five-point strategy toward historic-site sustainability and calls on all those with an interest in American history and historic sites to think carefully about the future role of preserved sites such as Mount Vernon.

American historic preservation both originated with and gained momentum from nineteenth-century patriotic women's organizations like the Mount Vernon Ladies' Association. In the United States, historic preservation has always been concerned with the civic meaning of the places and not solely with the artistic quality or architectural sophistication of unique or grand buildings. As such, the field continues to evolve steadily, as the cultural priorities of American society evolve. Preservation is always political. Memory is a contested ground in a democratic society, and the symbols of the past can connote different meanings to different groups. For many people, Mount Vernon has long stood for freedom and the principles of American independence—and it still does. The current interpretation of the site needs, however, to acknowledge and reconcile the stories of freedom with those of the individuals who toiled on the plantation in the eighteenth and early nineteenth centuries.

The future of American historic preservation will be vastly different from the historic sites and historic house museums of the nineteenth and twentieth centuries. Institutions will be called upon to serve as training grounds for the next generation of preservationists while also supporting holistic site preservation. Resources will continue to be in short supply, particularly as the definition of historic preservation increasingly overlaps with the principles and methodologies of land conservation. Institutions will, therefore, be required to adapt their priorities and wishes to emerging needs, and historic sites will need to continually reinvent themselves, a perhaps ironic aspect of the requirement to remain sustainable and relevant in a free and open society. The editors of this volume hope the essays that follow will impress upon readers the importance of finding new and compelling ways to energize the preservation of American historic sites so that they may

DOUGLAS BRADBURN AND CAROL BORCHERT CADOU

continue to unlock the past and serve to educate and inspire present and future generations.

Notes

1. The early members of the MVLA contributed to a periodical entitled the *Mount Vernon Record* in which their language demonstrates the belief that Mount Vernon was critical to American patriotism, principles, and the preservation of the union. As they wrote in 1858, "Let us teach our descendants to be proud of their proprietorship in one sacred spot where pilgrims from every part of the Union may assemble, and where the sectional animosities which at times threaten our political existence shall soften down and mingle into Love and peace." Hannah Blake Farnsworth, "Appeal to the Ladies of the State of Michigan for the Purchase of Mount Vernon," *Mount Vernon Record* 1, no. 8 (February 1859): 74.

2. Michael Wallace, "Visiting the Past: History Museums in the United States," in *Presenting the Past: Essays on History and the Public,* ed. Susan Porter Benson, Stephen Brier, and Roy Rosenzweig (Philadelphia: Temple University Press, 1986), 139.

3. "The Following Conclusion of Mr. Bowler's Ingenious Treatise upon Practical Husbandry, Lately Published in Rhode Island," *New Hampshire Gazette* (Portsmouth), November 2, 1786, 1.

4. Noah Webster, *An American Selection of Lessons in Reading and Speaking. Calculated to Improve the Minds and Refine the Taste of Youth* (Hartford: Hudson and Goodwin, 1789), 148.

5. For one example of the regular use of this phrase, see the *Boston Gazette and Weekly Republican Journal,* May 22, 1797, 3, in an advertisement for a public benefit in Boston where, in addition to music and comedy acts, there would be "a beautiful view of Mount Vernon, the seat of the illustrious Washington," presented to the audience.

6. Elkanah Watson, Memoirs, January 23–25, 1785, in John P. Kaminski, ed., *The Founders on the Founders: Word Portraits from the American Revolutionary Era* (Charlottesville: University of Virginia Press, 2008), 491–93.

7. "Mr. Pintard Dines with Mrs. Washington, Friday July 31, 1801," typescript, notebook 16, NLSGW.

8. William Faux, *A Journal of a Tour to the United States* (London: W. Simpkin and R. Marshall, 1823), 469–73, 472 (quotation).

9. Joseph Story to Mrs. Joseph Story, February 27, 1821, in *The Life and Letters of Joseph Story* (Boston: Charles C. Little and James Brown, 1851), 1:398–99.

10. Faux, *Journal of a Tour,* 469.

11. On the growing desperation to remember the founding generation in the nineteenth century, see Alfred F. Young, *The Shoemaker and the Tea Party: Memory and the American Revolution* (New York: Beacon Press, 1999); Sarah J. Purcell, *Sealed with Blood: War, Sacrifice, and Memory in Revolutionary America* (Philadelphia: University of Pennsylvania Press, 2010); and Janice Hume, *Popular Media and the American Revolution: Shaping Collective Memory* (New York: Routledge, 2014).

12. William Ferguson, *America by River and Rail: Notes by the Way on the New World and Its People* (London: James Nesbit, 1856), 175.

13. Louisa Cunningham to Ann Pamela Cunningham, Fall 1853, quoted in Marion R. Wilkes, *Rosemont and Its Famous Daughter: The Story of Rosemont Plantation, Laurens County, South Carolina, and Ann Pamela Cunningham Who Saved Mount Vernon for a National Shrine* (Washington, DC: M. R. Wilkes, 1947), 18.

14. Ann Pamela Cunningham, "To the Ladies of the South," *Charleston Mercury,* December 2, 1853.

15. Gerald W. Johnson, *Mount Vernon: The Story of a Shrine* (Mount Vernon, VA: MVLA, 1991), 26. Although Cunningham's movement began as a southern organization and undertaking, it was officially renamed the Mount Vernon Ladies' Association of the Union when chartered by the Virginia legislature in 1856. The official name remains that but is usually shortened to Mount Vernon Ladies' Association.

16. Ibid., 52.

17. For examples of whole place preservation, see Stephanie K. Meeks et al., "Bridging Land Conservation and Historic Preservation," *Forum Journal* 25, no. 1 (Fall 2010).

18. Harriet V. Fitch, "An Appeal to Indiana," *Mount Vernon Record* 1, no. 11 (May 1859): 138.

19. For a history of the preservation of the Mount Vernon viewshed, see Robert Ware Straus, *The Possible Dream: Saving George Washington's View* (Accokeek, MD: Accokeek Foundation, 1988).

20. For information on historic building information management (HBIM), see Gideon Fink Shapiro, "How Tech Is Transforming Preservation," *Architect* 104, no. 4 (April 2015): 81–86.

DOUGLAS BRADBURN AND CAROL BORCHERT CADOU

New History in Old Buildings

Architectural Research and Public History in the Chesapeake

CARL R. LOUNSBURY

When I first started visiting museums fifty years ago, historic sites such as Mount Vernon, Monticello, Gunston Hall, the home of the father of the Bill of Rights, George Mason, and Colonial Williamsburg still seemed deeply wedded to the oldest form of historic preservation: commemoration. They were driven by belief in a moral imperative that visitors should recognize and draw strength from a tangible link between the past and the present. This theme was made explicit in a 1960s travel brochure that proclaimed "a visit to Kenmore revives the flames of patriotism and brings a revaluation of the ideals and sacrifices of the intrepid men who established the foundations of the United States."[1] Well-dressed, white, middle-class families chose these places to enhance their civic education—to see the very spots where George Washington, Thomas Jefferson, and George Mason discussed the values that motivated their generation to throw off the shackles of British colonial rule, or where John Smith's dictum of work or die at Jamestown dramatically reshaped old world emigrants into self-sufficient American pioneers. Because we saw Jefferson's portable writing desk, viewed the key to the Bastille given to Washington, or stood where Patrick Henry spoke his defiant words, we knew we were treading on sacred ground, and that these objects, like religious icons, had numinous qualities. A leaflet for Mount Vernon described the mansion to be "of prime interest and importance," but "none should leave the estate without making a pilgrimage to the Tomb," which was to be undertaken in "silence and respect."[2]

Patriotic education was not new in the early 1960s but had been a prime objective of many historic sites since the beginning of the twentieth century if not earlier.[3] It certainly motivated the man who underwrote the restoration of Williamsburg. After the colonial Virginia capitol had been reconstructed in 1934, John D. Rockefeller told members of the Virginia General Assembly, who had gathered there in special session, that it was tempting to "sit in silence and let the past speak to us of those great patriots whose farseeing wisdom, high courage, and unselfish devotion to the common good will ever be an inspiration to noble living."[4] It was a very Whiggish teleology, which saw these patriotic places as shrines that marked the road toward greater liberty and democracy.

Of course, history and historic preservation did not necessarily work together in all places with such quasi-religious overtones. Even at Kenmore, Stratford Hall, and other house museums associated with the American Revolution or colonial past, the connections sometimes were hard to discern.[5] Where civic lessons lagged, there was always antiquarianism with its emphasis on the old, odd, and out of fashion. Somnolent tour guides pointed out an array of objects and recounted their origins and ownership in room after room. Most ten-year-olds like me, with their hands glued by their sides, found it hard to understand how this parade of things would make us better citizens. Perhaps it was by enduring the heat and boredom.

If the storyline was similar at these places, so too was our experience of them. The central focus was on the main house. A few service buildings may have been open—a barn or a kitchen—but the main attraction was the dwelling and its principal entertaining rooms with perhaps a glimpse of a bedchamber or two. Cellars and attics were inaccessible and often crowded with modern heating systems and

CARL R. LOUNSBURY

ductwork. If outbuildings survived, many of them served modern roles for staff members or tourists as lounges, offices, toilets, or visitors' centers. Jefferson's stone workman's house or weaving cottage—the only surviving building on Mulberry Row at Monticello—operated as the gift shop. As late as 1966, the National Trust for Historic Preservation gutted the relatively intact service wing of the Decatur House in Washington to create offices.

Few museums restored or recreated the historic landscape in which these patriots lived and worked. Except for fanciful gardens—some appropriately divided into parterres with flowering beds and many more overblown approximations of colonial gardening practices—the traditional curtilage received little consideration.[6] Some places had lost their historical context to later intrusions. Elsewhere, administrators erected parking lots, restaurants, hotels, and ticket booths that were convenient for visitors but altered original settings. In the late 1930s, for example, Colonial Williamsburg built two hotels on the southern edge of the town, which severed the traditional connection between the pastures and farmland that had spread unbroken beyond it and created in its place a formal vista at the end of one of the narrow cross streets where none had existed. By placing the inn and the lodge within a stone's throw of the restored buildings, foundation officials unwittingly hemmed in the boundaries of the historic area so that Tazewell Hall, the most imposing house in the capital and the residence of the colony's last attorney general, John Randolph, was inconveniently wedged in their midst. Rather than leave it, they dismantled the house and sold it, a move perhaps made easier by the fact that Randolph was an ardent Tory who never wavered in his allegiance to the crown rather than support the Revolution, a principled stand that did not sit easily with the main patriotic storyline.

In cities, the connection between merchants and their warehouses, wharfs, or shops no longer existed, and in rural settings, few fields showed any signs of agricultural production. How these patriots went about their everyday business, how they cared for their homes or managed their storehouses and plantations—the sources of their wealth—and how they dealt with the vast number of enslaved and free people who worked for them and made their households run efficiently was rarely on display or discussed. If noted at all, guides referred to the loyalty and hard work of servants who faithfully attended their masters.[7] Few interpretations broached the role of servitude at these sites. Even as the civil rights movement began to dominate public discourse, the moral dilemma of the relationship of the founding fathers to slavery never arose.

Two decades later, this historical narrative and approach to interpretation and preservation had changed dramatically. Some historic houses were ripe for rethinking as a new generation of scholars and administrators entered the museum field. Money became available to undertake bold, ambitious projects in a number of places. From the mid-1970s through the early 1990s, many house museums underwent major restorations, which sometimes radically transformed the appearance of iconic structures that had once seemed fixed in our imaginations. Some such as Gunston Hall; Jefferson's retreat Poplar Forest; Bacon's Castle, built in 1665 in Surry County; the Wickham-Valentine House in Richmond; and the Matthew Jones House in Newport News were thoroughly investigated and overhauled in response to new findings. The discovery of evidence for long lost murals, wallpaper, wainscoting, paving, and other features suggested to directors at other museums that perhaps their buildings too, despite apparently thorough restorations undertaken in the 1920s or 1930s, still had mysteries to reveal. This work was made possible by new research tools and methodologies employed by curators, paint conservators, dendrochronologists, and archaeologists who interrogated evidence in ways unforeseen or unimagined by earlier historians.

Curators reconsidered the role of objects at historic house museums. In a traditional house tour, material items played a static role in the interpretation as a guide might identify their origins, functions, and associations with the site but rarely spoke of how they were used in the lives of their makers or owners. The new curatorial approach wanted to turn this residue of curiosities into sources of historical inquiry. Docents sought more dynamic interpretations that stressed the relationship of people and objects to private, domestic, and public patterns of be-

CARL R. LOUNSBURY

havior.[8] The combination and arrangement of artifacts in specific spaces revealed how people worked, dined, slept, played, socialized, worshipped, and participated in civic affairs. Curators carefully analyzed the form and provenance of furniture, fabrics, and other household objects and turned to bills of sale, accounts, letters, and estate inventories that described the type, arrangement, and relative value of such things.

Objects linked to texts led to context. Where once aesthetics—an appreciation of an object's craftsmanship, materials, and form—dominated the discourse in the decorative arts, curators now considered the historical circumstances in which these items appeared when making decisions about the appropriate furnishings for different rooms. This approach in 1981 led to the removal of many fine English furnishings that had filled the Governor's Palace in Williamsburg since its doors opened to the public in 1934. The curatorial staff replaced them with many less ornate American pieces that best fit the items enumerated in a lengthy room-by-room inventory of the possessions of Norborne Berkeley, 4th Baron Botetourt, the penultimate royal governor of the colony who died in office in 1770.[9] The transformation of the palace caused a temporary furor among some collectors who discovered that their taste for such exquisite objects did not match colonial reality.

This reappraisal of furnishings and building fabric in the fourth quarter of the twentieth century benefited from new techniques of paint analysis including polarizing light microscopy, which prompted houses to receive new colors that were sometimes bolder than anyone had thought, yet in other places duller than the straitjacketed palette established during the colonial revival heyday of the 1920s. For every luminously glazed room, there were dozens of others that were coated in grays, ochers, and reddish browns. Rather than two or three contrasting colors for exterior trim, doors, shutters, and weatherboards, most buildings sampled by paint analysts revealed a single color for all these elements—generally reddish brown or white, perhaps relieved by chocolate brown for doors.[10] Uniform, multi-colored liveries for houses, kitchens, and service buildings disappeared as paint research demonstrated that tar and whitewash were more appropriate for subsidiary structures. Hinges and other hardware picked out in black to contrast with surrounding woodwork also proved to be erroneous. To be sure, such discoveries upset old certainties about colonial aesthetics, especially those that arose during the colonial revival era.

Just as the application of microscopic analysis revolutionized paint research, it also transformed the chronology of the region's architecture by challenging old assumptions about the age of many structures. Over the past forty years, the sampling of framing timbers through tree-ring analysis has provided the means of establishing the precise dates of construction for more than two hundred buildings in the Chesapeake region along with scores of others in New England, Pennsylvania, New York, North Carolina, and South Carolina. The microscopic measurement of the climatic-induced variations in the widths of the annual growth rings of cored samples allows dendrochronologists to compare those patterns to previously established growth sequences of a particular species within a region to determine the year in which the timbers were felled.[11]

The results have demonstrated the weaknesses of ascribing the date of a building based on legend, significant events, deeds, land patents, and even inscribed dates. This scientific evidence has forced historians to question the validity of using oblique documentary references to establish construction periods and revealed problems with relying heavily on stylistic details without considering other criteria. The change in dates had modest implications in the interpretation of some places. Fielding and Betty Lewis erected Kenmore in 1772–76 rather than some twenty years earlier.[12] Westover was built by William Byrd III in 1750, some half-dozen years after the death of his more famous father, the diarist.[13] Long advertised as the birthplace of two signers of the Declaration of Independence, Stratford, the home of the Lee family in Westmoreland County, turned out not to have been built in the 1720s soon after Thomas Lee acquired the property in the Northern Neck, nor shortly after a 1729 fire destroyed Machodoc, his first home. Rather, dendrochronology indicates that it was under construction in the late 1730s when Richard Henry and Francis Lightfoot Lee were young boys. The new date of 1737–38 did nothing to diminish the importance of the Lees' later political achievements or lessen the architectural significance of the house; it only forced the museum to change its advertising hook.[14]

The exaggerated claims to primacy of age took a rough beating as dendrochronology firmly anchored a few anomalies to their proper eras. The testing of the original timbers at Newport Parish Church, known since the nineteenth century as St. Luke's Church in Isle of Wight County, confirmed that it was constructed a few years after 1677, a much more plausible date than 1632, the traditional one that had circulated for more than 150 years.[15] Its plan, buttressed walls, and curvilinear gables matched those of the first Bruton Church at Middle Plantation and Jamestown Church, two contemporaries from the last quarter of the seventeenth century.[16] Long in competition with the Fairbanks House, its New England rival for the sobriquet as the oldest English house in America, the Adam Thoroughgood House in Virginia Beach shed more than eighty years off the date of its construction when dendrochronologists determined that its framing timbers were felled around 1720.[17] The date nicely matched other houses in the region and firmly placed the glazed header pattern of its Flemish bond front facade firmly within the range of use in Tidewater Virginia.[18]

As dendrochronology reduced the number of seventeenth-century buildings to a mere handful, the explosive growth starting in the 1970s of archaeological excavations at places like Kingsmill, Martin's Hundred, Flowerdew Hundred, St. Mary's City, and sites along the lower stretches of the James River finally revealed why so few early buildings had survived.[19] Most inhabitants of the Chesapeake region lived in wretched houses. Often built without masonry foundations, these early buildings relied on an earthfast framing technology that simplified many of the practices used in England. Thatched roofs and mud walls soon gave way to clapboard coverings to take advantage of abundant forests. Cheaply fashioned and flimsy, riven clapboard construction seldom lasted more than a few decades without major repairs.[20] Given the often chaotic social and political conditions of the colony, where high mortality rates exacerbated the task of establishing and maintaining stable families, most planters were more than willing to build temporary structures rather than ones that would last for several generations. In a hardscrabble land, few thought of establishing permanent roots.[21] Buildings perished as readily as many of their inhabitants.

All of these approaches to investigating objects, buildings, and sites provided fresh insights into the region's material past. Important as they were, they refined our understanding of the colonial period but did not fundamentally change it. Except for archaeological excavations, scholarly inquiry focused on familiar landmarks—the places that had long drawn attention due to their association with significant historical figures or their architectural prominence. The corpus of well-studied buildings would have remained relatively small but for the fact that the intellectual premises of architectural history were reshaped, prompting scholars to seek out new material.

The most fundamental difference between the historic house museums of my youthful excursions and my early professional career as an architectural historian involved in public history was the emergence of a new ethos that redefined the meaning of the term "historic," one that gave value to buildings, landscapes, people, and events rarely considered integral in past histories. Its origins can be traced to a new type of historical scholarship. In the 1960s and 1970s, the "new social history" rejected the notion that the most important subjects for study were political leaders, wars, and public events, a perspective seen as too limiting. Its practitioners were interested in exploring how entire societies were organized and functioned.[22] This history focused on processes that affected the great majority of people alive at any given time and so turned to subjects considered in political histories as inconsequential. Those who studied the colonial Chesapeake, for example, explored the dynamics of familial patterns in an unhealthy environment with an unbalanced sex ratio or the impact of tobacco production on settlement patterns, race, labor, and wealth formation.[23] What underlying forces shaped them and what elements worked to change them over time? In posing these kinds of questions, the lowborn became as important as the mighty in the web of integrated communities. Skeptical of literary evidence produced by the elite, scholars turned to new sources to answer fundamental concerns about ordinary people who generally did not leave direct documentary evidence about their lives and beliefs.[24] They examined rent rolls; estate inventories; lists of slaves, freeholders, or newspaper subscribers; birth and death records; and other documents that revealed patterns of behavior in the unobserved lives of these men, women, and children. The new social history thrived with data that could be quantified to demonstrate long-term trends and assured readers that conclusions were truly representative.[25]

Taking their cue from the new social history, architectural historians began to turn their attention to a far larger range of buildings. They found that traditional architectural histories did not serve them well. They had been predicated on the principles established by art historians at the beginning of the twentieth century. The great pioneer in the field was Fiske Kimball, who established a national reputation with his 1916 monograph on Thomas Jefferson's architectural drawings.[26] This was followed in 1922 by *Domestic Architecture of the American Colonies and of the Early Republic,* which became a canonical text, one that laid out the evolution of early American architectural forms and features. Antiquarian curiosities had no place in this impressive survey of nearly two hundred houses from Maine to South Carolina. Taking up the story from where Kimball left off, Talbot Hamlin tracked the popularity of *Greek Revival Architecture in America* (1944), which described a national style and its regional variation in the antebellum period. More tightly focused was the work of Thomas Waterman, a brilliant draftsman responsible for much of the design of the reconstructed Governor's Palace and capitol in Williamsburg in the early 1930s. Waterman's 1945 masterpiece was *The Mansions of Virginia,* an examination of the evolution of the stylistic details of fifty prominent dwellings that was long considered the biblical guide to the great houses of Tidewater Virginia.[27]

Although trained as architects, Kimball, Waterman, and others applied the theoretical concepts developed by art historians to buildings of the colonial and early national periods.[28] Although the historical associations of buildings such as

Mount Vernon or those in Rockefeller's Williamsburg still mattered, such interests took a back seat to a perspective that primarily considered architecture as a fine art. Such scholars measured the significance of buildings according to how well they embodied a formal set of design rules. Their task was to explain a building's relationship to an evolving stylistic system that shared certain formal aesthetic criteria. They evaluated buildings according to Renaissance rules of architecture that emphasized symmetry, proportion, and the appropriate use of the classical orders and judged them according to how well the buildings fit those precepts. Architects praised those that exemplified stylistic coherence or conformity to European models of classicism and reproached others for straying from these ideals, either through perceived ignorance or poor craftsmanship.

Kimball and his generation were among the first to classify American buildings by a chronology of stylistic categories and traced those styles back to English and European precedents. They searched period architectural books and British buildings to find a plan or detail that corresponded to an American example and scoured colonial documents to find the names of architects whom they thought capable of translating those ideas into design drawings. Their approach was an anachronistic perception of the design process where ideas moved in a linear direction from the inspired mind of an architect to craftsmen on the building site who faithfully followed the architectural drawings. Shaped by contemporary art historical methodologies, this perspective was narrow and static in conception. It emphasized appearance over function. The old scholarship concentrated on a few buildings that best embodied a particular style and disregarded vast swaths of the early American landscape. It ignored the cultural reception of academic design sources. Basic questions such as why this detail for that particular house or whether the book from which the element was copied was even available at the time were seldom posed. In this exercise in genealogical sleuthing, it was enough to demonstrate the similarities between a plan, elevation, or particular feature and its source of inspiration. Like the airborne transmission of dandelion seeds, design ideas were ethereal, floating three thousand miles across an ocean before they took root in a new place. Few of these early twentieth-century historians thought seriously about the nature of the seeds' reception or the very different soil in which they grew. This ahistorical perspective made little of the gritty reality of building in the colonial period where attendant hardships, onsite negotiations between client and craftsman, and access to local materials had a powerful influence on the final form of a structure. This was the scholarly legacy that my generation inherited and found wanting.

Thanks to the intellectual tenets of the new social history, the aesthetic character of buildings no longer answered the most important questions that we were eager to explore. This became evident when a new government program appeared that provided the practical training for those who wished to test new methodologies and theories. In 1966, Congress passed the National Historic Preservation Act, which mandated that each state conduct an inventory of its historic resources and list significant buildings and sites on a national register of historic places.[29] The resourcefulness of the act was its flexibility in defining the meaning of "historic" and "significant." Rather than selecting a fixed year or major event as the principal determinant, the act chose a sliding chronological measure of fifty years. This meant that any building more than fifty years old was worthy of investigation no matter how humble. It also undermined a longstanding belief among many in the field, including Colonial Williamsburg's president, Kenneth Chorley, who emphasized that "historic preservation must center upon a building, object, site, or environment of SUBSTANTIAL historical or cultural importance," as if such importance was self-evident.[30] The act recognized that a building's architectural or historical importance might be judged on several different levels, ranging from purely local criteria to more transcendent state and national categories of significance. It democratized and politicized historic preservation—allowing for buildings and sites associated with ethnicities and groups once excluded from the dominant historical narrative and more modest structures that did not adhere to elite aesthetic standards to be assessed on their own merits.

The impact of the 1966 act was profound because it prompted the largest inventory of standing structures ever undertaken in the country. Thanks to Kimball and others, Monticello and the major monuments of early American architecture were well known. But what else was out there, and how did these other structures relate to those canonical buildings? In order to find out what stood down the road from Monticello, state preservation offices began intensive surveys of buildings within their jurisdictions. From the late 1960s through the early 1980s, hundreds of surveyors, many of them trained in history, geography, folklore, and American studies departments, inventoried the nation's historic buildings, structures, and landscapes, mapping their locations and recording their salient features in photographs, sketch plans, and written descriptions. Fieldwork challenged these scholars to refine their skills of observation and recording.[31] Some of the best state programs, like those in Maryland and North Carolina, sponsored multiyear projects in cities, counties, and regions that permitted systematic investigation of hundreds of buildings. These were not windshield surveys, whose participants checked boxes on prepared forms. Surveyors got out of their cars, talked their way into shuttered houses, clambered through attics, and crawled in cellars looking for diagnostic clues. The confined limits of the surveys forced fieldworkers to think about the impact of local conditions on building practices and ponder the meaning of regionalism when comparing their buildings to national or academic models.

By the very nature of their task and their academic training, most of these surveyors began to rethink the purpose of architectural history. Many found the stylistic categories presented in Kimball and other general surveys too restrictive or simply irrelevant when recording farm structures, shotgun houses, commercial buildings, factories, and even more exotic buildings. Their investigations included the buildings and landscapes shaped, owned, or occupied by unheralded small farmers, mill hands, and artisans, not just gentry houses or extraordinary architectural monuments that had been the focus of genealogists, historians, and historical architects for generations. From this new perspective of trying to piece together the arrangement of a plantation landscape, they allotted equal prominence to the

Carl R. Lounsbury
conducting fieldwork in
the slave quarter at Eno,
Durham County, North
Carolina. (Photograph
courtesy of Carl R.
Lounsbury)

slave quarters erected by the Carter family at Shirley in Charles City County, Virginia, as to the great house itself.[32]

This new approach pervaded a state-funded project that I worked on in the summer of 1980 with historian George McDaniel. We were asked to survey several thousand acres of land that had once been part of the Bennehan and Cameron family plantations in Durham and Granville Counties, North Carolina. The state had already purchased and restored one of the main plantation houses, Stagville, and a neighboring quarter called Horton Grove with four two-story, multifamily slave houses, an overseer's house, and a very large barn. These formed the nucleus of a state historic site, but officials were unsure about how it would be used or interpreted. The other principal house, Fairntosh, and its associated

Two-story, multi-family slave quarters at Horton Grove, Durham County, North Carolina. (Photograph courtesy of Carl Lounsbury)

service buildings remained intact and well documented, but the full complement of nineteenth-century holdings was only vaguely understood. Through George's earlier work with the descendants of slaves and tenant farmers who had lived on this land for several generations, we knew that there once had existed a much more extensive and interconnected landscape of mills, tobacco houses, quarters, tenant farms, agricultural fields, pastures, roads, and paths which evolved over two centuries of occupation.[33] What of this had survived? We were hired by the state historic preservation office to locate, map, draw, photograph, and identify its remnants.

Although a small core had been preserved, the vast majority of the former Cameron plantation land had grown fallow despite its proximity to Durham and Raleigh. Many of the fields had reverted to woodland, and nearly all the buildings associated with the former slaves, tenants, storekeepers, and millers were abandoned and rapidly falling into ruin. Snakes, ticks, kudzu, and poison ivy thrived in these

CARL R. LOUNSBURY

places but little else. At our bidding, several former residents returned to Stagville where, with minimal coaxing, they were able to recall the layout of this overgrown landscape. Their memories stretched back to the 1920s and 1930s when Stagville was still an active farming community where wheat was ground in nearby mills and tobacco was shipped to the leaf warehouses in Durham. The informants told us where wells, woodsheds, and privies had been. They outlined the range of swept yards and fences that enclosed gardens and flower beds. They indicated where hogs were butchered every December, places where dances were held on Saturday evenings, and groves where the dead were buried. We learned who had the best wagons and the first cars, and which families decorated their houses with patterned wallpaper instead of old newspapers. Their vivid recollections described a vibrant, tightly knit community. Some spoke wistfully about their earlier lives, but none harbored any illusions about the circumscribed horizons they faced as sharecroppers. Dee Sutherland, the ninety-six-year-old son of a former overseer, pushed the living memory of this community back to the period just after the Civil War. He told us about the toil and pleasures of farm life from his boyhood in the 1880s and 1890s when families of white sharecroppers occupied former multifamily slave houses at Shop Hill quarter, a process that was repeated nearby at Horton Grove except that single families of black tenants inhabited each of the former quarters.

The mean quality of much of the surviving tenant housing confirmed the difficult conditions they remembered. Despite the extraordinary board-and-batten slave houses at Horton's Grove and Shop Hill, other surviving slave quarters and later tenant houses were crudely fashioned and sparsely finished. One-room houses erected in the early twentieth century were still fabricated in the traditional manner with hewn logs and mud-and-stick chinking. We discovered doors secured with wooden hinges and locks, slabs rather than shingles covering roofs, and sills set on wooden blocks instead of masonry foundations. One farmer had rebuilt a tobacco house in logs after the previous one had been destroyed by Hurricane Hazel in 1954. Occasionally we found remnants of a cook stove and only the presence of wire nails and machine-made windows provided postbellum dating evidence.

This could have been 1780 rather than 1980 so close were we to the older, rudimentary ways of building that had somehow hung on in the impoverished backwoods. We recorded certain forms that had survived here long after they were abandoned in other places and became intrigued by the ways in which industrialized building practices displaced traditional ones.[34]

Through our taped interviews, photography, and measured drawings, we were able to repopulate a landscape with the names of inhabitants and situate activities that occurred in and around these decayed homesteads. We recovered some of the more ephemeral aspects of the lives of these tenant families poised on the cusp of a modernizing industrial society, which would draw most of their children into the urban world of Durham and beyond. We laid out compelling reasons to preserve additional buildings and land of this former community.[35] But in the end, the state moved away from expanding its holdings or taking a role in preserving other parts of the plantation. The Division of Archives and History decided to develop a technical preservation training center at Stagville, turning away from the opportunity of making it the centerpiece for telling the story of the rise of slavery in the Piedmont and the legacy of Reconstruction and sharecropping—stories that had not been part of the traditional North Carolina narrative in textbooks or at historic house museums.[36] When the good intentions of the state faltered, greed prevailed as this scrubland was simply too close to the Research Triangle Park to remain undisturbed. An upscale country club community obliterated parts of it about a decade after we had completed our work. Much of what is left remains zoned for development, threatening to envelop Stagville in residential sprawl.[37]

Stagville may have been a major opportunity missed, but it was a battle and not the war. The fact that we were even hired to record its modest buildings indicates that architectural research had long moved beyond cataloguing a series of details from ornate or pretentious houses. It was the ensemble that had mattered, a demonstration of how the plantation worked in connecting great house to slave house and tobacco houses with tobacco factories. Our work raised issues about building technology, plans, and the spatial relationship of various elements in the

CARL R. LOUNSBURY

landscape. It demonstrated the impact of the new social history on architectural research. The moral compass had shifted.

As many of us moved from survey work to positions in museums and academia, this new perspective had a profound influence on the kinds of buildings we investigated, the questions we took into the field, and the manner in which we approached the restoration and interpretation of historic buildings. We considered architecture to be an expression of social behavior and cultural practices grounded in specific historical circumstances. Consequently, our research emphasized spatial analysis over stylistic pedigree. We drew lots of plans of many different kinds of buildings. Our focus moved from the aesthetics of form to the social manifestations of the buildings revealed in their arrangement and elaboration. Our interest in building technology expanded beyond the traditional antiquarian fascination with old tools or the romanticized arts-and-crafts appreciation of the aesthetics of hand craftsmanship to an exploration of how the preparation and finish of materials and ornament revealed clues about the relative importance of spaces.

The difference in this perspective from the older art historical methodology in restoration philosophy was evident in our different approaches to fieldwork.[38] For example, the first generation of Colonial Williamsburg's architects in the 1920s and 1930s traveled to Westover, Shirley, and other plantations to record mantels, stairs, cornices, doors, and other features, which they integrated directly into many of their designs for the reconstructed buildings in the historic area. Cribbing elements from the field, they followed the common practice used by architects working in the colonial revival style to give their new work a period authenticity. These early restoration architects developed a deep knowledge of eighteenth-century stylistic details gained from scouring the Virginia countryside but had only an imperfect understanding of how these various elements fit together in a system of design. Their notebooks are filled with dozens of examples of molded end boards, sash muntin profiles, and raised panel doors. The result of their fieldwork was a catalogue of formal design elements from which they could cherry-pick examples as needed. Intent as they were on recording a good chimneypiece at Shirley or a molded surbase at Sabine Hall, these scholars failed to note the relationship of these decorative elements to other details in a particular room or throughout a building. If a room had a modillion cornice, was it more likely to be accompanied by single or double architrave around the apertures? Why did one room have full paneling while another of comparable size did not?

Architectural forms and details might be interesting from an antiquarian or formal design perspective, especially if such items were going to be copied in a restoration or reconstruction, but recognizing that colonial builders employed them in a very systematic fashion to make distinctions about hierarchical relationships between spaces and structures leads directly to asking questions that are at the heart of social history. In contrast to our predecessors, we investigate historic buildings with the belief that architectural forms carry social meanings. Architecture gave physical shape to the way people perceived their place in the world and how they interacted with others. Without this perspective, we would be left wondering why a carpenter went to such trouble to secret nail the floor in one room and face nail it in another. It was not simply idiosyncratic behavior on the part of a craftsman but a conscious effort by the builder to distinguish the relative importance of the rooms.

Multiplied several times over, the walls, doors, and moldings literally tell us the social significance of each space. The best public rooms generally had the most elaborate finishes. The eighteenth- and early nineteenth-century world was filled with visual clues, props to orchestrate patterns of interaction and behavior in different environments. We spend much of our time in the field teasing out the small differences that are always there in the woodwork and brickwork. People designed some spaces to facilitate mingling whereas in other circumstances they carefully regulated access to prevent indiscriminant contact. The early American landscape communicated a variety of meanings that sometimes changed over time or were transformed by new ideas and attitudes. More often, the significance of a building was implied by its position in a landscape, its materials, its levels of finish, or its plan. However, these meanings were not static but often dynamic and could be interpreted in a variety of ways or contested by different members of society.

CARL R. LOUNSBURY

The restoration architects who preceded us were as skilled as anyone in recording and reconstructing lost parts of the early Chesapeake landscape. But they did not understand the system of hierarchical ornamentation that gave shape and meaning to the formal elements. As a result, the restorations in Williamsburg and at other museums from the 1920s through the 1970s had the same attributes of Garrison Keillor's Lake Wobegon where all the buildings were good-looking and all the details were above average. Theirs was a small slice of the eighteenth-century landscape. Nearly every reconstructed house and outbuilding in the early years of the restoration of Williamsburg had beaded weatherboards, boxed cornices, paneled doors, and sash windows. Yes, these forms could and were found in the field. But that was not all. Other buildings had riven clapboards, casement windows, and batten doors, which were also part of the colonial legacy.

Curious too was the manner in which the architects combined these and other elements in ways that would have struck colonial builders as awkward if not bizarre. For example, archaeological evidence suggests that colonists dug wells wherever there was a convenient space in the work yards of Williamsburg. Pumps and wellheads were considered utilitarian structures that facilitated the use of this much needed resource. Yet, in the 1930s, these features were often placed in the center of a formal garden, where any fetching of water or washing of tubs would have played havoc with the delicate border of flowers and boxwoods. It is analogous to having a can-opener as the centerpiece in the formal setting of a dining room table. Individual elements may have been around in the eighteenth century but not in these combinations. The grammar may have been eighteenth century, but the syntax was entirely modern. Today, our design takes into account the original context of these elements, using the clues left to us in the field.

Since the late 1970s, entire historic landscapes have been opened for scrutiny, not simply the style-conscious homes of the wealthy. New research and restoration projects frequently explore the physical dimensions of the lives of men, women, and children who have often been forgotten in traditional historical narratives—from craftsmen and laborers who shaped the buildings to the myriad individuals who lived and worked in them. This shift in the intellectual foundations of architectural research and public history has meant that scholars have embraced conceptual models of early American society that are far different from those held by the first preservationists and architects who rescued Mount Vernon and transformed Williamsburg.

This new perspective is evident in the types of buildings that have been restored since the 1970s as well as the kinds of stories that are now told at historic sites and museums. The unalloyed filiopietism still evident in my youth has been tempered by interpretations that acknowledge a much more complex historical record where ideals were often at odds with reality, resources were contested, groups of people and cultures clashed over values, and not everyone was free to enjoy the fruits of their own labor. Great men and women are still recognized for their achievements, but they have been contextualized—drawn back into their own times and examined, among other things, by the way they interacted with a variety of people, including those who labored for them on their plantations. Thus the interest in everyday life and the buildings that supported and exemplified the place of those interactions, from service buildings to tobacco houses and slave quarters, and in the public sphere—jails and courthouses, taverns, assembly rooms, and churches.

In interpreting this broader landscape of public and private engagements, buildings once forgotten or neglected suddenly became pressing preservation projects. The mansion at Mount Vernon continued to be studied, repaired, and restored—most recently the large "New Room" at the north end—but as much work since the late 1980s has focused on restoring or reconstructing service buildings and farm structures including the so-called greenhouse slave quarters, a sixteen-sided barn, a dung repository, a blacksmith's shop, a distillery, a gristmill and a slave cabin. Visitors now have a far better picture of the magnitude of the plantation and the effort it required from a large population of slave and free people to work and maintain such an estate. Washington the revolutionary leader we knew; Washington the plantation squire has only become manifest in recent decades.[39] In a similar vein, Colonial Williamsburg over the past thirty years has designed, reconstructed, or

Reenactment of life at Carter's Grove slave quarter, James City County, Virginia. (Photograph courtesy of the Colonial Williamsburg Foundation; photograph by David M. Doody)

restored an insane asylum, a slave quarter, a tobacco house, a kitchen and service buildings, a public armory, a coffeehouse, a courthouse, a theater, and a market house but not one gentry dwelling house. These choices have not been random or the result of merely filling in the missing pieces of the townscape but part of a conscious effort to redefine the stories we wish to tell about colonial society.

The work of this generation of architectural historians has substantially revised the histories of the colonial and early national periods penned by Fiske Kimball and Thomas Waterman in the first half of the twentieth century. This new scholarship has overturned or modified many traditional textbook views about design, building practices, and plan types. It has set aside the old artificial distinction between high style and vernacular design that had long defined and divided the study of early American architecture. Based on aesthetic criteria, the terms were too relative to have meaning. A building designated high style in one context might be considered vernacular in another depending on the perspective used to make such judgments. Our predecessors believed that the one-story wooden houses that line the streets of Williamsburg were modest and unremarkable homes compared to Christopher Wren's Hampton Court, elements of which were copied in some of their reconstructions. However, when measured against the housing standards of eighteenth-century Virginia, these surviving buildings reveal themselves to be extraordinary—far larger, better built, and more handsomely finished than the shoddy, impermanent, post-in-the-ground and log dwellings occupied by most colonists.[40]

Informed by new research methodologies and interpretations, historic house museums in the Chesapeake region have also changed dramatically. Some new sites have been established that reflect the impact of the new social history on places, issues, and people long overlooked such as the R. R. Moton High School Museum in Prince Edward County, a national historic landmark commemorating the civil rights movement. Even with revisions in the historical narrative, the attraction of monuments such as Mount Vernon and Monticello has not diminished. These places remain the grounds walked by the men who defined the meaning of the new American nation and shaped its political institutions and culture, even though their luster may have diminished when their occupants' foibles have been exposed or characters faulted when actions failed to live up to ideals. But even here, the story has expanded. We now recognize that Washington and Jefferson shared those grounds with scores of slaves who helped shape these places no less than their masters. Their buildings and spaces are no longer ignored. That kind of landscape was unimaginable fifty years ago when I first visited historic sites.

Notes

1. "Kenmore 1752, Fredericksburg, Virginia," travel brochure, 3, author's collection. Kenmore, built c. 1775, was the home of Fielding Lewis and Betsy Washington Lewis, sister of George Washington.

2. "Mount Vernon Virginia: The Home of George Washington, 1754–1799," travel brochure, 2–3, author's collection.

3. Charles Hosmer, "Private Philanthropy and Preservation," in *Historic Preservation Today* (Charlottesville: University Press of Virginia, 1966), 158.

4. John D. Rockefeller, Jr., address to a special session of the Virginia General Assembly, held in the House of Burgesses in the capitol in Williamsburg, February 24, 1934, cited in Howard Dearstyne, "The Capitol: Architectural Report," 3 vols. (unpublished report, 1954), 1:iii, Colonial Williamsburg Foundation Library, Williamsburg, VA.

5. Stratford Hall in Westmoreland County, Virginia, was built in 1738 as the home of the prominent Lee family. Robert E. Lee was born at the plantation in 1807.

6. Williamsburg's gardens have been much discussed as examples of colonial revival design rather than faithful recreations of the colonial landscape. Charles Hosmer, "The Colonial Revival in the Public Eye: Williamsburg and Early Garden Restoration," in *The Colonial Revival in America,* ed. Alan Axelrod (New York: Norton, 1985), 52–70; Edward Chappell, "The Museum and the Joy Ride: Williamsburg Landscapes and the Specter of Theme Parks," in *Theme Parks and Landscapes: Antecedents and Variations,* ed. Terrence Young and Robert Riley (Washington, DC: Dumbarton Oaks, 2002), 119–56.

7. The idea of the imperceptible role of blacks in colonial society permeated most pieces in the popular press about historic houses and museums in Virginia. For example, African Americans are scarcely noticed in articles about the restoration of Williamsburg that appeared over a thirty-year period in one major periodical. See W. A. R. Goodwin, "The Restoration of Williamsburg," *National Geographic,* April 1937, 402–43; Beverley M. Bowie, "Williamsburg: Its College and Its Cinderella City," *National Geographic,* October 1954, 439–86; and Joseph Judge, "Williamsburg, City for All Seasons," *National Geographic,* December 1968, 790–823.

8. Barbara G. Carson, "Interpreting History through Objects," *Journal of Museum Education* 10 (Summer 1985): 2–5.

9. Graham Hood, *The Governor's Palace in Williamsburg: A Cultural Study* (Williamsburg, VA: Colonial Williamsburg, 1991).

10. For a summary of trends in painting in the colonial period, see Susan Buck and Willie Graham, "Paint," in *The Chesapeake House: Architectural Investigation by Colonial Williamsburg,* ed. Cary Carson and Carl Lounsbury (Chapel Hill: University of North Carolina Press, 2013), 356–75.

11. Daniel Miles, "The Interpretation, Presentation and Use of Tree-Ring Dates," *Vernacular Architecture* 28 (1997): 40–56.

12. "Tree Rings Help Date Home of Washington's Sister," *Richmond* (VA) *Times-Dispatch,* August 18, 1991, C-1, 7.

13. Carson and Lounsbury, eds., *The Chesapeake House,* 404 (appendix).

14. Ibid., 406.

15. D. W. H. Miles and M. J. Worthington, "The Tree-Ring Dating of Timbers from Newport Parish Church (St. Luke's or Old Brick Church), Smithfield, Isle of Wight County, Virginia" (Oxford Dendrochronological Laboratory for the Colonial Williamsburg Foundation, unpublished report, August 2010). Traditional claims for its antiquity can be traced back to as early as the 1840s. For example, in the collections at the Museum of Early Southern Decorative Arts in Winston-Salem is a baluster with a label pasted to it noting that "the banister from the chancel of an ancient church near Smithfield Isle of Wight Co., Virginia, made in England in 1631 (in May 1845) obtained at the above church (said to be the second erected in Virginia) by Elisha M. Benham of New Haven, Ct. and by him forwarded to the Conn. Hist. Soc. J. W. Barber Aug. 1845." A few years later an antiquarian minister wrote that the church dated from 1632. Lewis P. Clover, "The Old Smithfield Church," *Church Review* 5 (January 1853): 571–76.

16. For a study of these early Virginia churches, see Carl Lounsbury, "'To Build up the Walls of Jerusalem': Anglican Churches in Seventeenth-Century Virginia," in *Parish Churches in the Early Modern World,* ed. Andrew Spicer (Farnham, England: Ashgate, 2015), 361–83.

17. Tradition had long held that the Thoroughgood House was constructed by Adam Thoroughgood between 1636 and 1640. D. W. H. Miles and M. J. Worthington, "The Tree-Ring Dating of the Adam Thoroughgood House, Virginia Beach, Virginia" (Oxford Dendrochronology Laboratory for the Colonial Williamsburg Foundation, unpublished report, June 2005). The Oxford lab also sampled two other one-story brick houses with large exterior chimneys in the region. The Lynnhaven House dated from 1723–25 and the Keeling House from 1734–35. D. W. H. Miles and M. J. Worthington, "The Tree-Ring Dating of the Lynnhaven House, Virginia Beach, Virginia" (Oxford Dendrochronology Laboratory for the Colonial Williamsburg Foundation, unpublished report, March 2009); D. W. H. Miles and M. J. Worthington, "The Tree-Ring Dating of the Adam Keeling House, Virginia Beach, Virginia" (Oxford Dendrochronology Laboratory for the Colonial Williamsburg Foundation, unpublished report, December 2006). Even the date of the Fairbanks House in Dedham, Massachusetts, was revised slightly after dendrochronology from 1637 to 1641 for the first phase of construction. D. W. H. Miles, M. J. Worthington, and Anne Andrus Grady, "Development of Standard Tree-Ring Chronologies for Dating Historic Structures in Eastern Massachusetts, Phase II" (Society for the Preservation of New England Antiquities and Oxford Dendrochronology Laboratory, unpublished report, May 2002).

18. Carl Lounsbury, "Brickwork," in Carson and Lounsbury, eds., *The Chesapeake House,* 246–47.

19. For a summary of the results of this effervescence of archaeological investigations in the 1960s and 1970s, see Cary Carson et al., "Impermanent Architecture in the Southern American Colonies," *Winterthur Portfolio* 16 (Summer–Autumn 1981): 135–96.

20. On early building technology, see Willie Graham, "Timber Framing," in Carson and Lounsbury, eds., *The Chesapeake House,* 206–38.

21. Cary Carson, "Plantation Housing: Seventeenth Century," in Carson and Lounsbury, eds., *The Chesapeake House,* 86–114.

22. Cary Carson, "Doing History with Material Culture," in *Material Culture and the Study of American Life,* ed. Ian Quimby (New York: Norton, 1978), 47–51.

23. Thad Tate and David Ammerman, eds., *The Chesapeake in the Seventeenth Century: Essays on Anglo-American Society* (Chapel Hill: University of North Carolina Press, 1979); Lois Green Carr, Russell R. Menard, and Lorena S. Walsh, *Robert Cole's World: Agriculture and Society in Early Maryland* (Chapel Hill: University of North Carolina Press, 1991).

24. Henry Glassie, *Folk Housing in Middle Virginia* (Knoxville: University of Tennessee Press, 1975), 11.

25. Laurence Veysey, "The 'New' Social History in the Context of American History Writing," *Reviews in American History* 7 (March 1979): 4–5.

26. Lauren Weiss Bricker, "The Writings of Fiske Kimball: A Synthesis of Architectural History and Practice," in *The Architectural Historian in America,* ed. Elisabeth Blair MacDougall (Washington, DC: National Gallery of Art, 1990), 215–35.

27. Fiske Kimball, *Domestic Architecture of the American Colonies and of the Early Republic* (New York: Charles Scribner's Sons, 1922); Talbot Hamlin, *Greek Revival Architecture in America* (New York: Oxford University Press, 1944); Thomas Waterman, *The Mansions of Virginia, 1706–1776* (Chapel Hill: University of North Carolina Press, 1945).

28. An earlier version of these observations on the pedagogical development of early American architectural history appears in my introduction in *Essays in Early American Architectural History: A View from the Chesapeake* (Charlottesville: University of Virginia Press, 2011), 3–5.

29. *With Heritage So Rich: National Trust for Historic Preservation* (New York, 1966; reprint, Washington, DC: Preservation Press, 1983), 199–221.

30. Kenneth Charley, *What's Wrong with Historic Preservation* (Williamsburg, VA: Colonial Williamsburg Foundation, 1955), 4.

31. An ad hoc group that formed in 1980 to discuss fieldwork methodology was the Friends of Friendless Farm Buildings. Orlando Ridout V, "The Chesapeake Farm Buildings Survey," in

Perspectives in Vernacular Architecture I, ed. Camille Wells (Annapolis, MD: Vernacular Architecture Forum, 1982), 137–49.

32. Ibid., 143–44.

33. George W. McDaniel, "Stagville: Kin and Community" (North Carolina Division of Archives and History, unpublished report, 1977; revised edition, Durham, NC: Historic Stagville Foundation, 1997).

34. These observations informed my dissertation research, which was turned into a chapter entitled "The Wild Melody of Steam: The Mechanization of the Manufacture of Building Materials, 1850–1890," in Catherine Bishir et al., *Architects and Builders in North Carolina: A History of the Practice of Building* (Chapel Hill: University of North Carolina Press, 1990), 193–239.

35. Carl Lounsbury and George W. McDaniel, "Recording Plantation Communities: Report on the Architectural and Historic Resources at Stagville" (North Carolina Division of Archives and History, unpublished report, 1980).

36. Kristin Deiss, "'To Different People, It Was a Different Treasure': The Creation and Development of Historic Stagville, 1976–1981" (M.A. thesis, University of North Carolina, 2010). A few years after our work at Stagville, efforts began to interpret the lives of slaves at Somerset Place in Washington County in the eastern part of the state. Dorothy Spruill Redford with Michael D'Orso, *Somerset Homecoming: Recovering a Lost Heritage* (Chapel Hill: University of North Carolina Press, 1988). See also Kimberly Taft, "Silent Voices: Searching for Women and African-Americans at Historic Stagville and Somerset Place Historic Sites" (M.A. thesis, North Carolina State University, 2010).

37. Julia Walter, "A Viewshed Protection Plan for Cultural Resources at Stagville, Durham, N. C." (M.R.P. thesis, University of North Carolina, 2006).

38. The following four paragraphs on fieldwork methodology are based on my essay on "The Changing Perceptions of the Restoration of Williamsburg," in *Essays in Early American Architectural History,* 253–55.

39. Thanks to Esther White and Thomas Reinhart of the MVLA for compiling a list of preservation projects carried out at Mount Vernon over the last thirty years.

40. On housing standards in America at the end of the eighteenth century, see Carole Shammas, "The Housing Stock of the Early United States: Refinement Meets Migration," *William and Mary Quarterly,* 3rd ser., 64 (July 2007): 549–90.

"Distinguished by the Name of the New Room"

Reinvestigation and Reinterpretation of George Washington's Grandest Space

THOMAS A. REINHART AND SUSAN P. SCHOELWER

In 2011, Mount Vernon's Historic Preservation and Collections staff began a reexamination of the mansion's largest and most elaborate space, the large, first-floor room at the dwelling's north end. Long known as the Large Dining Room, the space reopened in 2014, rechristened as the New Room, restored and interpreted on the basis of new archival and forensic research.

George Washington created the New Room in three stages over a span of more than two decades. Each stage represented not only a different phase of Washington's life, as his social position changed from ascending Virginia gentleman to national hero to first citizen of the United States, but each period of work also embodied Washington's changing conception of himself. The initial phase (1776) established the basic structure of the wing, while Washington was away fighting for political independence; the second phase (1784–87) completed the interior finishes and ornamentation of the room, directly overseen by the general, newly home from war; the final phase (1796–99) saw the room freshly installed with furnishings and art procured by Washington during and after his terms as president.

George Washington's New Room from the west door as installed, 2014. (MVLA; photograph by Gavin Ashworth)

During Washington's life, the room functioned as a showpiece, frequently mentioned in visitors' accounts, and since the opening of the mansion as a museum in 1860, it has received multiple examinations, restorations, and reinterpretations. One might think that after 150 years of scrutiny there was nothing more to learn. Yet by 2011, with the room showing the accumulated wear of the thirty years since its previous restoration, Mount Vernon's Department of Historic Preservation and Collections saw an opportunity not only to refresh the space but also to assess its condition, reexamine its fabric with improved technologies, and reassess our thoughts on what the room was and how it functioned. What functions was the room intended to serve? How was it finished and used at the time of Washington's

THOMAS A. REINHART AND SUSAN P. SCHOELWER

death? What did the space tell us about Washington and his place in the Chesapeake region and the new nation? And how closely could we restore its architecture and furnishing to the state when Washington last viewed it?

The overall form and plan of the room, as well as its principal architectural features, had survived intact, but the finishes of the room, which carry such visual weight, invited more thorough investigation. Several features set the New Room apart in the eyes of eighteenth-century visitors, not only from other rooms at Mount Vernon but from eighteenth-century American households generally: size, especially the ceiling height, which conspicuously rises above the adjacent rooms; the figure-carved marble mantelpiece; the grand Venetian window; and the avant-garde neoclassical stucco work, most strikingly displayed on the high curved, or coved, ceiling.

How Washington in 1775 envisioned the use of this grand space remains a tantalizing question. The space was a bold statement: the framing of the wing clearly indicates that from the start Washington intended a single first-floor room with an uncommonly high ceiling.[1] In negotiations for plastering the room in 1785, Washington described the space as 32 by 24 by 16 feet high, or a length:width:height ratio of 4:3:2. Architects and builders of the seventeenth and eighteenth centuries would have recognized these proportions as a variant of a "cube room," a space so named because its volume was calculated on that of a cube.[2] The tradition of double cube rooms (a 2:1:1 ratio) is generally traced to Wilton, the Wiltshire country house of the earls of Pembroke, where Palladian architects Inigo Jones and John Webb in the 1650s designed a grand formal stateroom with imposing dimensions (60 × 30 × 30 feet), an emphatically symmetrical plan, a coved ceiling, a two-story Venetian window, and a carved marble mantel centered on the interior wall, opposite the window.[3]

By George Washington's time, the architectural tradition of cube and double cube rooms was well established in the British Atlantic world. Often called saloons (after the French *salon* or the Italian *salone*), these spaces were characterized by formal elements that combined to make them feel outside ordinary experience: har monious proportions, great volume, height exceeding that of surrounding rooms, a strict adherence to symmetry, and a coved ceiling. In conceiving such a space in the mid-1770s, Washington verified his membership in Virginia's upper class and associated himself with gentry across the Atlantic who had such spaces, although his status and architectural expression were more modest than some. While such monumental spaces were rare in eighteenth-century America, Washington was not alone in making this statement. There were a number of such spaces in houses that Washington is known to have visited in the early 1770s. The dwellings of the royal governors of both Virginia and Maryland do not survive, but both had large entertaining rooms that Washington experienced. Whitehall in Anne Arundel County, Maryland, home of Maryland's penultimate royal governor, Horatio Sharpe, features a tall pavilion with a coved ceiling; Washington visited there in 1773.[4]

It was not only the homes of British officials that featured such impressive spaces; the great hall at Stratford Hall, Westmoreland County, Virginia, circa 1737-38; the 1760s ballroom at Hampton Plantation, Charleston County, South Carolina; and the drawing room at Elmwood in Essex County, Virginia, built around 1774, were all similar statements of British architectural affiliation in the colonies.[5] Stratford's great hall, thirty by thirty by fifteen feet high, topped with an arching cove ceiling, offers an early American expression of the grandeur of the cube room; while lacking the academic height of the type, it captures the monumentality. The ballroom of Hampton Plantation shares not only the grand scale and strict symmetry of a cube room; it also features the high cove ceiling, a hallmark of the type. The drawing room at Elmwood, a twenty-by-thirty foot space at the west end of the house, features a symmetrical plan with mantel centered on the interior wall, but it lacks the New Room's Venetian window and its graceful cove ceiling. Often the grandest in a series of spaces, as at Hampton and Elmwood, such rooms were not intended for daily use; they represented architectural features easily recognized as assertions of wealth, taste, status, and power.[6]

The timing of Washington's architectural statement adds further questions. At

THOMAS A. REINHART AND SUSAN P. SCHOELWER

a time when political turmoil was engulfing the colonies, he planned and constructed a large and elegant space with clear pretensions to nobility, intended to host extraordinary social activities. He thus moved to emulate the very British establishment against which he was leading an armed rebellion.

Two of the principal architectural features of the New Room, the Venetian window and the sculpted marble mantel in the center of the south wall, provide the axial symmetry required in a cube room. The elegant Venetian window, though inspired by a forty-year-old pattern published by British architect Batty Langley, acquired new vitality and style through the enrichment of its interior pilasters with cutting-edge ornament.[7] The marble mantel came as a gift from English merchant Samuel Vaughan, whom Washington met in December 1783. Upon returning to Mount Vernon, Washington expressed his desire to install a marble mantel in the New Room. He must have shared this thought with his friend, who comprehending Washington's monumental intentions for the room, wrote to offer one, which arrived a year later.[8] The agrarian subjects of the mantel's sculpted plaques gave vivid expressions of the bucolic themes articulated by the room's neoclassical finish.

Neoclassical detailing also enriched the ceiling and woodwork. Washington wrote Vaughan in January 1784, "I incline to do it in s[t]ucco, (which if I understood you right, is the present taste in England)."[9] Stucco referred to both ornamental plasterwork and composition ornament, a putty of glue and chalk pressed into molds to create finely detailed applique decoration. In choosing it, Washington determined that he did not wish to finish the room with paneling and a cornice made of wood, as in the other public rooms of the house; by the 1780s, that style of finish was out of fashion. Instead, he sought to execute the work in the lighter neoclassical style that was establishing itself as the height of taste on both sides of the Atlantic, principally due to the efforts of the Scottish architect Robert Adam. This style emphasized large panels of flat plaster decorated by delicate ornament inspired by the wall paintings being uncovered at the archaeological excavations in Pompeii.[10] That Washington was concerned about what was in fashion is no surprise to anyone who has read a biography of the man. But the specific notation about the English taste reveals that at a time when Washington had just successfully led his new nation to independence from his old, he was extremely concerned that his new room represent the height of elegance as defined by his former enemies/countrymen. Despite political realities, the great American had yet to declare cultural independence.

To attain the elegant stuccowork he desired, Washington undertook an agreement with the Baltimore plasterer John Rawlins. Rawlins had emigrated from England to Annapolis, Maryland, around 1770, describing himself in a February 1771 advertisement as a plaster and stucco-worker "late arrived from London" and offering "work being done as neat as in *London*."[11] In Annapolis, he executed perhaps the finest surviving ornamental plasterwork in the colonial Chesapeake, at the Chase-Lloyd House, which Washington likely saw on visits to the city in 1784 and 1785. Stylistic similarities suggest that Rawlins also probably created the now lost plasterwork of the Senate chamber of the Maryland Statehouse, where Washington resigned his commission to Congress in December 1783.[12] In September 1785, Washington met with Rawlins in the New Room to discuss the work. They settled on a design sympathetic with the new mantel, rich with agrarian symbolism harkening back to the idealized, bucolic life of republican Rome. In any other house, the symbolism of scythe, wheat, and spade would have ended there, but not so with General Washington's house. The theme of the New Room is Washington's response to what his countrymen were saying of him after he resigned his commission to Congress in 1783. In this act, Americans saw emulation of Cincinnatus, the Roman nobleman who left his plow to lead Rome to victory in battle, returning to his fields only sixteen days later, having given up absolute dictatorial power over the republic. The agrarian imagery of the New Room is Washington's quasi-private acceptance of the mantle of American Cincinnatus; the hero had returned to the plow after securing victory for the American republic.[13]

Missing from visitor descriptions but no less integral to the room's appearance were more ephemeral elements: the colors of the room's wooden and plaster surfaces. Consideration of documentary and physical evidence has been a part of restoration projects at Mount Vernon since the 1860s, and each successive restoration of the New Room (occurring about every thirty years) has brought new discoveries and approaches to the question of how the room looked at the end of Washington's life. The most recent project was no exception. Careful rereading of the archival record, close study of surviving physical evidence, and consideration of the conclusions of previous restoration teams were the foundation of the project, but the creation of the Department of Historic Preservation and Collections brought a new holistic approach. Additional research and forensic investigation injected the most up-to-date knowledge and advanced technologies.

From its start, the MVLA took seriously the quest to unravel what colors Washington had used in the New Room to replicate them. As early as 1869, MVLA founder Ann Pamela Cunningham expressed a desire "to reach the color of the room in General W's day" and not "try to modernize" his home.[14] When it proved impossible to answer the color question, the room received a neutral gray.[15] Later restoration campaigns continued research on color both for the walls and the woodwork. Documentary evidence indicated that in 1787 Washington ordered the trim to be painted "buff... of the lightest kind, inclining to white," and scraping revealed the first layer of paint to be an off-white, which painters in the 1940s replicated.[16] In 1980–81, preceding another round of refurbishment, Matthew J. Mosca conducted a groundbreaking comprehensive paint study of the mansion that represented one of the first holistic scientific paint investigations of a historic house and involved taking approximately two thousand samples, which were examined microscopically. Mosca concluded that few of the original finishes of the New Room survived into the twentieth century, but he did affirm off-white as the earliest color, identifying on top of it chrome yellow, a pigment first commercially available around 1820.[17]

For the most recent investigation, Dr. Susan L. Buck and conservator Amelia B. Jensen conducted additional paint microscopy.[18] Technological advances since Mosca's day allowed for the identification in the New Room of approximately seventeen paint layers, and documentary evidence ties most of these to specific dates. The first three layers of paint identified by Buck on the room's woodwork proved critical to determining the paint colors seen in 1799. For generation one, Buck read a cream present on all wood surfaces throughout the room. Generation two consisted of two colors: a darker cream that appeared on the architraves, chair rails, baseboard cap, and dado below the chair rail, and a dark verdigris green on the friezes of the cornice and doors and on the panels of the pilasters of the Venetian window. In both generations one and two, whitewash picked out the composition ornament in all locations (pilasters, friezes, and all trim). Buck's generation three was the same 1820s chrome yellow identified by Mosca that uniformly covered all of the architectural trim.

For the finish of the walls, Washington's writings indicate that he actively investigated wallpaper in the mid-1780s through contacts in Philadelphia.[19] He intended some of this paper for the New Room, for he specifically instructed that when the woodwork of the New Room was painted in 1787, that the walls were "not to be touched."[20] Even more pointedly, he inquired for "India Paper for my new Room," although no record of any wallpaper purchase for the room survives. Forensic investigation, however, has filled in some of the gaps in the documentary record. Fragments of two generations of wallpaper were first discovered in the New Room in 1869, with further discoveries in the twentieth century.[21] A skim coat of plaster bearing the circa 1820 chromium yellow paint covered the fragments, placing them in a sealed eighteenth- or very early nineteenth-century context. The earlier fragment, a vibrant pattern painted in red and pink, sat directly on the eighteenth-century plaster. A plain green paper, overlaid with a border also executed in green, covered the first paper.

The two generations of early wallpaper align nicely with the two cream paint layers found beneath the 1820s yellow paint, and Washington's letters help identify fairly tight dates for these first two decorative campaigns. Painting occurred in the room in July 1787, when Washington requested the buff inclining to white for all woodwork. This work corresponds with the first-generation light cream

THOMAS A. REINHART AND SUSAN P. SCHOELWER

paint identified in the paint microscopy. The first-generation red/pink wallpaper applied directly to the plaster was presumably installed at the same time. Surprisingly, there is a complete absence of documentation for this wallpaper as well as any window treatments or furniture at this time. The July 1787 reference indicates that this was only to be a temporary situation, noting, "Tis more than probable it will receive a finishing colour hereafter," suggesting that decisions on final finishes, furniture, and fitments were to be deferred until a later date.[22]

Washington's election to the presidency in 1788 likely delayed that redecoration until the family returned to Mount Vernon permanently in the late 1790s. At this time, the darker cream paint covered the first-generation finish on the wooden elements of the chair rail, window and door architraves, and cap of the baseboard. Coarsely ground verdigris paint decorated the pilasters and friezes of the window and door surrounds. Whitewash picked out the composition ornament embellishing all of these features. For the most recent restoration, conservator Erika Sanchez Goodwillie replicated these paints using linseed oil and hand-ground pigments. The coarsely ground copper acetate pigment of the verdigris paint creates a visible texture and a deep, vibrant green that starkly contrasts the whitewashed ornament that adorns the friezes and pilaster panels. The second-generation wallpaper, a light green field paper with a figured border paper, covered the walls in the post-presidency period. Susan Buck's analysis of the surviving fragments of field paper show the paper to be flax and the principal pigment in the paint to be green verditer, an early synthetic of copper carbonate bound in hide glue to make a soft distemper paint.[23]

Over the years, the MVLA has utilized several different approaches to imitate this green wallpaper. In 1932, the room's plaster was painted a pale green; in the 1950s, wallpaper was hung in continuous rolls and painted in place; and in the 1980s, rectangular sheets of paper were hung in a grid pattern then painted in situ. Research conducted for the most recent restoration indicates that neither of these two presentations of wallpaper were correct for the period of interpretation. Staff examined an almost identical green-verditer paper dating to the 1780s from

Pendleton House in Elizabeth City, North Carolina, and now in the collection of Colonial Williamsburg.[24] The Pendleton House paper was hung in rolls that had been assembled from rectangular sheets of laid paper and painted prior to hanging. Washington's inquiries in the 1780s about the price of "plain blue, green and yellow paper pr piece, with the number of yards in a piece" confirms that he was interested in rolls of paper that were produced and painted by a professional wallpaper maker and that the North Carolina example represents the exact sort of wallpaper that was available to him.[25] This research prompted the production of replica green-verditer wallpaper to eighteenth-century standards: 11-yard-long rolls made out of 19-by-23-inch sheets of laid paper. These rolls, fabricated by Adelphi Paperhangings, were then hand-painted in Mount Vernon's preservation lab, using a hand-ground green verditer also made by Erika Sanchez Goodwillie but using an acrylic binder for the durability needed to withstand the wear of over one million annual visitors.[26]

Investigation of the fragment of border paper led to the discovery of the complete border in a 1780s catalogue of wallpapers by the French manufacturer Réveillon, providing further evidence to date the border and associated green wallpaper to the Washington period.[27] Using the Réveillon catalogue, Adelphi reproduced the complete border, restoring details missing from the fragments surviving at Mount Vernon and enabling the first installation of the full border in the New Room since the eighteenth century. The resulting combination of green-verditer wallpaper, French border, darker buff and verdigris paints, and whitewashed composition ornament represents the complete finish of the room in 1799.

The most noticeable change during this restoration appears in the cove. Earlier investigations had identified the cove as being gray or blue-green, but systematic sampling determined that this surface was originally whitewashed to match the ceiling. A white cove dramatically alters perceptions of the room, tying this element to the ceiling, increasing the impression of height in an already lofty space.[28]

As the work to understand and reintroduce accurate finishes to the room's architecture proceeded, other research investigated just what the room was and how

Detail of the New Room's Venetian window showing decorative finishes of 1799, restored in 2014. (MVLA; photograph by Walter Smalling, Jr.)

it was used by the Washingtons. The space had been interpreted for decades as "the large dining room" and in recent years had been used to showcase a long dining table set out with porcelain, silver, and faux foods. Washington, however, only referred to the room as a dining room once, when in 1796 he specified "the large dining room" in contrast to the "small dining room."[29] During Washington's

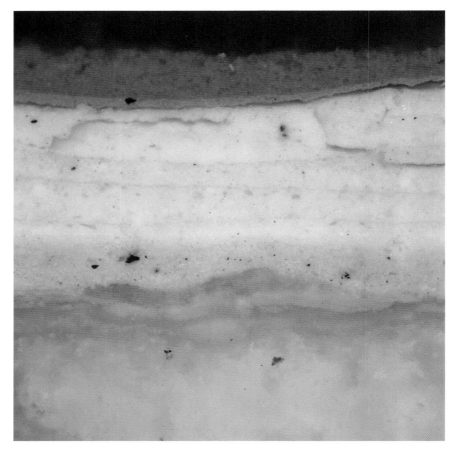

Microscopic image of a paint sample from the cove of the New Room, 2011. The sample shows no evidence for green paint during the George Washington period. (MVLA; photograph by Susan Buck)

lifetime, the space was most frequently identified as the "New Room." Washington first called it that in 1776 when in fact the unfinished space was very new, but this name seems to have stuck and is the most frequent identifier in the construction records for the space in the late 1780s. Outside of Washington's correspondence with his carpenters, the most notable appearance of this designation is found in the

THOMAS A. REINHART AND SUSAN P. SCHOELWER

contract executed between Washington and the Baltimore plasterer John Rawlins, whose shop designed and carried out the remarkable plaster work in "a Certain room at Mount Vernon, in the state of Virginia, and distinguished by the Name of the New Room."[30] In all, from the raising of the frame in 1776 to the time of his death in December 1799, Washington referred to the space in writing as "the" or "my" "New Room" at least fifty-seven times, and the name outlived him, used in both his and Martha's probate inventories.

The interpretive association of the room with eating can be traced back through the twentieth century to the early decades of MVLA presentation. The Mount Vernon guidebook designated the space as the "Large Dining Room" in 1974,

The New Room staged for a dining scenario, 1991. (MVLA; photograph by Hal Conroy)

commenting that "this two story room is most frequently designated in General Washington's writings as 'the large dining room,' occasionally as 'the New Room,'" although as noted above, this statement is demonstrably untrue.[31] According to MVLA historian Mary V. Thompson, the adoption of the title Large Dining Room was an attempt by Mount Vernon curator Mary Christine Meadows to move away from the grandiosity of the name Banquet Hall, which had been the identification of the room since the early years of the MVLA, encouraging flights of fancy about lavish parties and balls (for which there was no evidence).[32] More broadly, the change coincided with the scholarly movement known as the new social history, which beginning in the 1960s had wrought dramatic changes in how the past was researched, taught, and presented at historic sites and museums. Historians turned their attention to the study of nonelite groups, drawing on demographics and statistics to write "history from the bottom up." Historic house curators recognized that room presentations were generally filled with too much high-style furniture, turning to probate inventories to reshape furnishing plans. Material culture joined decorative arts as a framework for research and interpretation. Architectural historians conducted fieldwork on vernacular structures, and investigations of how buildings were used overshadowed sources of architectural influence and classical prototypes. The identification of Mount Vernon's north wing as the large dining room effectively democratized both the room and its residents. Whereas the banquet hall was clearly an out-of-the-ordinary place, inhabited by the great and mighty, the large dining room was just an oversized version of an ordinary dining room, to which anyone could relate.

The term "Banquet Hall" evidently originated with Colonel David Humphreys, one of Washington's Revolutionary War aides, who stayed at Mount Vernon for six weeks in the summer of 1786: he described the space as "a banqueting room" in a draft manuscript biography of the general.[33] Humphreys's self-proclaimed goal was to cast Washington's exertions for his country "in the true point of light in which posterity ought to view them," and his encomium to Washington's life at Mount Vernon was heavily laden with poetic flourishes but short on concrete details.[34] Humphreys's use of the term "banqueting room" is unique among known eighteenth-century accounts of Mount Vernon, suggesting that the inspirations for this title may have included the author's exposure to royal and aristocratic residences during his service as a diplomatic aide in England and France in 1784–86, his taste for ornate language, and his desire to portray Washington in the most heroic light possible.[35]

Humphreys did not publish his Washington biography, but he did evidently leak some passages to a fellow Connecticut author. The Mount Vernon description appeared, without attribution, in Jedediah Morse's *The American Geography,* first published in 1789 and reissued many times as a popular school textbook. From there, Humphreys's description went viral, reprinted in both reference works and periodicals.[36] This singular identification of Washington's New Room as a "banqueting room" thus became widely accessible at a very early date, even before Washington had actually completed furnishing the room. Ironically, the omission of Humphreys's byline in Morse's and subsequent geographies had the effect of enhancing the sense of veracity, transforming the description from an individual writer's observation to established fact. Like Parson Weems's more famous cherry tree fable, the vision of the banqueting room was firmly imprinted in the minds of Americans long before the MVLA began preserving the estate.

By 1869, the MVLA was applying Humphreys's banqueting title to the north wing. Support for this terminology came from two vice regents whose Washington family connections enhanced their credibility. Elizabeth (Betsey) Clapham Price Mason, the vice regent for Virginia in 1872–73, was the daughter-in-law of one of George Washington's four inventory-takers. In November 1870, Mason reportedly told Ann Pamela Cunningham that the "Banquet Hall [was] so-called by General Washington."[37] Additionally, Ella Moore Bassett Washington, vice regent for West Virginia from 1870 until her death in 1898, published an 1871 account of a visit to Mount Vernon that radiated an aura of inside knowledge, as she descended from the families of both George and Martha Washington: "From the west parlor we entered the banquet-hall, the handsomest room on the first floor, used by Washington on state occasions, as a reception or dining-room, and in which his body was laid in state—after his death."[38] Despite their pedigrees, both women were at best indirect witnesses, having late and insubstantial connections to the estate. In calling the north wing a banquet hall, both were likely adopting language already used by the association. The 1886 Mount Vernon guidebook designated the space as the "Banquet Hall," and this title persisted in guidebooks until the 1974 switch to the "Large Dining Room."[39]

The idea of a banquet evoked antiquity and aristocracy, both desirable attributes to many in Reconstruction-era America. Distancing Washington from messy everyday life, political controversy, and social strife pushed him farther into the pantheon of the past, reinforcing his image as "an unchangeable, inherently conservative force, a symbol and guardian" of America.[40] A banquet hall was also surprisingly modern, as barons of industry and commerce across the nation built grand houses with impressive formal reception rooms, glittering ballrooms, and cavernous dining rooms. The women of the MVLA were certainly familiar with these grand piles; some were even proud proprietors of mansions where fashionable gowns of the late 1870s and 1880s, echoing the open robes of a century earlier, were on display. It cannot have been difficult for the *grandes dames* of Gilded Age society to picture themselves stepping figuratively into Washington's world.

The late twentieth-century change to "large dining room" was thus primarily a repudiation of pretension, not a rejection of function. At least one eighteenth-century visitor explicitly had identified the space as a dining room. The British architect Benjamin Henry Latrobe observed, "The center is an old house, to which a good dining room has been added at the North end."[41] As an architect, Latrobe likely conceptualized the house in terms of floor plan, and as a newcomer to America, it is hardly surprising that he interpreted a large, unfurnished room in terms of the current British architectural and social practice of building formal dining rooms, a fashion adapted relatively recently from France and the rest of Europe.[42] Certainly, the New Room could have been pressed into service for dining when large numbers of guests or visitors of high rank were present, such as the Novem-

THOMAS A. REINHART AND SUSAN P. SCHOELWER

ber 1797 dinner for the British envoy Sir Robert Liston.[43] According to Washington's diary, in 1798 and 1799 (when the New Room was furnished and ready for use) dinners exceeding the number that could fit in the mansion's so-called Small Dining Room (ten) occurred relatively infrequently: there were eight large dinner parties in 1798 and eighteen in 1799, the latter coinciding principally with the February nuptials of Martha's youngest granddaughter, Eleanor (Nelly) Parke Custis and George's nephew Lawrence Lewis.[44]

Other observers did not make the same association, even after the final furnishing in the late 1790s. In 1787, master plasterer John Rawlins invoiced Washington for "the Composition work, in your Salloon room"; a decade later, Julian Ursyn Niemcewicz, a Polish count, saw a large salon, English businessman Joshua Brookes reported a drawing room, and English landscape architect George Isham Parkyns called it a withdrawing room.[45] As demonstrated, Washington rarely if ever used these names for the space, relying mostly on "New Room," but unlike "saloon," "parlor," "dining room," "study," or "bedroom," "New Room" offered no familiar clues to room usage and, by extension, to furnishings and meaning. Once it was determined in 2011 to return to the room's original name, the interpretive challenge remained: if not a dining room, just how was this space used?

The north wing arguably served first and foremost as a necessary architectural element, maintaining exterior symmetry. Function may have been secondary; what mattered most was that the north wing existed to balance the south wing, whose spaces answered practical needs for a more private study and bedchamber. Eighteenth-century visitors' descriptions corroborate the focus on form, and the variety of names conveys a fluid, multipurpose functionality. The current interpretation of the New Room stresses this adaptability, inspired in part by the strong architectural similarities to eighteenth century British saloons—evident in numerous country and city houses, and most strikingly at Saltram, the Devonshire estate of John Parker II, Baron Boringdon.[46] Deeply embedded in eighteenth-century social structures and practices, the uses of saloons are elusive to modern audiences. Like the Elizabethan great chambers that preceded them, saloons typically exhibited "certain definite characteristics: highly architectural in treatment, a magnificent setting for great gatherings rather than for everyday life. . . . The German word *prunksaal* or show-room perhaps describes it best."[47] Furnishings generally included large-scale works of art, with a set of seating furniture, often monumental in scale, arranged with tables around the walls. Following in this tradition, Mount Vernon's New Room was more commonly *experienced* as a visual sight, rather than *used* as a living space. Several accounts suggest that the typical visitor's encounter with the New Room was limited to a formal tour of the house, with the sole firmly documented activity being the laying out of George Washington's body, as recorded by his aide Tobias Lear: "The Corps[e] was brought down and laid out in the large Room."[48] This was, in fact, just the sort of solemn state occasion for which this formal room was perfectly suited.

George Washington's probate inventory, taken soon after his death, provides a snapshot of the New Room at its culminating moment. Notably, no tables are recorded therein, either in George or Martha Washington's probate inventories, nor are any mentioned in any of the known eighteenth-century visitors' comments. The only two dining tables in the inventories are those listed in the dining room. These are presumably the two tables that Washington ordered from London in 1757: "Two neat Mahogny Tables 4½ feet square when spread and to join occasionally." There is no documentation in Washington's extensive records of his subsequently acquiring any additional dining tables.[49] The Washingtons evidently continued to follow the practice—prevalent in both English and Virginia houses since the mid-eighteenth century—of dining on smaller, relatively portable tables that could be moved from room to room when needed, and folded up and arranged against a wall when not in use. The alternate custom—of having a large table permanently set up in the center of a dining room—was still relatively novel in late eighteenth-century England and would not become prevalent in American homes until around the second decade of the nineteenth century, well after the Washingtons' deaths.[50]

Perhaps the most striking aspect of the inventory listing for this room is a strong sense of symmetry (which is not repeated in any other room in the house). Virtually every item has a counterpart: two large looking glasses, two sideboards, two candle stands, three pairs of painted landscapes, two pairs of battle scenes, two portraits, two religious pictures, two pairs of classical subjects, and two copies of a celebrated British print, *The Dead Soldier* (after a painting by Joseph Wright of Derby). The only picture lacking a counterpart is the "Painting—'Moon light,'" described by Joshua Brookes as hanging "over the mantle."[51] Occupying the exact fulcrum of the room's installation opposite the great Venetian window, the "fine moonlight piece" anchors the symmetrical arrangement that George Washington so clearly articulated in his early instructions for the layout of the New Room. On September 30, 1776, he stressed to farm manager Lund Washington: "The chimney of the new room should be exactly in the middle of it—the doors and every thing else to be exactly answerable and uniform."[52] The inventory testifies to both the care with which this vision of symmetry was carried out and also to the strong impression that it made. This was no haphazard assortment of furnishings, accumulated over the years (as suggested by some of the other mansion room listings), but a select grouping of objects installed accordingly to a precisely controlled plan. If the mansion's exterior was marred by the asymmetry of its west facade (a defect presumably occasioned by its construction in multiple phases), this flaw was studiously excised in the precise symmetry of the New Room's interior.

In addition to highlighting that symmetry, the new installation showcases the New Room's function as a picture gallery—a function echoing the furnishing of English saloons and one certainly encouraged by the marvelous north light admitted by the Venetian window. This is the room use for which we have the strongest and most concrete corroboration—not only the documentary evidence of the inventory but also physical evidence of the surviving works of art. If the room was sometimes used for dining, it was after 1797 permanently fitted out as a picture gallery. Washington signaled his strong personal involvement in developing this aspect of the room, describing the pictures he brought home after the presidency as "all . . . fancy pieces of my own chusing."[53] The inventory lists a total

South wall of the New Room, 2014. (MVLA: photograph by Gavin Ashworth)

of 21 pictures in this space—nearly 20 percent of the 115 hanging throughout the house, and close to one-third of the 74 displayed on the main floor. Most were in impressive and expensive gilt frames, and all but two were relatively new, acquired after the beginning of the presidency.[54] All but one painting has been identified, and these twenty were all represented in the 2014 reinstallation, more than at any time since 1802. The "salon-style" hang, from chair rail to the cornice, often in vertical columns, creates a massed effect that heightens the perception of the room as a picture gallery.

Two iconographical themes—the American landscape and American history—link the major pictures in the room: three pairs of landscape paintings, two portraits, and two pairs of John Trumbull's Revolutionary War battle engravings. The landscape paintings were most conspicuously of Washington's "own chusing," as during the presidency he sought paintings of specific American scenes by two emi-

THOMAS A. REINHART AND SUSAN P. SCHOELWER

grant English painters, William Winstanley and George Beck.[55] Washington's pursuit of American landscapes diverged significantly from late eighteenth-century aesthetic theories as well as actual preferences of American consumers. Aesthetic theories held history paintings and classical subjects to be the most elevated genres, while portraits predominated in American homes. Washington's acquisition and display of American scenes preceded by nearly a full generation the vogue for landscape painting spurred by Thomas Cole and the Hudson River School, beginning in the mid-1820s. Moreover, Washington's river views brought together in one room scenes from the three distinct regions of the country—the Potomac, from the South; the Hudson, from the North; and the Genesee, from the West—just as, out of doors, he deliberately sought out plants from throughout the new nation.[56]

The New Room's two portraits were both gifts to the Washingtons, but their display offers further evidence of the president's iconographic program. The engraved portrait of *Louis Seize, Roi de France,* an official diplomatic gift, seems at first glance an anachronistic partner to John Trumbull's *George Washington at Verplanck's Point,* a personal gift from the artist to Martha Washington.[57] Yet both images depict national leaders in formal, full-length poses traditionally associated with authority, and each man wears the official garb associated with his rank. In combination, the two portraits celebrate America's revolutionary history and the successful alliance that defeated the British. More subtly, given the violent excesses of the French Revolution, the deposed king's portrait may have also served as a warning of the dangers of tyranny as well as of factionalism and popular democracy.

The content and chronology of the New Room's creation, decoration, and furnishing yield vital keys for unlocking the room's original use, meaning, and significance. Washington created a room that was in the first class of old-world fashion at a time when his cultural and political futures were about to change. He crafted the design to express his evolving status and his reputation among his fellow countrymen, and he fitted out a space that showcased the beauty of his new nation and its hopeful, fledgling status in the world. To the Washingtons and their inner circle, the room was literally and repeatedly new; more importantly, it was always a public-facing room, and its meaning changed with its owners' role in their society. Newly begun with steadfast optimism in the volatile 1770s, this unusually grand and ambitious space announced a Virginia planter's entry into the broader stage of the Atlantic world. Newly decorated in the 1780s, the room's display of stylish neoclassical details expressed a victorious general's embrace of the new republic and a new American identity, rooted in ancient ideals and the promise of the land. Newly furnished in the 1790s, the room's carefully crafted iconographic program embodied a retired statesman's farewell message to the nation he had led, balancing his vision for its future with a celebration of its past and a warning of the challenges ahead. The room also continues to be new to visitors today, due to fresh research and investigation. Far from being an empty name, the New Room is rich in meaning, offering twenty-first-century visitors a tangible metaphor for Washington's life, leadership, and indispensable role in the creation of America.

Notes

1. Each wall frame of the addition incorporates an intermediate girt to carry the ceiling joists of the room at a height of sixteen and a half feet, about three feet below the framing of the third floor.

2. Curtis Thomas, *The London Encyclopedia, or Universal Dictionary of Science, Art, Literature and Practical Mechanics,* 22 vols. (London: T. Tegg, 1829), 2:612–13; Scott Campbell Owen, "George Washington's Mount Vernon as British Venetian Architecture" (M.A. thesis, University of Virginia, 1991), 10-11; Charles E. Brownell, "Laying the Groundwork: The Classical Tradition and Virginia Architecture, 1770-1870," in *The Making of Virginia Architecture,* ed. Charles E. Brownell et al. (Richmond: Virginia Museum of Fine Arts, 1992), 39-42; Joseph Manca, *George Washington's Eye: Landscape, Architecture, and Design at Mount Vernon* (Baltimore: Johns Hopkins University Press, 2012), 50.

3. Gervase Jackson-Stops and James Pipkin, *The English Country House: A Grand Tour* (Boston: Little, Brown, 1985), 84–86.

4. Washington's diaries record that he dined at the Governor's Palace in Williamsburg many times and that he lodged with Governor Robert Eden of Maryland on several visits to Annap-

THOMAS A. REINHART AND SUSAN P. SCHOELWER

olis; the diaries also record the visit to Whitehall. The ballroom of the Governor's Palace was reconstructed from 1931–35 and was based partially on the drawing room of the Miles Brewton House in Charleston. Graham Hood, "The Ballroom and Supper Room," in Graham Hood, *The Governor's Palace in Williamsburg* (Williamsburg, VA: Colonial Williamsburg Foundation, 1991), 168–93; Edward A. Chappell, "Reconsidered Splendor: The Palace Addition of 1751—A Report to the Program Planning and Review Committee" (Colonial Williamsburg Foundation, unpublished report, 1984), 6–9, http://research.history.org/DigitalLibrary/View/index.cfm?doc=ResearchReports%5CRR0149.xml; A. Lawrence Kocher, "The Governor's Palace (An Architectural Report)" (Colonial Williamsburg Foundation, unpublished report, 1952), 56, http://research.history.org/DigitalLibrary/View/index.cfm?doc=ResearchReports%5CRR0133.xml; Thomas Tileston Waterman, *The Mansions of Virginia, 1706–1776* (Chapel Hill: University of North Carolina Press, 1945), 42, 51–54. The inventory of Governor Eden lists a "Long Room" that featured a marble chimney piece: "An Inventory of Houshold Furniture the Property of Sir Robert Eden, Baronet, Left in the Possession of His Excellency Thomas Sim Lee, Esq.," Maryland State Papers (Red Books) MSA S 989 MdHR 4557 Book 1, Item 7, http://msa.maryland.gov/megafile/msa/speccol/sc3500/sc3520/000300/000391/pdf/edeninv.pdf, Maryland State Archives, Annapolis. The square pavilion of Whitehall has a coved ceiling and highly enriched trim and carved decoration. Charles Scarlett, Jr., "Governor Horatio Sharpe's Whitehall," *Maryland Historical Magazine* 46 (1951): 8–26.

5. Waterman, *The Mansions of Virginia,* 298–300; James Dillon, "National Register of Historic Places Inventory—Nomination Form: Hampton Plantation" (April 1, 1976), http://www.nationalregister.sc.gov/charleston/S10817710016/S10817710016.pdf; SCIWAY, South Carolina's Information Highway, "Hampton Plantation—McCellanville—Charleston County," South Carolina Plantations, http://south-carolina-plantations.com/charleston/hampton.html; Virginia Historic Landmarks Commission Staff, "National Register of Historic Places Inventory—Nomination Form: Elmwood" (March 11, 1970), http://www.dhr.virginia.gov/registers/Counties/Essex/028-0011_Elmwood_1970_Final_Nomination.pdf.

6. Jackson-Stops and Pipkin, *English Country House,* 82-99.

7. Batty Langley, *The City and Country Builder's and Workman's Treasury of Designs* (London: S. Harding, 1741), plate LI.

8. GW to Bushrod Washington, January 15, 1784, PGWDE; GW to Samuel Vaughan, April 6, 1784, PGWDE; GW to Samuel Vaughan, February 5, 1785, PGWDE.

9. GW to Samuel Vaughan, January 14, 1784, PGWDE.

10. Damie Stillman, *The Decorative Work of Robert Adam* (London: St. Martin's Press, 1973), 28.

11. *Maryland Gazette,* February 14, 1771, http://msa.maryland.gov/megafile/msa/speccol/sc4800/sc4872/001281/html/m1281–1224.html.

12. *Maryland Gazette,* February 14, 1771, http://msa.maryland.gov/megafile/msa/speccol/sc4800/sc4872/001281/html/m1281–1224.html; Marcia Miller, "The Chase-Lloyd House" (M.A. thesis, George Washington University, 1993), 140; Mark R. Wenger, "Report on the Architectural Investigation of the Old Senate Chamber in the Maryland Statehouse" (Mesick Cohen Wilson Baker Architects, unpublished report, forthcoming). A somewhat ironic aspect of the execution of the plasterwork is that when John Rawlins arrived to begin the work on April 19, 1786, he was accompanied by Richard Tharpe, an Irish plasterer that Irish politician Edward Newenham had recommended Washington indenture the previous year. Rawlins intended Tharpe to execute the project that he and Washington had scoped the prior fall and contracted for in February 1786. Washington objected to the change, and Rawlins (who apparently was no longer actively plastering himself) convinced Washington to accept the substitution. As Washington wrote, "It became evident it must be *him,* or no *work,* there being no other, Rawlins said, who was competent to the undertaking." Washington noted that Tharpe "demeaned himself soberly & well." GW, Diary, April 19, 1786, PGWDE; GW to Edward Newenham, June 10, 1786, PGWDE.

13. Dennis J. Pogue, "George Washington and the Architecture of Personal and National Identity," 2008, AMVLA, NLSGW.

14. Ann Pamela Cunningham to Mrs. Nathaniel Norris Halsted (Nancy Wade Marsh Halsted), August 18, September 3, 1869, Early Records of the Mount Vernon Ladies' Association, AMVLA, NLSGW.

15. Ann Pamela Cunningham to Mrs. Nathaniel Norris Halsted (Nancy Wade Marsh Halsted), September 16, October 13, 1869, Early Records of the Mount Vernon Ladies' Association, AMVLA, NLSGW.

16. GW to George Augustine Washington, July 1, 1787, PGWDE; MVLA, Minutes, 1942, 11, 45–46.

17. Matthew John Mosca, "Introduction: The Paint Analysis Reports, Mount Vernon, Virginia," n.d., MVLA Preservation Files; Matthew John Mosca, "The Paint Analysis of the Large Dining Room, Mount Vernon, Virginia," October 21, 1980, MVLA Preservation Files; Roger W. Moss, *Paint in America* (Washington, DC: Preservation Press, 1994), 282.

18. Susan L Buck, "Cross-Section Paint Microscopy Report: The Large Dining Room Woodwork and Plaster Paints, Wallpaper Fragments, Mount Vernon, Virginia," 2011, MVLA Preservation Files; Amelia B. Jensen, "Paint Microscopy Report: The New Room, Further Investigation," 2013, MVLA Preservation Files.

19. GW to Clement Biddle, March 10, 1784, PGWDE; GW to Robert Morris, October 2, 1787, PGWDE.

20. GW to George Augustine Washington, July 15, 1787, PGWDE.

21. Harrison Howell Dodge, wallpaper fragment and note, RP3233.001, NLSGW; Superintendent's Diaries, March 14, 1902, AMVLA, NLSGW; MVLA, Minutes, 1951, 58–61.

22. GW to George Augustine Washington, July 1, 1787, PGWDE.

23. Buck, "Large Dining Room," 32–33; Moss, *Paint in America,* 286.

24. The authors thank Margaret Pritchard, the former curator of prints, maps, and wallpaper at Colonial Williamsburg, for her invaluable insight, advice, and assistance. Stephen & Francis, P.A. Architects, and Peter Sandbeck, "Pendleton House Historic Structure Report," 1996, MVLA Preservation Files.

25. GW to Clement Biddle, March 10, 1784, PGWDE.

26. Thomas Reinhart, "Research Report on the New Room Wallpaper," 2013, MVLA Preservation Files.

27. The border's Réveillon origin was found by Véronique de La Hougue, curator in chief at the Department of Wallpapers, Musée des Arts Décoratifs, whom the authors gratefully acknowledge. "Wallpaper Border—Emails." October 2011–July 2012, MVLA Preservation Files.

28. Buck, "Large Dining Room," 22–31.

29. GW to Tobias Lear, March 25, 1797, PGWDE. Washington's November 1796 request for measurements in the "new dr[awin]g room" has mistakenly been transcribed as "new di[nin]g room" in the PGWDE, but inspection of the original manuscript reveals that the second letter is an "r" rather than an "n." GW to William Pearce, November 20, 1796, manuscript collection, NLSGW, transcribed at Founders Online, National Archives, http://founders.archives.gov /documents/Washington/99-01-02-00018. Other references in Washington's papers to the "large dining room" clearly refer to the president's house in Philadelphia, not Mount Vernon.

30. John Rawlins and Tench Tilghman, "Articles of Agreement," February 25, 1786, Library of Congress, Washington, DC, https://memory.loc.gov/cgi-bin/query/P?mgw:8:./temp /~ammem_AoE1.

31. *Mount Vernon: An Illustrated Handbook* (Mount Vernon, VA: MVLA, 1974), 42. This commentary inexplicably reversed the language that had appeared in the guidebooks since 1947: "The banquet hall is most frequently designated in General Washington's writings as 'the New Room,' occasionally as 'the large dining room.'"

32. Mary V. Thompson, personal conversation, June 2014.

33. David Humphreys to GW, September 30, 1784, PGWDE; Rosemary Zagarri, ed., *David Humphreys' "Life of General Washington" with George Washington's "Remarks"* (Athens:

University of Georgia Press, 1991), xiii–xxii. Humphreys visited Mount Vernon on three other occasions, in 1781, 1783, and 1787–89; see Elswyth Thane, *Potomac Squire* (Mount Vernon, VA: MVLA, 1963), 196, 207–8, 260-62, 277, 291.

34. David Humphreys to GW, September 30, 1784, PGWDE.

35. For further evidence of Humphreys's florid style, his heroic view of Washington, and the influence of his European travels, see his 1785 poem "Mount-Vernon, An Ode," in Frank Landon Humphreys, *The Life and Times of David Humphreys,* 2 vols. (New York: G. P. Putnam's Sons, 1917), 1:223-25, https://archive.org/details/miscellaneouswooowashgoog. On Humphreys's literary context, see Leon Howard, *The Connecticut Wits* (Chicago: University of Chicago Press, 1943).

36. Jedediah Morse, *The American Geography; or, A View of the Present Situation of the United States of America* (Elizabethtown, NJ: Shepard Kollock, 1789), 127–32. For examples of contemporary reprintings, see William Guthrie, *New System of Modern Geography,* 2 vols. (Philadelphia: Mathew Carey, 1794-95), 2:495-96; William Winterbotham et al., *An Historical, Geographical, Commercial, and Philosophical View of the American United States of America,* 4 vols. (London: For the Editor, 1795), 3:97; and "American Advices," *Osborne's New-Hampshire Spy* (Portsmouth), April 19, 1791, 10. George Washington himself owned copies of Morse's and Guthrie's geographies. Amanda Isaac, *Take Note! George Washington the Reader* (Mount Vernon, VA: MVLA, 2013), 112-13. On the publication history of Humphreys's biography of Washington, see Zagarri, ed., *David Humphreys' Life,* xxvii-xxxi, 94n46, and William S. Baker, ed., *Early Sketches of George Washington Reprinted with Biographical and Bibliographical Notes* (Philadelphia: J. B. Lippincott, 1904), 124-25. On the passage related specifically to Mount Vernon, see Manca, *George Washington's Eye,* 84-85, 268n4.

37. Sarah Tiffey to Mrs. Nathaniel Norris Halsted (Nancy Wade Marsh Halsted), August 18, November 24, 1869; Elizabeth "Betsey" Clapham Price Mason to Sarah Tiffey, "Reminiscences," October 23(?), 1869, Early Records of the Mount Vernon Ladies' Association, AMVLA, NLSGW. Betsey Mason's husband, Judge Thomson Francis Mason, had grown up at Hollin Hall, a plantation adjoining George Washington's River Farm.

38. Ella B. Washington, "A Day and Night at Mount Vernon," *Appletons' Journal: A Magazine of General Literature,* April 29, 1871, 488-90.

39. Elizabeth Bryant Johnston, *Visitor's Guide to Mount Vernon,* 13th ed. (Washington, DC; Gibson Brothers, 1886), 26. From 1877 to 1902, the space was also known as the New York Room, referring to its stewardship by the vice regent for that state.

40. Karal Ann Marling, *Washington Slept Here: Colonial Revivals and American Culture, 1876-1986* (Cambridge, MA: Harvard University Press, 1988), 65-66.

41. Benjamin Henry Latrobe, *The Virginia Journals of Benjamin Henry Latrobe, 1795-1798,* ed. Edward Carter II, 2 vols. (New Haven, CT: Yale University Press for the Maryland Historical Society, 1977), 1:163.

42. Michael W. Fazio and Patrick Snadon, *The Domestic Architecture of Benjamin Henry Latrobe* (Baltimore: Johns Hopkins University Press, 2006), 83-182. On the evolution of dining rooms, see Mark Girouard, *Life in the English Country House: A Social and Architectural History* (New Haven, CT: Yale University Press, 1978), 162, 203, 239; Jackson-Stops and Pipkin, *English Country House,* 120-37; and Mark R. Wenger, "The Dining Room in Early Virginia," *Perspectives in Vernacular Architecture* 3 (1989): 156-59.

43. GW, Diary, November 13, 1797, PGWDE.

44. Jessie MacLeod, "Large Dinner Parties," August 15, 2012, MVLA Curatorial Files; Mary V. Thompson, "'That Hospitable Mansion': Welcoming Guests at George Washington's Mount Vernon," in *Dining with the Washingtons: Historic Recipes, Entertainment, and Hospitality from Mount Vernon,* ed. Stephen A. McLeod (Mount Vernon, VA: MVLA, 2012), 11-12, 216n8.

45. John Rawlins to GW, March 10, 1787, PGWDE; Julian Ursyn Niemcewicz, *Under Their Vine and Fig Tree: Travels through America in 1797–1799, 1805, with Some Further Account of Life in New Jersey,* trans. and ed. Metchie J. E. Budka (Elizabeth, NJ: Grassmann, 1965), 96–97; Joshua Brookes, index entry for "Washington, Gen. George," manuscript journal, 1798-1803, 521, 524, New-York Historical Society Mss Collection (BV Brookes, Joshua). George Isham Parkyns's commentary accompanies a rare 1799 print, the earliest known engraving of Mount Vernon's west front, issued as the first print in his planned series, *Sketches of Select American Scenery, No. 1* (Philadelphia: John Ormrod, 1798), John Carter Brown Library, Early American Imprints, series 1: Evans, 1639–1800, no. 48951. See Eleanor M. Peck, "George Isham Parkyns: Artist and Landscape Architect, 1749-1820," *Quarterly Journal of the Library of Congress* 30, no. 3 (July 1973): 175-78, and Emily T. Cooperman, ed., *The Country Seats of the United States: William Russell Birch* (Philadelphia: University of Pennsylvania Press, 2009), 8, 13-14, 21, 36n37. Whether Parkyns actually saw Mount Vernon personally remains in question, as no visit has been documented. Parkyns's text on Mount Vernon echoes David Humphreys's earlier description with some additions; Parkyns's depiction of the west front similarly draws on Edward Savage's painted version of the subject, c. 1787-92, which was on display in Philadelphia in the late 1790s. Carol Borchert Cadou, *The George Washington Collection: Fine and Decorative Arts at Mount Vernon* (Manchester, VT: Hudson Hills Press, 2006), 206-7, 289n118.

46. Saltram's saloon was designed by Robert Adam in 1768. Siân Evans, *Saltram, Devon, A Souvenir Guide* (London: National Trust, 2012), 6, 16–17, 40–41; Robert F. Dalzell, Jr., and Lee

Baldwin Dalzell, *George Washington's Mount Vernon: At Home in Revolutionary America* (New York: Oxford University Press, 1998), 85–89.

47. Jackson-Stops and Pipkin, *English Country House,* 82. See also Girouard, *Life in the English Country House,* esp. 126-29, 201-3.

48. Julian Niemcewicz describes one such tour, in 1798; see *Under Their Vine and Fig Tree,* 84–94, 96–97. Tobias Lear, "The Last Illness and Death of General Washington," journal account, December 15, 1799, PGWDE. Niemcewicz provides an ambiguous reference to an afternoon dinner with "the table in the great hall set out with a Sèvres porcelain service with places for 20" (106–7). This reference has generally been interpreted as a dinner in the New Room; however, in describing his tour of the mansion, the Polish nobleman uses the term "hall" to designate the central passage, while calling the New Room "a large salon." The matter is further complicated by a different translation of Niemcewicz's original Polish text, in W. M. Kozlowski, "A Visit to Mt Vernon a Century Ago: A Few Pages of an Unpublished Diary of the Polish Poet J. U. Niemcewicz," *Century Magazine,* February 1902, 517, 521. Mount Vernon's curators and historians continue to debate the location of Niemcewicz's dinner.

49. GW, Invoice to Richard Washington, April 15, 1757, PGWDE.

50. Gerald W. R. Ward, "The Intersections of Life: Tables and Their Social Role," in *American Tables and Looking Glasses in the Mabel Brady Garvan and Other Collections at Yale University,* ed. David L. Barquist (New Haven, CT: Yale University Art Gallery, 1992), 22-24.

51. "Inventory and Appraisement of the Estate of Genl. George Washington Deceased," transcription, Gunston Hall Plantation Probate Inventory Database, http://www.gunstonhall .org/library/probate/WSHGTN99.PDF; Brookes, index entry for "Washington, Gen. George," 524.

52. Brookes, index entry for "Washington, Gen. George," 524; GW to Lund Washington, September 30, 1776, PGWDE.

53. GW to Mary White Morris, May 1, 1797, PGWDE.

54. "Inventory and Appraisement of the Estate of Genl. George Washington Deceased"; GW, Prints Purchased, February 1797, George Washington Papers, 1741-99, series 4, General Correspondence, 1697-1799, Library of Congress; GW to Clement Biddle, frame orders, May 28, September 15, 1797, June 17, 1798, PGWDE; Jessie MacLeod, "Acquisition of Objects in the New Room," November 12, 2012, MVLA Curatorial Files.

55. "Household Accounts," *Pennsylvania Magazine of History and Biography* 29, no. 4 (1905): 391; 30, no. 2 (1906): 177; 31, no. 3 (1907): 338 (entries for April 6, 1793; April 28, 1794; January 31, 1797); J. Hall Pleasants, "Four Late Eighteenth Century Anglo-American Land-

THOMAS A. REINHART AND SUSAN P. SCHOELWER

scape Painters," *Proceedings of the American Antiquarian Society* 32 (October 1942): 195-214, 301-24.

56. Andrea Wulf, *Founding Gardeners: The Revolutionary Generation, Nature, and the Shaping of the American Nation* (New York: Knopf, 2011), 21-23.

57. GW to Jean-Baptiste Ternant, December 21, 1791, PGWDE; GW, Diary, July 8, 1790, PGWDE.

"We Have Done Very Little Investigation There; There Is a Great Deal Yet to Do"

The Archaeology of George Washington's Mount Vernon

LUKE J. PECORARO

On May 14, 1937, Morley Jeffers Williams, the newly minted director of research and restoration, addressed the board of the Mount Vernon Ladies' Association (MVLA) for the first time in his role. He gave a carefully laid out, lengthy address on the challenges his department faced, what was known about George Washington's plantation, and how he intended to go forward. One of the nagging issues Williams wrestled with was the property itself: "We are trying to accumulate data so the place can be put back as it was, insofar as possible. You can not catch the atmosphere of the plantation and have the public on the grounds. We are faced with the problem of having the public, which destroy the atmosphere, and at the same time try to show that very public the thing Washington knew." The report went on to enumerate what had been achieved through archaeological and architectural investigations but indicated that Williams was a long way from being able to tell the story of George Washington's life at Mount Vernon. As Williams succinctly stated toward the end of his assessment of the historic core of the plantation, "We have done very little investigation there; there is a great deal yet to do."[1]

In many ways, the observations Williams made in his 1937 report were echoed by those who preceded and followed him, and the work is ongoing. In the over 160-year history of the MVLA's stewardship of the house and grounds, archaeological fieldwork has made contributions toward understanding daily life on Washington's plantation. The vestiges of his formal plantation arrangement and English-style gardens, grasslands, and tree plantings are preserved and protected on the MVLA's 423 acres, which encompass most of what was Mansion House Farm.[2] Mansion House Farm was only one small portion of Washington's larger Mount Vernon estate, an optimized, agricultural system made up of four other farms on roughly eight thousand acres. Toward the end of Washington's life, financial constraints prompted him to try to rent some of his farmland, which ultimately proved unsuccessful. Washington's heirs, entrusted with the management of Mount Vernon, faced the same concerns. Over a period of fifty-six years, Washington's heirs gradually parceled off or sold all but 1,025 acres. The MVLA's purchase of the mansion and 200 acres in 1858 preserved Washington's home, but the remaining 825 acres of the estate of John Augustine Washington III were put up for sale at the close of the Civil War. More recent twentieth-century suburban development on the land that composed the so-called Five Farms has all but obliterated the traces of Washington's grand plantation design.[3]

Although Mount Vernon welcomes over a million visitors to the mansion and preserved gounds annually, the story of the larger plantation and Washington's tight connection to agriculture and land improvement is often difficult to relate to the public. The plantation system propelled Washington forward in his social and political life, and the day-to-day operations of the farms were his paramount concern. The narrative of his relationship with the landscape is critical to understanding his carrer and the changing nature of his hopes and interests. As historian David McCullough commented at the opening of the Fred W. Smith National Library for the Study of George Washington in 2013, the emphasis of Washington's writing on Mount Vernon and its environment makes his plantation the most salient reminder of his character.[4]

The MVLA's early commitment to saving a portion of the grounds around the mansion ensured that a small piece of the estate was saved. In subsequent years, the efforts of the association, its employees, and visiting scholars worked to bring the landscape back to a fatihful representation of that which Washington saw. The changes that the stewards of the property wrought were products of their time and reflections of trends in the growing field of historic preservation. As we continue to adopt the best practices to ensure stewardship in a new era where digital technologies are increasingly enhancing our management and research stratgies as well as public outreach, it is useful to take a look into the past to determine the best road for the future. To that end, this essay revisits the formation of the archaeology program at Mount Vernon and the role it has played in researching and restoring Washington's estate. It also introduces the larger cultural landscape along with new initiatives that tell the story of multiple generations of site occupants and visitors.

Early Research Efforts (c. 1859–1930)

When the MVLA acquired the the estate from John Augustine Washington III, the field of archaeological inquiry in the United States was in its infancy and grounded firmly in antiquarian traditions. Archaeologists conducted excavation, but the interpretation of finds generally focused only on those artifacts that were very unusual, rather than considering a complete assemblage. At Mount Vernon, the resident superintendent collected objects recovered from Mount Vernon's grounds either through maintenance work or from visitors making an occasional surface find. No formal policy nor research strategy existed, however, for treating these artifacts. The material collected formed the nucleus of Mount Vernon's "Old Collection," which consisted of finds from across the historic estate, as well as additional sites that bore a connection to George Washington. Oddly enough, the first scholarly interest in archaeological material from Mount Vernon did not focus on the Washington family's occupation but on the site's prehistory. Children living on the property collected prehistoric projectile points and pottery, which the

MVLA sold in the gift shop, and in the 1890s, the association granted permission to local antiquarian William Hunter to collect similar artifacts. Hunter later made a gift of his collection to the Smithsonian Institution; William H. Holmes, the chief of the Bureau of American Ethnography accessioned the finds and worked them into his prehistoric survey of the Potomac drainage basin, published in 1897.[5]

During this period, the MVLA worked toward cleaning up the grounds and attending to deferred maintenance issues that threatened the historic fabric of the estate. In his capacity as Mount Vernon's resident director, Colonel Harrison Howell Dodge performed the first act of building reconstruction in 1895 when he uncovered the buried foundations of the coach house, which had been destroyed by fire in the mid-nineteenth century. Dodge's efforts were driven primarily by a map of the historic estate drawn by Samuel Vaughan, an English visitor who stayed at Mount Vernon as a guest in 1787.[6] Although the use of the Vaughan Plan to aid restoration was a step in the right direction, Dodge's work complicated matters because the features and buildings depicted on the map did not work in concert with the interpretation of the estate to the year 1799, the year of George Washington's death. American travel writer Benson J. Lossing, who visited Mount Vernon in 1858, also confounded efforts in his well-known text; Lossing's descriptions were fraught with inaccuracies that took several decades to realize.[7]

The Path to Authenticity (1931–1976)

The national effort to preserve historic houses and restore sites based on archaeological evidence (notably through federally funded recovery programs) coincided with the centennial celebration of Washington's birth in 1932 and efforts underway at Mount Vernon.[8] In 1931, Harvard-trained landscape architect Morley Williams arrived at Mount Vernon as part of a study he was conducting of southern plantations and their associated landscapes.[9] Williams began a robust program of historical research using the eighteenth-century plantation records, plats, and surveys held in the MVLA archives to determine a chronology of building campaigns

Samuel Vaughan's plan of Mount
Vernon, 1787. (MVLA)

at Mount Vernon beginning with Augustine Washington's work circa 1734. Over the course of the next three years, Williams determined a sequence of the changes to landscape that ocurred between when George Washginton took control of the plantation in 1753 and when his ownership ended in 1799. Although Williams was not a trained archaeologist, his engineering background provided him with the skillset to produce field drawings, record the locations of his test trenches, and take photographs of his work.[10]

By 1936, Williams was named the director of research and restoration. While in this capacity, Williams's newly formed department compiled primary documents related to the plantation operations as well as sourced other known Washington materials not owned by the MVLA. He also oversaw restoration and repairs to the mansion, stable, new tomb, smokehouse, and lower garden. The lower garden was restored based on contemporary work being done elsewhere and remains today as a surviving example of a colonial revival garden plan. One of the elements of Williams's interptetation plan for the estate was to remove anachronisms from the historic core. Beginning with the MVLA's ownership, the outbuildings had been used as estate offices, restrooms, maintenance shops, and storage facilities, all things that diminished the site's historical integrity. In the later years of the 1930s, these functions were moved elsewhere on the grounds, and plans were put in motion to think of reconstructing the eighteenth-century blacksmith shop that Williams had located during his excavations.[11]

A dispute with the MVLA led to Williams's dismissal in 1939. He was succeeded by Walter Macomber in 1941. Macomber's background was solidly within the nascent field of historic preservation. Prior to coming to Mount Vernon, he had served as an architect with the Colonial Williamsburg Foundation and was a well-known practioner in the field, collaborating with landscape desinger Beatrix Farrand and others. Carrying on with the tasks of his predecessor in the march toward authenticity, Macomber's hallmark contribution was the reconstruction of the greenhouse (1787) and greenhouse slave quarters (1791–92). The eighteeenth-century greenhouse and quarter complex had burned in 1835, and though some of the original walls survived, a modern greenhouse had been erected in its place. A combination of archaeological evidence of the building's foundations and the discovery of an early nineteenth-century insurance document worked in tandem to ensure one of the most authentic reconstructions undertaken by the MVLA during the postwar period.[12]

A Permanent Archaeological Program (1976–Present)

Macomber's service at Mount Vernon ended in 1976 with one of his last projects, a continuation of the search for evidence to restore the blacksmith shop. Despite the archaeolgical work that he undertook to reveal the forge, Macomber was unable to convince the board that there was enough evidence to reconstruct the building. It is interesting to note that this juncture coincided with a period of increased archaeological fieldwork in the United States and the rise of archaeology as a professional discipline; excavations at places like Kingsmill and Carter's Grove near Williamsburg, Virginia, were establishing plantation archaeology as a subdiscipline, and academically trained students were entering the field.[13] New historical trends as well as renewed effort by the MVLA to safeguard their below-ground cultural resources resulted in a contract with the Virginia Historic Landmarks Commission to conduct a feasibility study for the establishment of an in-house archaeology program and a conditions assessment of the archaeological collections held at Mount Vernon. To complete this task, Alain C. Outlaw, the state archaeologist and chief of the Virginia Research Center for Archaeology (VRCA), began a two-year study that included both fieldwork and archival research.

When the assessment ended, some of the locations within the historic core that Williams had uncovered were revisited and new discoveries were made, including a cellar for the "House for Families" slave quarter. Archaeologists also delineated twenty-four previously unknown sites on the MVLA's acreage with dates ranging from prehistory to the twentieth century.[14] Several recommendations were proposed in the VRCA report, foremost among them being immediate excavation work in the historic area to mitigate features that would suffer from the installation of new infrastructure. The research initiatives that Outlaw proposed and the promise of new avenues for exploration were sufficient to revive interest in a permanent program, which became a reality in 1987. In keeping with the commitment of the board members to safeguard and preserve Mount Vernon, Mrs. Clifton M. Bockstoce, vice regent for Connecticut, provided the funds to establish the program.[15]

Mount Vernon's archaeology program began its work under the direction of Dennis Pogue, and a combination of mitigation and research-driven excavations took place. In 1994, the program was transformed into the Department of Restoration—a body consisting of personnel trained as archaeologists, architectural historians, and conservators. Under this department, archaeological research designs with specific focus on plantation slavery, explorations of Washington's entrepreneurial pursuits, and the Washington family at home resulted in building reconstructions and replicas, as well as revising the historical narrative about life at Mount Vernon. Legacy archaeological projects on the estate's historic core included revisiting the blacksmith shop (1987–90); exploring the fruit garden and vineyard enclosure (1988–91); and completing excavation of the House for Families cellar (1989–90), the south grove midden (1990–93), the dung repository (1992–94), and the upper garden (2005–2010). Mount Vernon archaeologists also investigated the grounds surrounding a gristmill that was operated by Washington, uncovering the foundations to a whiskey distillery that has since been reconstructed based on archaeological and architectural research.[16]

As the archaeology program at Mount Vernon matured, efforts toward applying data from the archaeological and historical records led to the authentic reconstructions of the blacksmith shop and dung repository to support the estate's mission to interpret the historic area to the benchmark year of 1799. The archaeology staff took the lead in developing the Pioneer Farm site, a living history demonstration area south of the historic core, developed in 1996 to showcase Washington's abilities as an agricultural innovator; the main feature of this complex is a faithful replica of a sixteen-sided wheat treading barn that was on Washington's Dogue Run Farm and no longer extant. A slave cabin was also built on the site based on gathered archaeological and photographic evidence from Mount Vernon and elsewhere and furnished accordingly based on recovered artifacts in 2007.[17]

In 2012, the Department of Restoration was folded into the newly formed Department of Historic Preservation and Collections, representing the programs of archaeology, architecture, horticulture, collections management, and object curation. Within the new department framework, the archaeology program's mission to safeguard the estate's below-ground cultural resources and disseminate findings to the public to the highest standard remains in step with the program's founding.[18] Although much has been undertaken since 1987, the statement Morley Williams made eighty years ago still has weight behind it, and excavations on Mount Vernon's grounds have much to reveal. While the current research focus of the archaeology program is to fill in the gaps in the historical development of the historic core, a plan is underway to investigate the eight-thousand-acre extent of Washington's holdings, and to do so does not always involve excavation. What follows is a discussion of the landscape research initiatives and efforts toward viewshed preservation that the archaeology program is carrying out currently.

The Cultural Landscape

In 1751, a nineteen-year-old George Washington was abroad on the Caribbean island of Barbados with his ailing older brother, Lawrence. This trip was noteworthy primarily because it was the only time Washington traveled internationally. It was also significant because of the journal he kept, recording his daily activities, shedding light on the future commander and statesman's values. On November 5, Washington's entry relates, "In the cool of the evening we rode out accompanied by Mr. Carter to seek lodgings in the country, as the Doctor advised, and were perfectly enraptured with the beautiful prospects, which every side presented to our view—the fields of cane, corn, fruit-trees, &c. in a delightful green. We returned without accomplishing our intentions."[19] For Washington, the aesthetic of an improved, agricultural landscape was a thing of incredible beauty, and over the four decades of his ownership of Mount Vernon, he worked to leave his imprint on the land. His inheritance of the plantation and expansion of land holdings increased his agricultural production, in turn leading to his ascendancy among Virginia's landed gentry. Periods of warfare hampered the transformation of Mount Vernon from a marginally productive farm to an English-style country estate, and throughout the 1770s and 1780s, Washington guided his farm managers toward shaping the land on his terms and design.

A visit to Mount Vernon today takes a visitor by automobile or boat transportation to the MVLA's preseved estate; the George Washington Memorial Parkway connects the site to points north, and those arriving by boat may travel aboard the "Spirit of Mount Vernon" from Washington, DC. If a visitor approaches from the nearby interstate highway system from either the north or the south, portions of U.S. Route 1 are traversed. This roadway follows sections of old colonial roads that would have been used by Washington and his neighbors and connects with Mount Vernon Memorial Highway, providing a direct route to the estate and intersecting with the parkway. Along this route are modern subdivisions, with names like Gristmill Woods, Union Farm, Mount Vernon Forest, Sulgrave Manor, and West Gate—all located on Washington's former eight thousand acres and all references to historic Mount Vernon–related places (or in the case of Sulgrave Manor, the Washington family's ancestral home in England). The area surrounding Mount Vernon abounds with landmarks and lore of Washington's ownership of the place, where the legacy of one individual is the defining characteristic of this small section of the county.

Studies of people, relationships, and interaction with land are common in humanities fields such as anthropology, history, and geography and require a multidisciplinary approach to understanding landscapes of the past and the memories with which they are imbued. The research of archaeologists Cornelius Holtorf and Howard Williams on the relationships between landscape and memory suggest a need to explore how "memories (including mythologies and genealogies, as well as cultural, community, and personal histories) were inherited . . . through landscapes." Individuals, wittingly or unwittingly, leave on the land "prospective memory," which may endure over generations and which is certainly the case of the area encompassing Mount Vernon.[20] For example, a donation website for the Neighborhod Friends of Mount Vernon (a local group who provides support for major projects at the estate) reads, "Do you live on one of George Washington's original Five Farms in the 22308, 22309 or 22121 ZIP codes? If so, join this exclusive group of supporters, the Neighborhood Friends of Mount Vernon with benefits that you and your family can enjoy throughout the year!"[21] This statement draws on the cultural capital that residents place on living on Washington's former property, attaching modern homeowners to the history of the place. Landowners in the surrounding area frequently contact Mount Vernon with queries about how land where their property sits was used:

> We live in a neighborhood that used to be George Washington's property. We recently moved to a new home. The home has a large wooded area in the backyard that has overgrown over the years and wasn't utilized by the previous owners. While exploring this area recently, I discovered a well that seems to be very old. It is about 42 inches in diameter and about 20 feet deep. It is filled with water. I don't know the origins of the well and have no idea if it has any historical significance. It is not on our survey. I have no reason to believe it dates to George Washington, but thought I would check and see if you have any records of such a well around this property. We live in the [name omitted] subdivision at [address omitted]. Thank you in advance for your assistance.[22]

Although more often than not these questions of validation lead to dead ends, they afford us a unique opportunity to educate others about Washington's plantation and how the land has changed over time.

Despite the radical changes that have been made to the Mount Vernon plantation landscape since the eighteenth century, we have the ability to determine what it may have looked like and to engage in research like Holtorf and Williams suggest. Through studying the "cultural landscape"—the terrain modified to a cultural set of plans ranging from a small homelot, gardens, and field systems to neighborhoods that all "bear the imprint of a shared set of values"—Washington's plantation in its entirety becomes more tangible. According to archaeologist James F. Deetz, "The cultural landscape is the largest and most pervasive artifact in which we as archaeologists must deal, yet much remains to be done, and much thinking about the ways to do it must be indulged."[23] The two case studies that follow draw on cultural landscape studies as we focus on the macro scale of the plantation through surveying the site of Mount Vernon's slave cemetery and the preservation of place through efforts to save Washington's view from the eastern vantage of Mount Vernon across the Potomac River.

Mount Vernon's Slave Cemetery and the Plantation Neighborhood

Constraints of scale are paramount when considering George Washington's cultural landscape. As architectural historian Dell Upton has observed, "A thorough understanding of the early Virginia scene requires concurrent analysis of both the gentry world and overlapping lower-class sphere, for gentry, poor whites, and slaves often shared the same physical structures but constructed very different mental landscapes from them." The two levels of landscape comprehension based on class lines require the observer to read the physical signals in the environment, experienceing it across space and time. Traveling through Virginia in 1795, architect Benjamin Henry Latrobe asked a slave for directions to a nearby plantation. The instructions were bewildering to him, requiring Latrobe to "make minute enquiry after all the byeroads and turnings which I am to avoid. By this mode of enquiry I in general astonish my directors by discoveries of difficulties they never thought of before."[24] The slave's descriptions of a patchwork collection of fields, farm lanes,

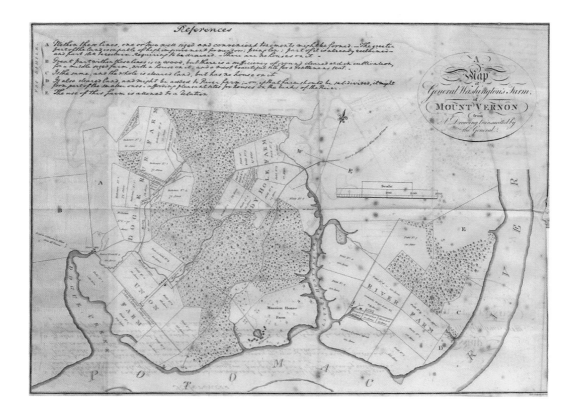

George Washington's
map of his five farms,
1793. (MVLA)

waterways, and fences ran counter to Latrobe's notion of a systematic, ordered route where clear boundaries marking possesion and control were the norm.

The landscape that confounded Latrobe presents a challenge to visually represent the world of the enslaved population who provided the bulk of Mount Vernon's labor force. When George Washington's Five Farms Map of 1793 is viewed in this context, the agricultural fields, slave quarters, and barn sites are all clearly

LUKE J. PECORARO

defined. Similarly, the roadways that crossed through Washingotn's holdings are depicted, as are secondary pathways, differentiated by a lighter-weight line stroke.

One noticeable element that is very clear from the map is the large expanse of land forested in the middle of the Mount Vernon neck. This forest seperated four of Washington's five farms from one another, with at least three of the primary roads traversing this space. If we take Latrobe's obervations at face value, there were likely smaller paths and alternative circulation routes that were used by plantation tenants, the enslaved population, and perhaps even Washington himself. These in-between spaces on the landscape often escaped notice but were used nonetheless, and occasionally were locations where the enslaved population established cemeteries. With sets of slave quarters on each of the five farms, we have not yet positively identified any cemeteries associated with these quarters, which likely existed for the occupants.[25]

On Mansion House Farm (largely controlled by the MVLA), a slave cemetery exists approximately five hundred yards south of George Washington's "New Tomb." Historical documentation on this place is sparse; there are no known references from Washington's writings, and the first records we have come from nineteenth-century visitor accounts.[26] Oral history suggests that William "Billy" Lee, Washington's body servant during the Revolutionary War, was buried there around 1828, and that the final internment occurred in 1863 when West Ford, a slave of Bushrod Washington's who was freed in 1829, passed away.[27] In the more recent past, a memorial placed by the MVLA in 1929 to the memory of the enslaved population was dedicated, and another was placed in 1983 consisting of a brick archway heading a gravel pathway that leads to a sunken ring of three circles. On each circle are inscribed the words "Faith," "Hope," and "Love." At the center of the memorial stands an incomplete column bearing the inscription, "In Memory of the Afro Americans Who Served as Slaves at Mount Vernon, This Monument Marking Their Burial Ground Dedicated September 21, 1983, Mount Vernon Ladies' Association."

Despite the memorialization, there was little investigative work on the site to determine the cemetery's extent and number of burials present until the twenty-first century. In 2014, Mount Vernon archaeologists began a systematic survey to learn more about the cemetery, stripping away the topsoil to expose the outlines of graveshafts without exhuming any remains. To date, after three seasons of field-work, sixty-two burials have been located, and the eastern, northern, and southern extents are delineated; this accounts for about 40 percent of the area thought to compose the slave cemetery. This ongoing survey project has yielded a few historic artifacts, and these have a temporal range from the last quarter of the eighteenth century to the second quarter of the nineteenth century.

The timing of the visitor accounts, the two known internments, evidence from artifacts, and the location of the cemetery in relationship to Washington's New Tomb provide compelling evidence for reinterpretation. While still up for debate, a strong case can be made that the cemetery was used after Washington's death for the enslaved and free African American community who lived on the Mount Vernon estate in the nineteenth century.[28] The question of what happened to the slaves Washington emancipated in his will and those who remained in bondage under his subsequent heirs is cloudy to say the least, and archaeological investigations of the larger eight-thousand-acre landscape can illuminate the period from 1831 to 1863. While conducting research on the slave cemetery before excavation, archaeologists discovered documents in the MVLA archives referencing *another* slave burial ground off of the MVLA property but associated with the estate. A written description by MVLA research associate Worth Bailey, who in 1947 visited the cemetery, gave a few descriptions of the space, estimating that there were about twenty-five to thirty graves showing up, though most of the stone markers were broken or vandalized by neighborhood youths. Twenty years later, in 1967, the *Washington Post* reported on a cemetery near Mount Vernon that was slated for sale and development by the U.S. Plywood Corporation; ten days were allotted for descendants to claim the remains. No claims were made — the developers surveyed the bounds of the burial ground to be impacted, and a local undertaker was hired to remove the remains, reinterring them in the City of Fairfax Cemetery.

Archaeologists used Bailey's account and the newspaper piece, concluding that both referred to the same burial ground, which led to efforts to determine the site location. A visit to the county courthouse yielded the plat with an outline of where the burials had been exhumed, along with coordinate reference points. Using GIS (geographic information software), the archaeology team was able to accurately georeference the location into Mount Vernon's plantation GIS database. The geo-referenced plot of the cemetery matches the descriptions from Bailey's memo, though it lies on two lots in the suburban neighborhood of Wessynton.

Although the burial ground is no longer visible on the landscape, its rediscovery provides a reference point toward reconstructing the larger Mount Vernon planta-tion. The cemetery lies near a quarter site shown on a map from 1858 shortly after the land transfer of part of Manison House Farm to the MVLA, and the burials likely relate to that particular quarter cluster. The deployment of GIS technology and integration of historical documentation will enable Mount Vernon archaeol-ogists to explore the larger plantation landscape at periods ranging from Washing-ton's tenure to the present without immediate excavation.

Preserving Washington's View

Telling the whole story of Mount Vernon cannot be done without placing it in the context of the cultural landscape, and the preservation of this is an immense task indeed. Mount Vernon has taken steps to carefully preserve the view that George Washington enjoyed eastward into Maryland from the mansion piazza, a view that struck Latrobe as more awe-inspiring than his drive to the mansion: "Toward the east, nature has lavished magnificence. Before the portico a lawn extends on each hand from the front of the house to the edge of the riverbank. Down the steep slope trees and shrubs are thickly planted. They are kept low so as not to inter-rupt the view but merely to furnish an agreeable border to the extensive prospect beyond."[29] Latrobe's comments on the view are as appropriate today as they were 217 years ago, but the viewshed has been threatened on multiple occasions in the

1950s, 1960s, and 1980s. If development had been allowed to proceed, a much different vista would be seen today.

The program of viewshed preservation is an ongoing cooperative effort between Mount Vernon and several conservation-minded groups on the Maryland side of the Potomac. Two Maryland groups formed in the 1950s—the Moyaone Association and the Alice Ferguson Foundation—with core missions to counter an increased threat of suburban development through conservation and responsible development.[30] In 1955, a different threat came when a nearby farm directly across the river from Mount Vernon came up for sale. An oil tank farm was proposed for the 485-acre tract, but quick thinking by the Maryland conservation groups, with some help from Ohio congresswoman and MVLA vice regent Frances P. Bolton, stopped the project. Bolton bought the land outright with the intent to preserve the property as undeveloped space, but this initial purchase was just a start.

Acknowledging that future problems were likely to arise, Bolton met with Robert Straus, chairman of the Moyaone Association to discuss the Maryland organizations' plans for preserving the area. According to Straus, "We agreed that to achieve Mount Vernon's purpose and the chartered purpose of our organizations, the whole six-mile stretch of riverfront from Piscataway Bay through Marshall Hall, the Mount Vernon prospect, should be brought under control so it could not be adversely developed. We both felt this threat was quite real due to the flight from the city, the opening of suburbia, and the fact that some of this land, like that which she [Bolton] already owned at Bryan Point and the adjoining properties, would continue to be threatened by industrial or commercial development."[31] The meeting resulted in the creation of the Accokeek Foundation in 1957, incorporating the interests of the groups, with Bolton as the president from 1957 to 1976. The foundation pursued a campaign of purchasing property along the riverfront with some success, meeting with resistance at times, but steadily increasing the acreage under protection.

A serious challenge came in 1960 when the Washington Suburban Sanitary Commission (WSSC) proposed a sewage treatment plant at Mockley Point across from Mount Vernon at the mouth of Piscataway Creek. When the Accokeek Foundation approached the WSSC to reconsider the site for the plant, citing historic and conservation-related factors, the WSSC's response was "there's nothing here." The local and state government had little power to slow the process for re-evaluation, as the WSSC's operating structure allowed it to function without governmental oversight. A contentious battle ensued over the proposed plant; help was solicited from Congress to create a new national park, which was the only recourse to block efforts to develop the shoreline. A bill was proposed in which the federal government would purchase or be awarded by deed of gift 1,100 acres to be held in fee (full ownership), with an additional 2,800 acres east of the shoreline to be placed under scenic easement.[32] This bill was passed and signed into law on October 4, 1961, by President John F. Kennedy, forming what would become Piscataway National Park.

For the next seven years, additional conservation easements and land purchases were sought, and Piscataway National Park was officially dedicated in 1968. Although the ensuing decades brought other challenges to the viewshed area, the cooperation between private conservation groups and the federal government is a remarkable achievement and has served as a model for subsequent parks. Today, Piscataway National Park encompasses 4,695 acres managed entirely by conservation foundations and private citizens. The Accokeek Foundation, for example, controls two hundred acres, overseeing a small educational farm and other conservation-related programs. Mount Vernon's efforts to support the institutions who manage the land is ongoing as the MVLA seeks to be an active voice in development of the viewshed area, further supporting the visual preservation of the cultural landscape.

This essay has introduced the growth of Mount Vernon's archaeology program and the strategies being deployed to understand Washington's plantation outside of the MVLA borders through cultural landscape study. The way the plantation grew, the farms and appurtenances of the neighbors that George Washington bought out, and the rerouting of neighborhood circulation roads to get to Mount Vernon composed a radically different landscape from that of today. If development had occurred on the east side of the Potomac in Maryland, the viewshed would have changed significantly as well. The MVLA's important first step toward preserving a portion of Washington's Home Farm in 1858 laid the foundations for studying the cultural landscape, but there is much more still to accomplish.

Landscape architect Charles Birnbaum writes, "Reading the landscape, like engaging in archival research, requires a knowledge of the resource and subject area as well as a willingness to be skeptical. As with archival research, it may involve serendipitous discoveries. Evidence gained from reading the landscape may confirm or contradict other findings and may encourage the observer and the historian to re-visit both primary and secondary sources with a fresh outlook. Landscape investigation may also stimulate other forms of research and survey, such as oral histories or archeological investigations, to supplement what appeared on-site."[33] Exploring the cultural landscape from a digital perspective enables us to become stewards of the entire eight thousand acres of farmland, which is an exciting prospect for strengthening the site's cultural context. The landscape is complex, and in order to understand it as a lasting legacy of George Washington, it needs to be approached on different scales across time—holistically and not piecemeal. With more tools and technologies at our disposal, we are poised to take further steps to better understand Washington's Mount Vernon and his neighborhood.

Notes

1. Morley J. Williams, "Report of Morley Jeffers Williams," MVLA, Minutes, 1937, 47.

2. John Milner and Associates, *Mount Vernon Estate and Gardens: Cultural Landscape Study,* 2 vols. (Charlottesville, VA: John Milner and Associates, 2004).

3. Lorena S. Walsh, "Slavery and Agriculture at Mount Vernon," in *Slavery at the Home of George Washington,* ed. Phillip J. Schwarz (Mount Vernon, VA: MVLA, 2001), 47.

LUKE J. PECORARO

4. David McCullough, "Keynote Address," September 27, 2013, NLSGW, Mount Vernon, VA.

5. William H. Holmes, *Stone Implements of the Potomac-Chesapeake Tidewater Province: Extract from the Fifteenth Annual Report of the Bureau of Ethnology* (Washington, DC: U.S. Government Printing Office, 1897), 79.

6. Alain C. Outlaw, "Exploring Mount Vernon's Buried Past: A Study of the Potential for Archaeological Research" (Virginia Research Center for Archaeology for the MVLA, unpublished report, September 1984).

7. Dennis J. Pogue, "Preserving and Restoring Mount Vernon," in *The Mount Vernon Ladies' Association: 150 Years of Restoring George Washington's Home,* ed. Stephen MacLeod (Mount Vernon, VA: MVLA, 2010), 128–34.

8. See Carl R. Lounsbury, "New History in Old Buildings," this volume.

9. Dennis J. Pogue, "Archaeology at George Washington's Mount Vernon, 1931–1987" (Dennis J. Pogue for the MVLA, unpublished report, 1987).

10. Ibid., 3.

11. Ibid., 6.

12. Pogue, "Preserving and Restoring Mount Vernon," 129.

13. See Lounsbury, "New History in Old Buildings," and Carter L. Hudgins, "Mount Vernon and America's Historic House Museums," this volume.

14. Outlaw, "Exploring Mount Vernon's Buried Past," 58.

15. Pogue, "Preserving and Restoring Mount Vernon," 133.

16. Dennis J. Pogue and Esther C. White, "Archaeology at Mount Vernon," in *Encyclopedia Virginia* (Virginia Foundation for the Humanities, 2016), https://www.encyclopediavirginia.org/Archaeology_at_Mount_Vernon.

17. Rather than review all the work undertaken by Mount Vernon's archaeology program to date, this essay is focused on current efforts and the direction the program is taking. Several reports, monographs, journal articles, and other peer-reviewed works have been undertaken on the same subject matter. See Pogue, "Archaeology at George Washington's Mount Vernon"; Dennis J. Pogue, "Mount Vernon: Transformation of an 18th-Century Plantation System," in *Historical Archaeology of the Chesapeake,* ed. Paul Shackel and Barbara Little (Washington, DC: Smithsonian Institution Press, 1994), 101–14; Dennis J. Pogue, "Slave Lifeways at Mount Vernon: An Archaeological Perspective," in *Slavery at the Home of George Washington,* ed. Phillip J. Schwarz (Mount Vernon, VA: MVLA, 2001), 110–35; Dennis J. Pogue, "The Domestic Architecture of Slavery at George Washington's Mount Vernon," *Winterthur Portfolio* 37,

no. 1 (2002): 3–22; Dennis J. Pogue, "Archaeology at George Washington's Mount Vernon, 1931–2006," *Quarterly Bulletin of the Archaeological Society of Virginia* 4 (2006): 165–75; Dennis J. Pogue, Esther C. White, and Eleanor E. Breen, "Digging for Trash and Finding Treasure at Mount Vernon," *Magazine Antiques* 168, no. 3 (2005): 88–95; James C. Rees, "Preservation: The Ever-Changing Frontier," in *George Washington's Mount Vernon,* ed. Wendell Garrett (New York: Monacelli Press, 1998), 218–44; Esther C. White, "Reconstruction Dilemmas at George Washington's Blacksmith Shop," in *The Reconstructed Past: Reconstructions in the Public Interpretation of Archaeology and History,* ed. John H. Jameson (Walnut Creek, CA: AltaMira Press, 2004), 77–89; and Morley J. Williams, "Washington's Changes at Mount Vernon Plantation," *Landscape Architecture* 28, no. 2 (1938): 63–73.

18. From the Mount Vernon Archaeology Program description, the mission is to preserve and maintain Mount Vernon to the highest standards applicable in the related fields of archaeology, collections management, and historic preservation. In addition to managing the below-ground cultural resources, Mount Vernon is committed to preserving the historic landscapes and viewsheds. To fulfill this goal Mount Vernon uses research and data sets to advocate for the restoration or reconstruction of appropriate buildings and features on the estate to enhance the authenticity of the visitor experience. In support of these efforts, Mount Vernon conducts research pertaining to all aspects of the Mount Vernon estate, and as a consequence of preservation activities generates and curates archaeological artifact collections as a resource for research and education.

19. Jared Sparks, ed., *The Writings of George Washington,* vol. 2 (Boston: Hilliard, Gray, 1834), 424.

20. Cornelius Holtorf and Howard Williams, "Landscapes and Memories," in *The Cambridge Companion to Historical Archaeology,* ed. Dan Hicks and Mary C. Beaudry (Cambridge: Cambridge University Press, 2006), 237, 244.

21. MVLA, "Compare Neighborhood Friends Membership Levels," http://www.mountvernon.org/membership/benefits/neighborhood-friends.

22. Anonymous, personal correspondence, November 29, 2012.

23. James F. Deetz, "Prologue: Landscapes as Cultural Statements," in *Earth Patterns: Essays in Landscape Archaeology,* ed. William M. Kelso and Rachel Most (Charlottesville: University Press of Virginia, 1990), 2, 4.

24. Quoted in Dell Upton, "Imagining the Early Virginia Landscape," in Kelso and Most, eds., *Earth Patterns,* 74.

25. Esther C. White, "The Landscape of Enslavement: His Space, Their Places, " in *Lives*

Bound Together: Slavery at George Washington's Mount Vernon, ed. Susan P. Schoelwer (Mount Vernon, VA: MVLA, 2016), 89–93.

26. One such account reads, "Observing some servants busy in a little grove, in front of the new tomb, we went thither. They were enclosing with a paling a grave very neatly sodded, and some sweet briar was still clinging to its native turf upon it. It was the grave of a favorite servant, an aged colored woman, whose good and amiable character had won respect and regard.—'When did she die?' we enquired. 'She parted from us last Sunday,' was the reply. There are many graves in the grove, and one of the servants pointed out that of Washington's favorite servant, who was with him in his campaigns, fulfilling his simple duties faithfully and affectionately. The spot is not forgotten, though the tramp of passing years has leveled the little mound. Nor was the humble cemetery a mournful spot: the birds were singing merrily in the trees, and the hand of Spring was molding the wild flower, and training vines over the graves." "Visit to Mount Vernon," *Western Literary Messenger,* May 2, 1846, 201.

27. Joseph A. Downer, "Interim Report on the Summer/Fall 2015 Slave Cemetery Excavation (44FX116)" (Joseph A. Downer for the MVLA, unpublished report, 2016).

28. See Scott E. Casper, "Saving Mount Vernon, in Black and White," this volume.

29. Benjamin H. Latrobe, *The Journal of Latrobe* (New York: D. Appleton, 1905), 52.

30. Robert W. Straus, *The Possible Dream: Saving George Washington's View* (Accokeek, MD: Accokeek Foundation, 1988), 16.

31. Ibid., 22.

32. Ibid., 34, 37.

33. Charles Birnbaum, *Protecting Cultural Landscapes: Planning, Treatment and Management of Historic Landscapes* (Washington, DC: U.S. Government Printing Office, 1994), 19.

Mount Vernon's Historic Building Information Management System

Digital Strategies for Preservation in the Twenty-First Century

ROBERT L. FINK, THOMAS A. REINHART, AND ALYSON STEELE

The care and management of historic properties require systematically utilizing a wide range of data on a timely basis. No single source of information is adequate; the conscientious steward must access and synthesize reliable information from many diverse sources. Primary source documentation illuminates the intentions of the owner, builders, and inhabitants, while historical surveys, analyses, preservation drawings, and reports contain the collective knowledge of prior generations of stewards and demonstrate the myriad outlooks and techniques utilized in past preservation efforts. Surviving interior and exterior building elements of all types provide opportunities to directly engage with and assess historic materials and configurations, shedding light on forgotten original details or attesting to gradual changes due to settlement, weathering, and wear over time. The efficient access, use, and update of all such relevant information is crucial to effective stewardship. Stewards must also record from the field, where repair and research projects expose building and site elements temporarily and offer time-sensitive windows for exploration. The streamlined integration and organization of all documentation into existing data structures ensures successful transmission to future caretakers. Likewise, facilitated access to all data increases the ability to provide accurate information and interpretation to a wide range of audiences.

Mount Vernon's significance was known during George Washington's lifetime, and the plantation began to be officially maintained as a historic site a little more than sixty years after his death. This unusually long history as a consciously preserved site means that the volume of relevant records and generations of documentation amassed surrounding the origin and preservation of the estate's resources is significantly greater than that for many American historic structures or landscapes. We envisioned and developed Mount Vernon's historic building information management (HBIM) system out of a need to organize and utilize this vast archive, to capture a large historic landscape with many significant structures and site features, and to preserve an ever-growing record of staff preservation and maintenance efforts.

Stewardship in the Information Age

It is estimated that 90 percent of the world's information today has been generated in the last two years.[1] The efficiency afforded by digital technologies has significantly simplified the production of new information. As little as thirty years ago, architectural drawings were produced by hand using ink and Mylar, photographs required film, and reports were still principally written on typewriters. This manual recordation and production produced fewer documents than in today's era of computer-aided drafting (CAD), digital photography, and electronic word processing. Today's digital revolution also dramatically increases the access and use of historic data as existing analog information is made more accessible through digitization; the process, in turn, spurs more research, which creates more information. Historic preservation, while not always at the forefront of technological development, has keep pace in the digital revolution by adopting and adapting technologies that may have been developed for entirely unrelated reasons. As the field produces more and more digital data pertaining to historic properties, the way that data is managed and made available is a critical challenge to the long-term stewardship and viability of historic places.

The first major tool to bring architectural preservation into the digital age was computer-aided drafting. Two-dimensional CAD provides a robust means to develop and manage dimensional information about a place that could be scaled and used for a myriad of analytical, planning, design, and documentary purposes. The replication of two-dimensional forms as the basis for consistently addressing the issues associated with management of a historic site was invaluable. The subsequent development of three-dimensional modeling has improved the ability to visualize and document the construction logic of a building. As a virtual representation, three-dimensional modeling gives the viewer the ability to see through solid surfaces, revealing conditions and relationships outside of our usual experience. The power of this super visualization is considerable. Even so, it pales in comparison with the usefulness and power of a tool that combines visualization with relevant and usable information within the three-dimensional context.

Building information modeling (BIM) is that tool. BIM combines the super visualization of three-dimensional modeling with a database of information about the model's built elements. Like CAD, BIM was developed for architects and engineers designing new construction. It is, however, obvious that the utility of accessing building data visually is similarly applicable to the work of preserving historic structures.

Stewardship Challenges at George Washington's Mount Vernon

Given Washington's position in history and the role of Mount Vernon as one of the first historic house museums in the United States, the estate contends with an unusual set of challenges. Mount Vernon enjoys an annual visitation of over one million people and is open 365 days a year. These factors place continued stress on the site, place constraints on how and when restoration and maintenance work can be carried out, and necessitate that all work be done efficiently in order to minimize disruption for visitors. Project research is carried out in advance of work, but questions requiring additional investigation routinely arise as work progresses. Preservation staff rely on a number of varied record types to prepare for and respond to restoration work.

Eighteenth-century records are the primary source for knowledge of the construction, use, and alteration of Mount Vernon's cultural resources during Washington's lifetime. The first president was a prolific correspondent and meticulous record-keeper, and due to his continued prominence in the history of the United States, his papers have been preserved largely intact, if somewhat scattered. After careful preservation of them during his public life, Washington's hope to organize his papers for posterity never materialized. Bushrod Washington, George Washington's nephew, inherited the archive, which was fairly complete with the exception of the private letters between the general and Martha Washington. The archive was slowly dispersed in the beginning of the nineteenth century, and the bulk of it was sold to the U.S. Department of State by George Corbin Washington in two transactions in 1833 and 1844. Thus, the Library of Congress, where the corpus eventually ended up, holds the largest single collection of Washington's papers, amounting to approximately 65,000 items.[2] The distribution that occurred before the acquisition of the papers by the federal government means there are items in collections, public and private, worldwide; the MVLA itself owns about a thousand documents written or received by George and Martha Washington.[3]

Washington's voluminous letters were published in thirty-nine volumes starting in 1931 as part of the bicentennial celebration of Washington's birth.[4] In 1968, a collaboration between the University of Virginia and the MVLA launched the publication not only of letters Washington wrote (as did the 1931–44 endeavor) but also letters he received, as well as all other documents attributed to him, a total of 140,000 items. The project produced six hardcopy series between 1976 and 2017, representing sixty-three of a projected ninety volumes. Beginning in 2004, the project began digitizing the fifty-five volumes published at that point, as the Papers of George Washington Digital Edition (PGWDE).[5] In addition to the letters, the project is digitizing Washington's financial papers, account books, farm accounts, Mount Vernon ledgers, various property inventories, and store accounts.[6] The sundry document types provide information on life and work at Mount Vernon during the eighteenth century, often recording specifics of construction and decorative arts that have provided great detail to the HBIM model and database. Additional sources of information on eighteenth-century Mount Vernon include the papers of Martha Washington and reminiscences of the Washingtons' grandchildren. Mount Vernon was a pilgrimage site during Washington's lifetime and only became more popular after his death; numerous visitor accounts have survived.[7]

Records from the nineteenth century convey information concerning Mount Vernon after the general's death in 1799. The personal papers of the Washington heirs, Bushrod, John Augustine II, and John Augustine III, are not completely transcribed, but those that have been record more than half a century of upkeep and some alteration. Such information provides dated points in the historic record that can be tied to events identified in the historic fabric of the structures and landscape, such as paint campaigns or the erection of new structures, thereby helping to sort out undated work.

The archives of the MVLA begin with the creation of the association in the 1850s and provide more than 160 years of history of the preservation of the property. Once the plantation was recognized and protected by the MVLA, documentation of the estate was prepared professionally through careful surveys and measured drawings. Intensive survey and photographic documentation efforts expanded the archive in the 1930s, as has ongoing research, investigation, and construction documentation associated with repair and stabilization efforts throughout the decades.

The history of how the MVLA has approached preservation over time, and approached their documentation of preservation activities, can be traced through a number of documents and collections. The archive includes early correspondence of the MVLA, which contains a great deal of information about early preservation philosophy and work. Minutes of council meetings and annual reports give summaries of restorations and maintenance work, while financial documents track materials and labor on restoration projects. Departmental files for collections and restoration contain decades of reports, photographs, and drawings. Of particular note is a large collection of architectural drawings of the mansion and outbuildings from the nineteenth and twentieth centuries, as well as the early superintendents' records of Colonels J. McHenry Hollingsworth (1872–85) and Harrison Howell Dodge (1885–1937).

Mount Vernon also has two comprehensive reports that have provided important resource analysis and been a first stop for any research on the mansion or the landscape. The 1993 historic structure report for the mansion, compiled by Mesick-Cohen-Waite Architects, offers a summary of thought about the condition and history of the building over time. John Milner Associates' 2004 cultural landscape studies created all-encompassing narratives of the plantation and began to unify the naming conventions for buildings and places throughout the estate. Both works detail the history of Mount Vernon through the twentieth century.[8]

In addition to the historical records in the archive, Mount Vernon's Department of Historic Preservation and Collections' care of the resources on the estate is constantly producing new documentation, often through the application of new technology. Supplemental research and testing, such as ongoing archeological investigations, ground-penetrating radar, paint analysis, dendrochronology, high-resolution photography, and infrared photography, have produced a better understanding of specific resources and produced additional documentation. Since 2013, point clouds at the scale of the landscape (LiDAR), buildings, and architectural details (laser scans) have become a new source of information to help understand the natural and cultural systems throughout the estate.

What Is Mount Vernon's HBIM System?

Recognizing the need for more efficient access to Mount Vernon's vast amount of data, the institution's historic preservation staff created the HBIM system, the first known application of BIM technology to an historic structure. The HBIM system is a powerful tool for the management of historic resources and landscapes that provides the ability to fluently use and update reliable information in order to make good stewardship decisions. It is an elegantly structured, three-dimensional, searchable database that organizes data spatially, functioning essentially as a three-dimensional virtual file cabinet containing all documentary information about George Washington's Mansion House, associated buildings, landscapes, and infrastructure. Two commercially available software programs combine to make the system: Autodesk Revit, a three-dimensional building information modeling software that has an associated database, and Esri ArcGIS, a geographic information system used to create maps and compile and analyze geographic data.

The HBIM tool provides the ability to understand and organize information according to spatial frames of reference, such as location, scale, orientation, and repetition as well as analytical frames, such as period, name, manufacturer, and other data. The database is tailored to reflect the configuration, materiality, stewardship traditions, and anticipated needs of preservation staff within a holistic structure that can accommodate future adaptations and enhancements. While BIM has traditionally referred to information management associated with buildings alone, the development of the HBIM system has introduced the ability to integrate building and landscape information into a unified geographic information system (GIS) data environment. Through this unified environment, preservation staff can gain continuity in the management of stewardship information for architectural, archaeological, and landscape resources.

The Proof of Concept: The New Room

In 2013, Mount Vernon established a dedicated architecture division tasked with the preservation and documentation of its thirty-two historic and reproduction buildings. One of the goals of the new division was to explore the idea of utilizing BIM's full potential for this task. The objective was to adapt the technology to document, understand, and manage one of the nation's most important historic resources and to organize and streamline the use of the large quantity of documentation available. With this in mind, Mount Vernon partnered with Quinn Evans Architects (QEA) to attempt the creation of the world's first HBIM system. QEA brought a quantity of experience in the use of BIM and a longstanding partnership with Mount Vernon, having designed the reconstructions of Washington's threshing barn (1996) and distillery (2006), both using three-dimensional software.

The concept of creating three-dimensional models of buildings from laser scans has become fairly common, mostly through the efforts of CyArk, a nonprofit organization dedicated to preserving digitally cultural heritage sites through laser scanning.[9] Other institutions have championed the concept of creating a library of parametric historic components created from pattern books for incorporation into a processed point cloud of a structure; this idea was discussed as early as 2006, under the name of HBIM.[10] But these only created models, used for visualization of building surfaces and sometimes for preserving documentation of conditions or integrating limited diagnostic data, such as thermography, into the model.[11]

In 2014, Mount Vernon and QEA established a team to execute a pilot project on the HBIM concept using the mansion as the subject but with its north wing as the focus. The north wing was the focal point of the project because it contained the New Room, the large, first-story saloon room that had just reopened after a two-year restoration. The restoration project produced an extensive amount of research on the New Room, and that data was ready-made for integration in the proposed HBIM system. The goal of the project was to go beyond a simple three-dimensional model. The superior ability to generate digital geometry made Autodesk Revit the right choice for creating a model, but the team also wanted to maximize the power of BIM by utilizing Revit's ability to associate data with building elements. The idea of "retrofitting" BIM to a historic structure and utilizing the power of the program to manage both the preservation management of the building and the associated historical documentation had never been attempted.

The proposed HBIM concept posed some challenges. Revit's geometry access is limited to a select few who are trained in the program, so it was desirable to develop a more accessible interface that communicates with Revit to allow wider access to the model and its associated data, preferably through a web browser. The HBIM system was envisioned to serve several user groups with differing informational and functional needs. Despite the desire to provide access to a wide and diverse user community, not all members of that community should have the same access nor permission to make changes. While preservation staff need full access to all functions—modeling, data entry, and retrieval, including all types of data—other user groups, such as history interpreters, only need access to limited portions of the system. This need for controlled access made an interface even more necessary. The desired functionalities of the user interface were similar to the functions available on GIS, where a wide range of users can access data appropriate to a user's needs and role. Investigation into programs that demonstrated the desired integration and functionality became one of the pilot's priorities, but the development of a final user interface was not.

The team identified key functional priorities for the HBIM system pilot, including

- Accurately represent current conditions of resource location, size, and configuration, with the level of detail of modeled information dependent on available data, with greatest level of detail in the New Room focus area;
- Accurately represent current conditions of spatial relationships between landscape and building resources;
- List or graphically sort resource elements by historic installation date or period;
- List or graphically sort resource elements by other custom data as outlined in the data tree/branch diagrams;
- Provide access and viewing of up to three reference documents per element in Revit in which the first document may be a photo;

- Deliver the system as a dedicated directory with stable, prescribed file structure and naming on the Mount Vernon system;
- Provide the ability to pull and push custom data from the model as outlined in the data tree/branch diagrams;
- Be searchable by element metadata;
- Protect inherent model parameters and data from corruption and accidental modifications; and
- Demonstrate potential use for landscape analysis and landscape resource stewardship.

Creating the Model

The HBIM system consists of two principal parts, the model and the supporting data structure. Development of both progressed in tandem. The model began with data collected from a variety of sources, each with its own characteristic strengths to inform the as-built construction of the mansion. The various types of data included both digital and analog media. One of the most valuable data sets early in the modeling process was point clouds. A point cloud is a three-dimensional digital file of known points in space that represent the surface of a physical object. The points are generated with a laser scanner, which emits thousands of beams of light that hit the surface of an object and bounce back to the scanner; the scanner then locates each surface point based on the time each beam of light takes to travel out and back. Scans are taken from several vantage points, and then the captured points are registered to align the scans to their proper relationship to one another.

The team scanned the mansion to the greatest extent possible. Locations such as the exterior and individual rooms within the mansion were relatively straightforward to capture. But areas more difficult to access, such as attic spaces and an interstitial space between the New Room ceiling and the floor of the room above, were also captured. These hard-to-get scans captured many elements of the building's frame and proved to be invaluable when modeling the structure of the house. Point cloud accuracy can be within a millimeter, so the resolution of the scans varied according to the space being captured. In most cases, moderate resolution was adequate, but the carved chimneypiece and ornamental plasterwork of the New Room ceiling were captured in high resolution. The resulting master point cloud was linked into Autodesk Revit.

The advantage of point clouds is the accuracy to which the surface of something can be measured. But the scan can only capture what is exposed. The underlying structure, unless exposed, cannot be captured by laser scanning. This limits the use of a point cloud for informing the representation of construction logic in the model. For what could not be captured in the scans, existing documentation, such as photographs, drawings, and field survey notes, were consulted. Fortunately, Mount Vernon has a wealth of such documentation, both historic and recent. Between the use of historic photos showing the stabilization work done to the

Palladian window,
MVLA Archives.
(MVLA)

FINK, REINHART, AND STEELE

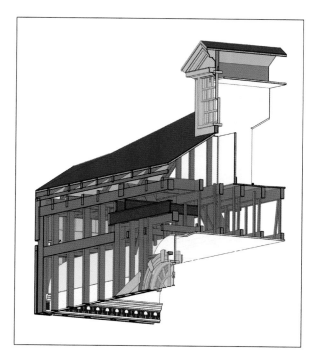

Palladian window, HBIM, 2017.
(MVLA)

mansion in the 1930s, historic survey drawings from the same period, and input from staff, an accurate model of the mansion's timber frame emerged. Photographs were essential to the basic interpretation of the point cloud. Point clouds can be difficult to read, as was the case in the attic and cellar, where cobwebs registered in the scans and obscured details of building elements. Photographs of these areas helped clarify what the scan had captured.

When modeling for an HBIM system, there is a higher demand for accuracy and detail than when modeling for modern building construction projects. The degree of accuracy, however, with which to capture the existing conditions depends on an institution's proposed use of the system and on the available supporting data. The model's purpose and the context in which the data would be accessed require prime consideration. Some institutions and projects might only use an HBIM system to track finish information and thus may not require rigorous efforts to capture construction logic. For Mount Vernon, it was considered essential to model the mansion to a very high level of accuracy, therefore each construction element was handmade. Capturing as many subtle details as reasonably possible enables the HBIM tool user to begin to interpret elements for their historical value. It certainly was not reasonable, or even possible, to model everything exactly, so the team devised a metric to inform users to what level of accuracy a particular element has been modeled as compared to the as-built condition. This metric is referred to as the Level of Development (LOD).

The LOD is represented by three numbers which correspond to three characteristics, location, shape, and material. The first numeral rates location:

1 = Approximate—Location is approximated by sight, or scaled from non-scaled drawings, or interpreted from written description.
2 = Two-dimensional—Location is correct in two dimensions, typically in plan, and is based on a reliable source, that is, measured drawings, point cloud, field verification, and so on.
3 = Three-dimensional—Location is correct in three dimensions and is based on a reliable source, that is, measured drawings, point cloud, field verification, and so on.

The second numeral rates shape:

1 = Approximate—Exact shape is unknown and is approximated by sight or scaled from nonscaled drawings or interpreted from written description.
2 = Assumed—Object shape is modeled based on an assumption, typical size, or similar known objects. As-built size information is included in the metadata associated with the object. Object shape does not reflect variations in shape due to bowing, warping, notches, and so on.

3 = Accurate—Overall object shape is correct, but the object shape does not reflect variations in shape due to bowing, warping, notches, and so on.

4 = As-built—Object shape is correct, matching the as-built condition, including variations in shape due to bowing, warping, notches, and so on.

The third numeral rates material:

1 = Generic—Material is unknown with no defining characteristics.

2 = General—General material is known: wood, plaster, paint, and so on.

3 = Specific—Specific material properties are known, such as wood species, type of stone, type of plaster, and so on.

4 = Very Specific—The majority or all physical properties of the material are known.

As development of the model progressed, validation of the model needed to occur. It must be emphasized that the validation exercise was critical to accurate modeling and the reliability of the system. When authoring the model, the team made every attempt to gather as much information about the materials and construction logic of the area of focus, but it had to make assumptions for conditions where documentation was not at hand. During the development of the model, the HBIM system team met every two weeks to review progress. This vetting process proved to be effective in making corrections to errant model conditions and for informing conditions in the model that had not yet been developed. It also spurred the retrieval of forgotten documentation records. As-built conditions were a focus of discussion, as were determinations of how accurately those conditions needed to be represented in the model. For example, doors inspired lengthy debate. Should the model represent door hardware? Is the hardware its own element or is it part of the larger door element? Some door openings have elaborate surrounds and trim: are they their own elements? The answer to these questions directly impacted not only the model but the organization of the associated data structure as well. The same held true for knowing how much detail needed to be in the model versus what information would be conveyed through linked documentation, such as photographs. Often these meetings would be followed by a visit to the house to investigate the conditions that had been reviewed that week.

At the end of the pilot, the model featured the mansion modeled to LOD 111, with the New Room and the room above it modeled to LOD 232. Since the completion of the pilot, the rest of the house has been brought up to LOD 232. It must be noted, however, that the development of the model is a perpetual process. As restoration and maintenance work on the mansion continues, incorporating newly obtained information in the model is essential. The HBIM system is never static; it will continue to change with our state of knowledge.

The team also devised a system to assign to each element in the model a unique mark that becomes an identifying tag for that element and the means by which to link all relevant documentation. For those familiar with Mount Vernon's preservation history, the mark conveys the spatial location, type, and sequence of the object itself. This is because the mark is a logically constructed fifteen-digit moniker that indicates the element's type, location, and identity within the sequence of Mount Vernon's preservation history. For the uninitiated, the mark system is the backbone of the long-term management and searchability of the database. The marks were created with the complexity of the mansion in mind, as the system would easily accommodate the estate's smaller structures.

Each mark is composed of the building identifier, room/zone identifier, element type, separator, and sequence identifier:

• Building Identifier: The first three letters of the mark indicate the building resource to which the element belongs. For this purpose, the HBIM system uses existing abbreviations developed by Mount Vernon preservation staff for the estate's historic structures. For example, element tags within the mansion all begin with the prefix "MAN."

The Mount Vernon
Mansion, HBIM, 2017.
(MVLA)

- Room/Exterior/Zone Identifier: The next three digits of the mark indicate a designation of one of three types of elements: (1) Interior elements are designated by the room number of the room within which they are located. Room numbers begin with the digits B through 4, representing the basement through the fourth level. For example, the mansion first-floor passage is MAN101; the second-floor passage is MAN201. (2) Exterior elements are designated by the identifier 000. (3) Structural elements are designated by a three-digit identifier beginning with "9" followed by the building level and building zone to which the structural element belongs. Zones locate an element in one of the three parts of the mansion: (1) center block, (2) south wing, and (3) north wing. For example, a structural member on the second level within the south wing includes the identifier MAN922.
- Element Type Identifier: Interior, exterior, and structural element tags next indicate the type of element. Unique three-letter abbreviations for each type of anticipated element are part of the lexicon. For example, the identifier for door surround is "DSR."

- Instance Identifier: A three-digit sequence that identifies how many instances of an element there are in a given location. For example, the little parlor on the first floor has two windows, MAN105WDW001 and MAN105WDW002.
- Separator: An underscore dash separates the instance and sequence describing portions of the tag and helps provide visual legibility for the mark.
- Sequence Identifier: A three-digit numeric sequence identifier designates the element's identity within generations of iterations of repairs, which can serve Mount Vernon stewards for future generations. For example, an original door surround in the New Room would be MAN104DSR001_001 (as an original it is 001). A repair to that surround would be MAN104DSR001_002.

Structure and Organization of Associated Data

The organization of data was critical to the success of the system. As the backbone of the three-dimensional filing cabinet, the data structure needed to reflect the spatial organization of the estate, seamlessly encompassing all types of site and building elements at all scales, addressing the logic and substance of Mount Vernon's stewardship traditions, and accommodating historic and new information about diverse topics from a wide array of sources.

A key precept of the HBIM system is the organization of data spatially in accordance with how the built landscape is understood and experienced. To achieve this, the structure of its data needed to be developed with a hierarchy that addressed the physical scale, as well as the interrelationships between site and built resources. Although the project focused initially on the mansion, it quickly became clear that the HBIM system had a utility and flexibility that allowed it to handle not only a single standing structure but multiple structures set in their landscapes. The MVLA manages the estate and the related viewshed across the Potomac through GIS; early in the creation of the HBIM system, the concept of linking the structural model of the mansion into the estates GIS system became a goal.

This aim of linking the BIM into GIS meant that at top of the hierarchy of the data structure was "Washington's World." Beginning hierarchy at a global scale would allow Mount Vernon to put Washington in the context of his world, tying in his connections throughout the United States and Europe, tracking the origins of his purchases, and charting his global influence, literally taking the system worldwide. It would also open the system to data produced by scholars throughout the globe.

The next level down was the estate's viewshed across the Potomac, which since the early 1960s has been managed through a partnership of the MVLA; federal, state, and local governments; and nonprofit organizations. Next was the neighborhood, which represents the entire neck of land on which the estate sits. Most of this land was part of the eight thousand acres that comprised Mount Vernon at the end of Washington's life.

At the scale of the estate, the HBIM data structure was developed in accordance with the logic through which landscape information has been collected and organized over recent decades. It reflected the six landscape areas identified by the 2004 cultural landscape study: the Primary Washington Area, Commemorative and Interpretive Area, Service and Support Area, Parkway Terminus, Maintenance and Operations, and Peripheral and Undeveloped Areas. The Primary Washington Area encompasses the historic core of the plantation, with outbuildings, gardens, walkways, and lawns arrayed with respect to the mansion overlooking the Potomac. While this historic core represents the most urgent stewardship need for the HBIM system, the data structure was established to be able to place information about the historic core in context with the other landscape areas. Ultimately, being able to access and assess data for these areas will be useful for comparative analysis, management, and research at a local and regional scale.

Within each landscape area, data was assigned to individual buildings and landscape resources, such as the bowling green. Most of the resources and buildings have multiple vertical levels that needed to be addressed. In the case of a landscape resource, above- and belowground levels were created to address above-ground structures such as walls and fences, plantings, and so on and underground resources

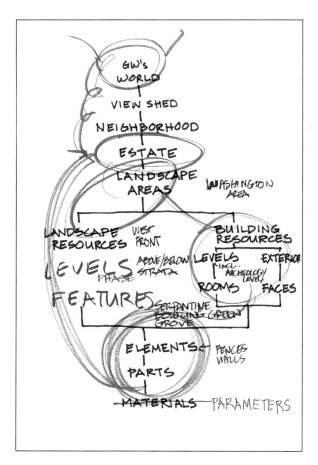

Data hierarchy and structure,
HBIM. 2017. (MVLA)

such as archaeological features or wells. In the case of buildings, there were interior
levels of multiple stories, from cellar to roof. Levels within a building were further
divided into rooms bearing identifiers like those that had been put in place for the
mansion, and landscape levels were divided into landscape features identified by
the cultural landscape study and archaeological investigations. Rooms (interiors),

FINK, REINHART, AND STEELE

faces (exteriors), and features (landscape) were subdivided into elements. Room elements, for example, include floors, walls, wainscots, doors, windows, ceilings, and cornices. Each of these subsets of a resource's construction and configuration was methodically integrated into the data structure so that relevant information may be fluently entered, accommodated, and accessed.

The structure of the data reflects the traditional understanding of how the Mount Vernon landscape has been understood. The naming of the resources, and the components and elements that comprise them, addresses the data structure as well as Mount Vernon's place naming conventions. The data structure incorporates names for Mount Vernon's places, resources, and subcomponents that reflect historical terminology. Naming conventions from Washington's papers, prior historic structures reports, the cultural landscape study, and glossary documents by Mount Vernon staff were cross-referenced with Carl Lounsbury's *Illustrated Glossary of Early Southern Architecture and Landscape*.[12]

The naming of resources and elements not only needed to be able to provide a recognizable frame of reference for people using the HBIM tool, but the approach to naming was developed in conjunction with a system of name abbreviations that can be used to create unique identifying marks for each component of the three-dimensional model. A unique identifier assigned to each component part ensured ties into standing traditions of Mount Vernon and regional feature names; the naming and identifier system was composed to become the Rosetta stone for the HBIM system as it expands and grows. All elements (interior, exterior, or landscape) were broken down into parts, the subcomponents that often explain the construction logic or material distinctions. Each of these parts has several assigned parameters. Parameters are the containers for data and information.

The model integrates two basic types of information about building elements: essential information (or parameters) and cultural information (more substantive documentation). Essential information, or the inherent properties of the building elements themselves, was embedded directly into the three-dimensional data structure hosted by Revit. It was incorporated into the system as custom data fields established by Mount Vernon preservation staff to quickly provide basic information about individual elements of the model. Parameters include date of original installation, material properties and data, associated craftsmen, manufacturers, products, repair activities, and maintenance dates. These custom parameters incorporate information from Washington's era through to the present.

Cultural information represents more substantive documentation that can be linked to elements, including historical references, photographs, analytical reports, construction and conservation information, interpretive summaries, and even myths and legends. Cultural information is associated with elements within the data structure but is hosted in another database, such as a content management system. In this way, users can quickly access basic information about the history and maintenance of an element or choose to go deeper and retrieve its complete archival record. All information thus will be readily and quickly available to guide future restorations and support ongoing stewardship at Mount Vernon.

There was a desire to communicate to users the level of confidence placed in individual pieces of documentation, just as was done with the LOD establishing the degree of confidence in the accuracy of objects in the model. This was accomplished through the creation of a similar ranking, the degree of reliability (DOR). Each generation investigated and took care of the Mount Vernon property, adding thousands of archival records, photos, surveys, and analyses organized with the singular perspective of that time. The passion and focus of each stewardship team resulted in particular achievements in the area of primary focus for each generation. Peripheral efforts or documentation from that era may not be as highly focused or may be invalidated. Thus, the documentation of each era may have high points of accurate recounting of newly understood conditions, histories, and associations. At the same time, there are examples of texts and accounts that have been discounted over time. To be truly useful, the HBIM system needs to provide a general sense of the known accuracy of the enclosed material. The DOR provides guidance on how accurate that document is known to be with respect to the element with which it is associated. It uses the following scale:

1 = Very Unreliable: the source is known to be inaccurate on multiple occasions and the data has been field-checked in the process of incorporation into the database and proven to be incorrect.

2 = Unreliable: the documentation comes from a source known to be inaccurate but has not been field-checked in the process of incorporation into the database, or there is no established record for the reliability of the source but the data has been field-checked in the process of incorporation into the database and proven inaccurate.

3 = Uncertain: there is no established record for the reliability of the source, or the source has an inconsistent record of accuracy and the data has not been field-checked in the process of incorporation into the database.

4 = Reliable: the documentation comes from a source known to be accurate but has not been field-checked in the process of incorporation into the database, or there is no established record for the reliability of the source, but the data has been field-checked in the process of incorporation into the database and proven to be accurate.

5 = Very Reliable: the documentation comes from a source known to be accurate, and the data has been field-checked in the process of incorporation into the database.

Addressing the Stewardship Challenges of Historic Museum Properties

Management and stewardship of a historic museum property involves making large and small decisions while considering the available information, balancing the protection of historic resources with the pressing institutional needs of today. Direct access to the most accurate and applicable information is the key to making sound decisions that address the balancing act between preservation and relevance for a property. Decades of historic preservation experience have taught that mistakes are made when people act on incomplete or inaccurate information, assumptions, or myths. In an irreplaceable context such as Mount Vernon, the cost of such mistakes increases the importance and value of a robust, holistic information management system, such as the HBIM system. The potential uses are myriad; however, a handful of ongoing information needs are foremost.

Visualization, communication, and coordination over space and time. For any planning and budgeting exercises, research and analysis, and refurbishment or repair activities, accurate information on massing, materials, relative ages of historic elements, and location and setting of modern infrastructure is critical. A searchable database of such information can support comparative analysis of similar elements throughout a property and provide other insights. Visualization is also critical to all these and other types of resource management activities as it delineates spatial relationships, provides volumetric information, and can allow for analysis of change in a structure over time. The HBIM tool ties together visualization and data organization in such a way as to aid these management functions

Historic stewardship. As historic resources change over time through settlement, weathering, material wear from use, and other natural processes, the ability to call up and review data by physical element can be useful. Sorting and comparing similar elements by location, age, orientation, and the like can reveal similarities and differences in how they have respectively changed over time. The impacts of location-specific activities and uses can be similarly tracked and understood.

Stewardship not only involves the physical preservation of structures; it includes public outreach and interpretation that are critical to maintaining a historic site's relevance in the public imagination. Access to historic preservation information, along with consistent, easy-to-grasp metrics regarding what information is known, conjectured, or unknown where modern elements have been incorporated into the structure, advance both the conservation and interpretive mandates of managing a public historical site. Interest in and the recognized relevance of a historic property to the public is crucial for its long-term survival. Public engagement, visitorship, and interpretation are important to maintaining that relevance. The ability to provide visualizations of alternative states such as earlier configurations and views through surfaces, over large areas, into inaccessible spaces, and even underground can bring clearer understanding of a site and encourage increased engagement with visitors. It can also allow offsite visitors to have more meaningful interactions with a historic site on the web. Along with three-dimensional imagery, the HBIM system can connect viewers with verified documentation supporting and explaining what they are experiencing.

Architectural and life safety. Using a management tool such as the HBIM system, data can be organized for reference and problem-solving. Existing condition information can be visualized in the context of the building and site resources to which they pertain. Work with local code authorities can be facilitated when needed information, such as size, volume, height, code section citations, material construction characteristics, quantification and itemization of elements of particular interest, and applicable testing results, can be easily retrieved. At the same time, meeting current building requirements—life safety codes, for example—to their letter may be physically impossible without excessive damage to character-giving historic features. A clear understanding of the age and significance of building fabric can protect important features and original materials when installing necessary modern infrastructure such as fire detection and suppression systems. In such cases, digitally mapping a route through a structure before drawing up final installation documents can save time and money. Developing and implementing innovative methods by which the intent of the codes may be met through a performance-based analysis is commonly the only way to address modern safety goals in historic facilities. In such cases, the analysis of and agreed-on means by which a historic facility meets current safety requirements is and will be key information for the next generation of facility managers responsible for public safety. If this information is lost, each generation is required to start over in the analysis and building of a systematic approach to safety in the historic setting.

Operations and emergencies. Reliable information is needed to operate historic sites responsibly and to support public visitation and long-term stewardship. Real-time information about space use, environmental conditions, material conditions,

Mansion structure,
HBIM, 2017. (MVLA)

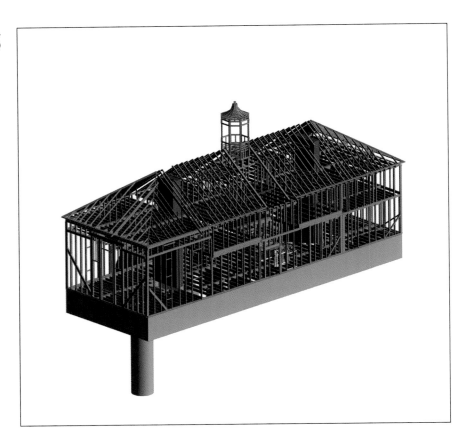

inspection records, maintenance activities, energy use, monitoring of movement, paint colors, manufacturers/model numbers, and craftwork resources all need to be updated and coordinated on a regular basis. A unified and mobile information management system can help streamline the use and management of operational information. By integrating information on the dimensions and conditions of sites and buildings within their context, the HBIM system's three-dimensional database can support realistic emergency visualization and planning exercises addressing a range of scenarios to safeguard the estate as well as visitors and staff.

Next Steps

With the mansion modeled, the proof of concept for the HBIM system established, and a data structure in place to incorporate information on all of Washington's world, there are several next steps to be taken. The development of a web-based user interface is in progress. The Esri ArcGIS database created to host the model allowed for the HBIM system to be accessed online though an Esri WebScene, a three-dimensional interactive environment used to display data.[13] Proof of concept has been successful, but integration of all desired functionality is ongoing. The web-based interface provides access to different user groups from anywhere and on multiple platforms.

Additional project goals have been identified and incorporated into the work plan of preservation staff; these include integration of landscape resource visualizations, incorporation of additional structures, establishing one or more content management systems, and continual maintenance of the HBIM system at hand.

While much of the landscape data structure was outlined during the information hierarchy discussions, putting it into practice will require a level of effort similar to what was put into the building elements. An area of interest has been identified in the estate's upper garden. It has been selected due to its scale, importance on the estate, diversity of character-defining elements, and recent restoration, which included extensive archival and archaeological research. Many of the landscape conditions that exist throughout the estate can be found in the upper garden.

Incorporating additional structures has already begun with the creation of a HBIM for the 1775 salt house, a small storage structure just to the north of the mansion. Point cloud data existed for the salt house, and its small scale made it an ideal candidate for testing on an outbuilding the data hierarchy and nomenclature

Accessing and using
the data, HBIM, 2017.
(MVLA)

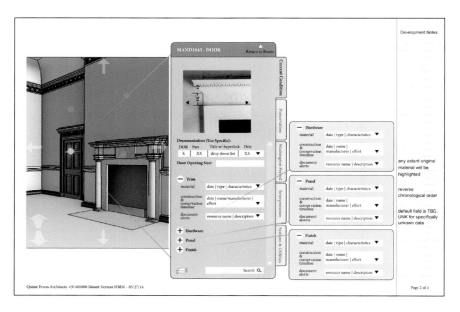

schema developed for the mansion and for integrating a second model into the
HBIM system. In addition to the mansion and the salt house, there are thirty additional historic and reconstructed buildings on the estate that have been identified
for incorporation into the HBIM system.

A key part of the system that will allow it to grow is the content management
system (CMS). Revit is powerful in that it can associate metadata with three-
dimensional data, but it is limited in the quantity of data it can manage. Revit
models can quickly become overwhelmed and unstable as more and more parameters are introduced into them. It is not reasonable to expect Revit to handle hundreds or even thousands of file associations for each element. For that, a CMS is
the right tool. Using the unique identifier assigned to each element as established
in the nomenclature guidelines, a CMS can associate as many digital records to
an element as there is digital storage space for the records. Selection of a CMS

must take into account the digital ecosystem of the estate. With Mount Vernon's GIS geodatabase acting as the hub where all the information intersects, it is important that any CMS implemented be compatible with it. In addition to its role as part of the HBIM system, a CMS may also have a standalone role in digital record-keeping for the MVLA. For these reasons, careful thought is being given to selecting the right CMS.

The ever-increasing amount of digital information, both new data and the digitization of existing analog data, presents a challenge to any institution tasked with the preservation of historic resources. Mount Vernon and QEA's creation of a HBIM system is a step forward in using digital technology to manage not only historic buildings and their associated records but also the cultural landscapes in which these structures reside. Combining BIM technology widely used in new construction with a web-accessible GIS creates an accurate digital landscape that provides an efficient means to manage and access data. The HBIM system provides a useful tool for historic site management in the twentieth-first century.

Notes

1. "Big Data, for Better or Worse: 90% of World's Data Generated over Last Two Years," ScienceDaily, May 22, 2013, http://www.sciencedaily.com/releases/2013/05/130522085217.htm.

2. "The George Washington Collection: About This Collection," Library of Congress, https://www.loc.gov/collections/george-washington-papers/about-this-collection/.

3. "The Papers of George Washington Documentary Editing Project," George Washington's Mount Vernon, http://www.mountvernon.org/library/research-library/washington-papers/.

4. George Washington, *The Writings of George Washington from Manuscript Sources, 1745–1799,* ed. John C. Fitzpatrick, 39 vols. (Washington, DC: U.S. Government Printing Office, 1931–44).

5. "About," Washington Papers, http://gwpapers.virginia.edu/about/.

6. "Researching George Washington," n.d., MVLA Preservation Files. For the PGWDE, see http://rotunda.upress.virginia.edu/founders/default.xqy?keys=GEWN-info-about.

7. Jean Butenhoff Lee, *Experiencing Mount Vernon: Eyewitness Accounts, 1784–1865* (Char-

lottesville: University of Virginia Press, 2006); "Visitors to Mount Vernon: Letters and Diaries Organized by Decades," n.d., MVLA Preservation Files; "Mount Vernon Visitor Accounts: Approaching Mount Vernon," n.d., MVLA Preservation Files; Dennis J. Pogue, "Approaching Mount Vernon," 2012, MVLA Preservation Files.

8. Mesick-Cohen-Waite Architects, *Mount Vernon Historic Structure Report,* 3 vols., 1993, MVLA Preservation Files; John Milner Associates, Inc., *Mount Vernon Estate and Gardens Cultural Landscape Study,* 2 vols., 2004, MVLA Preservation Files.

9. CyArk began scanning cultural landmarks in 2003, with a goal of recording five hundred sites. http://www.cyark.org/about/.

10. Maurice Murphy, "Historic Building Information—Adding Intelligence to Laser and Image Based Surveys," International Archives of the Photogrammetry, Remote Sensing and Spatial Information Sciences, vol. XXXVIII-5/W16, 2011, http://www.int-arch-photogramm-remote-sens-spatial-inf-sci.net/XXXVIII-5-W16/1/2011/isprsarchives-XXXVIII-5-W16-1-2011.pdf.

11. Francesco Chiona et al., "Integrated Building Information Modeling and Augmented Reality to Improve Investigation of Historical Buildings," *Conservation Science in Cultural Heritage* 15, no. 1 (2015): 133–65.

12. Carl Lounsbury, *Illustrated Glossary of Early Southern Architecture and Landscape* (Charlottesville: University Press of Virginia, 1994).

13. ArcGIS, "ArcGIS Online Help: Web scenes," n.d., http://doc.arcgis.com/en/arcgis-online/reference/what-is-web-scene.htm.

Stepping Up and Saving Places

Case Studies in Whole Place Preservation

GEORGE W. MCDANIEL

I recently went on a tour of Mount Vernon, George Washington's plantation home in Fairfax County, Virginia. Since I had been a historic site director, touring such a place was like going on a trip I had taken before yet seeing different things for the first time. I appreciated the well-kept grounds, the professional management of so many visitors, the well-stocked museum shop, the clean restrooms, and the careful restoration of the gardens and outbuildings. I thought back to the derelict condition of the main house in 1858 and to the debt our nation owes to Ann Pamela Cunningham and the organization she founded, the Mount Vernon Ladies' Association (MVLA). As I walked the grounds, I observed families with children and student groups enjoying themselves, creating memories that would last a lifetime. Inside the house, I was stirred to see anew the very rooms in which George Washington, his family, and his many guests had passed their time and to see the carefully revised arrangement of original artifacts and the repainted interiors that more accurately illustrated their way of life. When I exited the main house to enjoy the panoramic view across the Potomac, however, I was stunned. There across the

Conjectural rendering
of Mount Vernon's
viewshed, 2009.
(MVLA; photograph by
Patrick J. Hendrickson)

river stood an oil refinery. How could this be? I couldn't believe my eyes, so I took
a picture.

Now the story I have told is all true, except for the ending. There is no oil refinery, but there could well have been, because a refinery directly across the river was
proposed in the 1950s. Frances Payne Bolton, then the vice regent for Ohio, and

GEORGE W. MCDANIEL

Mount Vernon viewshed, 2009.
(MVLA; photograph by Patrick J.
Hendrickson)

other vice regents of the MVLA stepped up and stopped it. They developed a strategy in which Mount Vernon, the National Park Service (NPS), and the Accokeek Foundation each bought key portions of the land and secured conservation easements to protect others. The MVLA also earned support from the government of Prince George's County, Maryland, and won passage of preservation ordinances.

By doing so, they enabled the future we now enjoy.[1] Their actions made four key points, which serve as themes undergirding this essay:

1. Historic preservation is not so much about the past as it is about the future. What kind of future do we want?
2. Buildings don't preserve buildings. People do. People have to step up and make it happen. Preservation is not a given.
3. The preservation of our environs is often more about what we don't see than what we do see. In the view across the Potomac today, it looks as if nothing has happened, but it has.
4. Preservation is not just about saving buildings; it is also about saving places. Old buildings, their landscapes and gardens, and their environmental context are all of a piece. Imagining Mount Vernon with an oil refinery across the river is a case in point.

There are sites across the nation whose environs serve as examples—some well protected, most threatened, others lost. This essay features a selection of these sites and seeks to extract lessons from their campaigns that can benefit us all. I cite specifics in the hope that the reader will not only learn from those sites and be inspired but will also contact those sites to get the rest of the story. Since new opportunities and new threats constantly arise, their campaigns are by no means over. All of the sites and their campaigns teach a key lesson: be proactive rather than reactive. It is more effective and far less expensive.

When I refer to "whole place preservation," I mean the preservation not just of the historic site itself but also its environmental context, which is vital for a number of reasons. One is that it results in the preservation of the cultural landscape that the historical residents of the site knew. Those people, whose story the site interprets, both shaped that landscape and were shaped by it, so the preservation of the surrounding place with its natural resources, house sites, work places, communities, fields, and transportation routes enhances the site's capacity to research and interpret history.[2]

Whole place preservation is also important because it broadens visitors' experiences, which begin far before arrival onsite or at the beginning of the tour. The places through which visitors pass serve as transition zones that help them prepare for their experience. In his thoughtful reflections on why old places matter, Tom Mayes, National Trust for Historic Preservation attorney and preservationist, characterizes old places as transition zones that nurture a sense of memory and continuity for both visitors and local residents by providing them with a sense of orientation.[3] This means that when people pass through subdivisions, commercial strip developments, or urban blight as they approach a site, the visual and auditory cues they receive shape their minds accordingly; when visitors enter the site, their receptivity to site interpretation is diminished. As architect and architectural theorist Juhani Pallasmaa has written, "We are rooted in the continuity of time. We do not only dwell in space, we also dwell in time."[4]

Whole place preservation helps visitors to make connections between sites located in the same region, thereby providing insights that may otherwise seem disjointed both in time and space. It helps those experiencing sites to see themselves within what architectural critic Paul Goldberger characterizes as a "great sweeping arc, that is not narrowly defined, but broadly defined by its connections to other eras.... Successful preservation makes time a continuum."[5]

To accomplish this, site visitors need time to make transitions from the contemporary to the historical world, to loosen their minds from their twenty-first-century moorings so that they can be freer to receive information, to engage their imaginations, and to empathize with past ways of life. In addition, according to Estevan Rael-Gálvez, former vice president for historic sites at the National Trust for Historic Preservation, and Cindi Malinick, former senior director of sites stewardship of the National Trust, we should be much more aware of how important one's senses are to the power of place: "Historic sites hold the promise of awakening the senses," and what visitors see, hear, and even smell shape their ability to connect with the past. Imagine how the experience would be diminished if the oil refinery had been built across the Potomac River from Mount Vernon.[6]

I want to be clear that whole place preservation requires the management of change to a site's environs, not the prevention of change. Landscapes are dynamic, as are the economy and society of which our sites are a part. Since there is no way a site can stop change, the challenge becomes how to manage it so that the key elements that contribute to the historical and natural integrity of the environs and to a positive visitor experience remain intact. Since the location, threats, and resources of each site are different, one of the initial tasks should be to define the areas of concern. Criteria include the cultural landscape of the historical residents, the route of the visitors to the site, and the size of the area in which the site can reasonably seek to manage change.

Monticello: Collaboration with Conservationists

Monticello provides informative illustrations of the importance of whole place preservation and of strategies for dealing with it. As visitors tour the grounds and look to the east and south, they see a beautiful, pastoral view from the terraced vegetable gardens extending far into the distance—a view evocative of the one Thomas Jefferson saw. This view is not the result of happenstance. Instead, it is the result of years of work by the Thomas Jefferson Foundation, which owns and operates Monticello, and of the foundation being proactive within its community and collaborating with conservation organizations. In the 1990s, the foundation partnered with the Trust for Public Land and developed a viewshed analysis, which identified critical areas of concern and listed tools to assist in viewshed protection, in order to influence the look of growth emanating from Charlottesville, growth that continues today.[7]

In doing so, Monticello was ahead of the curve for many historic sites and continues to offer lessons in whole place preservation. For example, how do sites that seek governmental regulations, such as zoning or height controls, within their own viewsheds meet the arguments against governmental intrusion and in favor of private property rights elsewhere? How do they mitigate the perception that sites are being elitist and not bona fide community members? There are no easy answers, but the key is to play to the site's strengths. In this case, Monticello, which attracts several hundred thousand visitors a year, positioned itself as a major economic contributor to the region. As Kat Imhoff, former executive vice president and chief operating officer of the Thomas Jefferson Foundation explains, in the early 2000s, the foundation persuaded the county's planners and leaders to insert the value of the viewshed from Monticello into the economic development section of the Albemarle County Comprehensive Plan. This strategic move gave the foundation the basis on which to comment on proposed development projects, including re-zonings as well as visual impacts, which encompass color, height, communications towers, power-line transmission towers, and so forth.[8]

Since governmental regulations may be changed by shifting political tides, the foundation also worked on the private and more permanent side of viewshed pro-tection by securing easements, which are tied to the deeds and are in perpetuity. For Thomas Jefferson's childhood home, Shadwell, a site within Monticello's viewshed, the foundation secured an archaeological easement with the Virginia Department of Historic Resources. This land was along the Virginia State Highway 250, a po-tential major growth corridor with highly developable land. Had it not been for this easement, Imhoff noted, those lands would probably have been condemned to create a four-lane highway. The foundation also combined conservation and entrepreneurship by securing easements with the Virginia Outdoors Foundation on much of the Monticello mountain and Tufton Farm, one of Jefferson's quarter farms adjacent to the Monticello plantation. It then sold the Virginia state tax credits for that easement, a first for a nonprofit in Virginia and an excellent ex-ample of how a site can use easements in an entrepreneurial manner for financial advantage. Despite all of its efforts, Monticello was not always successful. One example, which Imhoff described, is the impact of mountainside development in the Southwest Mountains northeast of Charlottesville. In this case, the foundation did not secure a proposed mountaintop ordinance—a lesson to us that failures happen, so the key is to press on and never give up.[9]

The lesson in boldness is clearly illustrated by Monticello's most noteworthy accomplishment—the purchase of Montalto, Thomas Jefferson's beautiful "high mountain," rising 410 feet above Monticello and constituting Jefferson's first land acquisition in 1771. Under separate ownership, the property was a prime concern for the foundation. In 2004, when it came on the market at a price that generated strong interest among developers, the foundation's board along with Dan Jordan, president and CEO at the time, seized the opportunity. Within forty-eight hours, they bought the land at the full price of $15 million (notably, the same price as the Louisiana Purchase). They then launched a capital campaign and successfully paid off the debt. According to Leslie Greene Bowman, Jordan's successor, this courageous step of faith was the "high water mark of the foundation's ongoing efforts to safeguard the historic and scenic nature of the views from Monticello." Continuing its efforts in preservation, the foundation entered into a conservation agreement in 2008 with the Piedmont Environmental Council to preserve 150 acres on Montalto as open space.

As Bowman explains, all of these initiatives in whole place preservation are directly in keeping with Monticello's mission, because "land stewardship is a typically Jeffersonian concept." Today, both Monticello and Montalto are protected as a whole, and the retention of the beautiful view from Monticello toward Montalto (which visitors will now enjoy for generations to come) underscores the point that preservation is often more about what you do not see than what you do see. This preservation example also serves as an illustration of the perseverance needed by sites across the nation if they are to protect our environs. In this case, the price was high—perhaps more than most sites can raise—but the foundation focused on the goal, not the obstacles. And for other sites, the challenges may not be only the dollar amounts but the political risks or the potential disfavor of a donor or of the local community. The point is that both board and staff need to be united in the goal and have the courage to step up on behalf of the site's future.[10]

GEORGE W. MCDANIEL

Olana: Educate and Engage the Public

Another example of a site with decades of deep engagement in whole place preservation is Olana, the remarkable home and designed landscape of the Hudson River School artist Frederic Church overlooking the Hudson. Essential to visitors' understanding of Church's careful design is an appreciation of the 360-degree views from the main house, creatively designed in a Near Eastern style on the crown of the hill. One can look east to Vermont and to the Berkshires in Massachusetts, south down the Hudson River, and west to the Catskill Mountains in the distance. The creation and maintenance of such views were central to Church's art in his later years.[11]

In the 1970s, a tall, cylindrical nuclear power plant made of concrete was proposed just downstream. Fortunately, Olana and its allies stopped it. In the early 2000s, the threat loomed of a St. Lawrence Cement plant directly across the river. The plant plan called for a smokestack four hundred feet in height, the tallest structure between New York City and Montreal. After a hard-fought campaign, that too was stopped. But threats continued, this time communications towers. At Blue Hill today, which was painted multiple times by Frederic Church during his residency at Olana after the Civil War, one can discern a communications tower of slim design atop the crown. What is now being proposed is a bulkier tripod tower, of the same height but much more visible. Also looming is the threat of yet another

View of the Hudson River from Olana, historic home of Frederic Church. (Photograph courtesy of the Olana Partnership; photograph by Stan Ries NYC)

tripod tower. If Olana loses that fight and the precedent is set, a proliferation of towers could convert the scenic hilltop into a "communications tower farm."[12]

To meet these threats and to be proactive against future ones as yet unforeseen, the Olana Partnership, a nonprofit organization that supports the state-owned site, has developed a range of programs to reach diverse audiences and engage its local community. It has emphasized the value of Olana's outstanding school programs and its recreational and economic benefits to the community, and in 2008 and 2009 launched its Viewshed Tours. In 2011, the group launched a series of programs by producing an innovative symposium, *Framing the Viewshed: The Transformative Power of Art and Landscape in the Hudson Valley.* Attracting professionals from across the nation, the symposium and its accompanying booklet won a Leadership in History Award from the American Association for State and Local History. The next year, the series featured a panel discussion that brought together the major players from the campaign against the nuclear power plant, allowing attendees to look back and forth and to graphically see the need to be ever vigilant.[13]

The third in the series was a landscape event featuring contemporary artists who presented site-specific works in sound, text, installation, and movement along Olana's carriage roads. It was a creative event that won an interpretation award from the Museum Association of New York. Continuing the momentum, the Olana Partnership created programs for local and national audiences that featured diverse forms of social media as well as a revised website, www.olana.org, which includes a viewshed section. Integral to this has been the partnership's efforts to win support from local families and to engage younger children in understanding the importance of historic preservation. This kind of outreach makes the point that historic preservation is inclusive for all, regardless of age, because it is our common future at stake. Taken as a whole, the range and content of Olana's diverse programs offer creative, practical, cost-effective ideas for sites engaged in the preservation of their environs.[14]

Petroglyph National Monument: Perilous Partnerships in Managing Growth

Persistence is needed in abundance as suburban sprawl expands ever outward from urban centers and inevitably encounters once-rural historic sites, causing abundant problems in whole place preservation. No place represents the host of such challenges more graphically than the Petroglyph National Monument. Located on the outskirts of Albuquerque, New Mexico, this 7,236-acre park stretches 17 miles along the city's west mesa, a volcanic basalt escarpment that dominates the city's western horizon and contains approximately 24,000 rock carvings (or petroglyphs). The monument is co-managed by the city of Albuquerque and the NPS, a duality in governance that has generated far-reaching problems in whole place preservation due to a lack of agreement on goals and strategies. As a result, conflicts between the city and the park service, as well as with private developers, have been waged intensely for years and will continue in all likelihood far into the future. Site managers and boards from across the nation have much to learn from the park's experience, a key lesson being the importance of a unified governing authority.

Public access provides wonderful opportunities for education and inspiration but also presents serious problems for management. The entire boundary of the vast monument is secured only by a four-foot tall five-wire fence with numerous gateways for public access. Trails lead up and down hillsides and offer spectacular views of unspoiled open lands, especially to the northwest. They also lead visitors to the petroglyphs themselves, some of which date from the Pueblo IV period, 1300–1650 AD, with a few dating from the Spanish colonial period. A small gem is Boca Negra Canyon, an easily accessible seventy-four-acre site with numerous petroglyphs spanning hundreds of years. Amid this open-air setting, the rock carvings provide an almost spiritual sense of connection to the centuries of human beings who have known this site and who have stood where visitors now stand. The trails remain open year round, yet this lack of control over public access makes the monument vulnerable to vandalism and drains staff time as well as financial resources.[15]

As Acting Superintendent Diane Souder explained, when the park was established in 1990, it was seven miles from downtown Albuquerque. It seemed at the time to be a good idea for both the city and the NPS to co-manage the site because the city already owned a third of the land. However, a few years later, as suburban sprawl began to creep ever closer and then boomed at the turn of this century, the city refused to support the NPS's efforts in growth management. Subdivisions received building permits right up to the monument's boundaries, usually with no buffers or setbacks. With houses backing up to the monument, neighbors often tossed yard waste over their fences onto monument land. Coveting the large open spaces, residents even added swing sets, archery targets, trees, and patios on monument land. The land was often viewed as being suitable for all outdoor recreation—hot air balloon landings, cross-country running races, paint-ball games, falconeering, snake and native plant collecting, shooting fireworks, and dozens of other activities.[16]

Despite opposition from the NPS, the Nature Conservancy, the National Trust for Historic Preservation, and Tribal Councils, Albuquerque planned, designed, and fought to construct two roads through the monument on lands owned by the city—one a parkway and the other a four- to six-lane freeway. Impending is the city's proposed expansion of the small general aviation airport from 17,000 operations a year to 350,000 annually. The problem? The airport is immediately adjacent to the monument and to the five volcanic cones that continue to be sacred sites for Native Americans. All of this encroaching suburban development has drastically increased the amount of impervious surface and changed storm water patterns en route to the Rio Grande. Previously slow-moving runoffs have become torrents. They have eroded the fragile and loose soil, toppled and tumbled the petroglyphs clinging to the volcanic escarpment, and threatened the property owners at the base of the two- or three-hundred-foot basalt hillside.[17]

These experiences have forced park staff to become more adept in skills not

GEORGE W. MCDANIEL

usually taught in graduate programs for education and historic site management. Acting Superintendent Diane Souder, with a degree in urban planning, learned the hard way to persevere. Staff, she said, has learned how important it is to get involved early in the planning process, to be proactive, to become well-versed in the language of city planners, and to organize public support. Historians and educators have now learned about building codes, civil engineering, storm water management, traffic flows, air-quality measurement variances, height limitations, reflective surfaces, ambient noise measurements, light restrictions, and the like. Armed with this knowledge, they have been able to mobilize key sectors of their community and secure ordinances that restrict the height of homes adjacent to the park to a single story, include proper setbacks, and require color schemes that are respectful of the viewshed. These preservation professionals are learning about smart growth and how instead of continuing the consumptive patterns of sprawl, it is often better to allow higher density, mixed uses, and more height in order to confine growth to specific areas surrounded by green space.

Examples of success include the fact that park staff have been able to persuade the airport to build a control tower to route planes away from the monument. A small but important victory is that the monument has been able to require through an approved master plan more aesthetically pleasing see-though fencing of varying heights instead of a stark line of uniform, six-foot-high cinder block walls along the subdivisions' boundaries with the monument. They have also been able to restrict developed storm-water flows to historic nondeveloped levels by requiring the developers to construct water retention ponds upstream from the monument. As Souder explains, "Of course, all of this requires diligence. It has been one struggle at a time."[18]

On the near horizon, another grave threat has emerged to the monument's integrity. Immediately adjacent to Petroglyph National Monument is arising, with the city's blessing, a three-thousand-acre (about 4.7 square miles) "town center" with buildings several stories in height and miles of expansive, impervious-surfaced roads to replace today's view of open land stretching to the horizon.

While monument staff and their supporters failed to stop the creation of the town center, they did win some small measures. Vehicle speeds and traffic in the development are to be limited; the night sky will be "protected" by downward lighting and limited reflective surfaces; landscaping will feature native southwestern plants; the blight of billboards is restricted; and small neighborhood parks, rock outcrops, and open space lands will be connected by greenways and arroyos. Park staff is valiantly trying to turn these visual intrusions into teachable moments by incorporating them into their interpretation and educational programs. According to Souder, teaching the concept of stewardship is important—especially for children—because "in the fastest growing area of Albuquerque, each small effort is worth it. Who knows what the next challenges will be? No doubt there will be some losses, a few wins, and most likely, many compromises."[19]

Mount Vernon: Proactive Partnerships

As I reflect on campaigns for whole place preservation, it becomes clear how crucial it is for historic sites, preservation organizations, and environmental conservation organizations to partner and learn from one another. Mount Vernon has taken a leadership role and offers a national model. To protect its viewshed across the Potomac River, the institution has engaged in a range of partnerships with organizations local and national, private and public. The project to map its viewshed and identify priorities for conservation is a telling example. Beginning in 1989, Mount Vernon was proactive and conducted a study to assess opportunities and threats in its viewshed and to prioritize responses. In 2007, the study and recommendations were updated. They identified an area of primary concern outside the Piscataway National Park and noted specific places where buildings more than thirty-six feet tall or the destruction of tree cover could negatively impact the viewshed. The study also identified places at a higher elevation that, though further distant, would pose a greater threat if developed to the view from Mount Vernon than those areas in valleys or at lower elevations that are closer to the estate.[20]

GEORGE W. MCDANIEL

To protect its views, Mount Vernon crafted a range of informative strategies. One was the development of a close partnership with Prince George's County, Maryland, which agreed to assess new construction to determine if proposed plans would impact the view. In addition, Mount Vernon secured new and stronger easements and pushed the donation of key parcels of land to various agencies, both federal and state, as well as to private organizations like the Accokeek Foundation—all of which agreed to work on behalf of preservation. With this back-story in mind, it becomes clear that it was a visionary, long-term strategic investment in viewshed protection that secured the view we enjoy today, an approach that provides lessons for sites across the nation.

Mount Vernon also teaches us to be ever vigilant, for serious threats continue. According to staff and members of the MVLA, both Prince George's County and Charles County, Maryland, are under severe development pressure as metropolitan Washington, DC, expands southward and eastward along the Potomac River. One example is the recently developed National Harbor, where a popular casino has been constructed. While the casino itself does not impact the view, it is triggering needs for additional housing for casino workers and other related developments, all of which heighten threats to Mount Vernon's area of primary concern. As a result, there is more work to be done, which creates yet another opportunity for Mount Vernon and all of us to share knowledge and help if called upon.[21]

Ashley River Region: A Historic District's Future in the Balance

In advocating for whole place preservation, the most critical strategy is to be proactive and build coalitions both vertically at local, state, and national levels and horizontally to include community organizations that fall outside the realm of traditional historic preservation. To build such diverse coalitions requires developing a targeted media strategy to get others to care about your site and its mission and to see how they are connected and benefit. One site cannot win alone, so the time to act is now. This has been clearly illustrated by Drayton Hall in South Carolina, for over the last decades, one of its major challenges has been the encroachment of suburban sprawl from the cities of Charleston, North Charleston, and Summerville. The fundamental question is, what kind of future will come to this historic region? Consisting of a still-undeveloped swath of thousands of acres of forests and wetlands located on the west side of the Ashley River and replete with historical and archaeological resources, Drayton Hall is essential to the understanding of Charleston, South Carolina, and even the nation. Will it be overwhelmed and resemble the urban development on the opposite side of the Ashley River, or will change be carefully managed using preservation measures?[22]

An aerial view shows Drayton Hall amid the Ashley River region and illustrates how the site literally serves as a bulwark against suburban sprawl coming up the river. Over the decades, efforts to preserve the Ashley River region help us to understand answers to that key question: what kind of future do we want for our past? The region is nationally significant because within such close proximity to a metropolitan center, it encompasses a concentration of historical and natural resources perhaps unrivaled in the nation. As designations for the National Register of Historic Places and for National Historic Landmarks show, these resources include the early eighteenth-century Old St. Andrews Episcopal Church, a National Historic Landmark; Drayton Hall, a National Historic Landmark, established as a plantation by John Drayton in 1738, and the first fully executed example of Palladian architecture in America; its near contemporary, Middleton Place, a National Historic Landmark, which has the oldest formally landscaped gardens in America; the late seventeenth-century Magnolia Plantation and Gardens, which offers the nation's oldest romantic gardens and is still in possession of Drayton family descendants; and Colonial Dorchester, a late seventeenth- and eighteenth-century settlement with important archaeological resources, now a South Carolina State Park. Today the Ashley River Road is both a State and National Scenic Highway, and much of the region is on the National Register of Historic Districts. The cultural landscape of this region is replete with historical rice fields and work places, slave and tenant quarters, the remains of postbellum calcium phosphate mines,

African American cemeteries, and ecologically important maritime and upland forests. In fact, the presence of African Americans dates to the arrival of enslaved people directly from Africa, and these places would not have existed and flourished without the hands and minds of African Americans. Native American sites date to the time of the pyramids in Egypt and span thousands of years.

One graphic example of the explosive growth threatening the Charleston metropolitan area is the amount of impervious surface, the quantity of which is predicted to triple by 2030. Such predictions clearly demonstrate to the public eye that unless proactive measures are supported, the green swath of the Ashley River region, which they have come to value, will be engulfed by development.[23]

In 1994, soon after I became its director, a critical threat to Drayton Hall arose: a proposal to develop the land across the river, which consisted of about forty-two acres of uplands and was zoned for apartments at twenty-two units per acre, with no provisions for buffers. The owner offered it to Drayton Hall as a bargain sale. What to do? How were we to get our members, our limited donor pool, foundations, and other sources of funds to care enough about our future and envision it as we foresaw? Fortunately, a donor stepped up and enabled us to purchase the first parcel of 27 acres at $325,000 via a charitable remainder trust. We had a year to raise $300,000 to buy the second parcel of 15 acres.

At about that time, I attended a workshop at the National Trust offices in Washington, DC, about urban planning and Mount Vernon and learned about a new technology called "Photoshopping." It gave me an idea to "picture" the future. Back then, most cameras used film; few were digital. Adobe Photoshop 1.0 had only come on the market for Macintosh computers in 1990 and required that one take the processed film to a computer Xlab, where it was digitized so that the image editing could occur. I located the one computer technician in Charleston who had a Mac that could run Adobe Photoshop. Since color editing was prohibitively expensive, we used black and white.

Inspired by that workshop, I decided to use two images and a question as the centerpiece for our campaign. One image was of the "view today," that is, a

Drayton Hall—Suburban Sprawl,
Brad Nettles. (Courtesy of
Charleston Post and Courier)

photograph of the scenic river, marsh, and forests across from Drayton Hall. The other was of the same view but edited with apartments and other structures built out with no vegetative buffers and as zoning and height regulations would have permitted. The question was clear and simple: Which future do you prefer? Faced with that question and those images, donors from almost every state and six countries overseas responded, and we raised the money to complete the purchase of our viewshed.

While the Photoshop image may look crude by current standards, no site in the nation had used it before for a land campaign. It was state of the art at the time. A decade from now, today's technology will also seem crude. The point is to use whatever technology is available to "picture" choices for the future.[24]

For whole place preservation to be successful, it must involve partnerships throughout the region because such coalitions bring numbers of people, funds, and diversity to the cause and prevent your site from being outnumbered, stereotyped, and marginalized. Allies, of course, should include nearby sites and local historical or preservation organizations as well as state preservation organizations and the National Trust. Just as important, sites should look outward to nontraditional allies and connect with environmental conservation organizations, neighborhood associations, affinity groups, and others since they can bring a range of useful resources to the effort. For example, a little-known fact about sprawl, as documented by the National Trust for Historic Preservation and other respected organizations, is that it usually generates public expenses for new roads, schools, water and sewer extensions, and emergency services that are higher than the tax revenues produced by the development. A useful tactic therefore is to educate existing residents and conservative taxpayer groups to the fact that new subdivisions coming into the region will hurt them where it counts most—their pocketbooks through the taxes they pay. To do so, it is useful to hire economists from local, well-respected colleges or universities to produce an economic assessment of the proposed development.[25]

From 2005 to 2009, the Ashley River region faced a threat that, had it been successful, would have forever transformed the character of the region by obliterating natural woodlands, forcing construction of new highways, introducing thousands of residents, and setting the precedent for suburban sprawl throughout the area. That threat was Watson Hill, a 6,600-acre mega-development, which proposed 5,000 homes with a commercial district, golf courses, and more, all in emulation of the developers' projects in suburban Florida. It was to be located just past Middleton Place, fronting the Ashley River Road. It had strong political and financial support. To oppose it required a range of partnerships, public and private, local and national. It also required a lot of courage, vision, and luck.

One argument we wished to make was how expensive Watson Hill would be for taxpayers, since many county residents are financially conservative. Drayton Hall therefore allied with the South Carolina Coastal Conservation League, and together they funded a professional economic assessment, supported in part by a grant from the Southern Regional Office of the National Trust for Historic Preservation. We hired well-respected economists from the University of South Carolina who weighed the tax revenues to be generated by the proposed development against the public expenses it would cause. Their findings showed that Watson Hill would not pay for itself and would trigger higher taxes on everyone else in the county. We publicized the impact in the media and through public hearings, and this prompted taxpayers' associations, neighborhood associations, and financially conservative political leaders to jump on the bandwagon to protect their constituents.[26]

Too often arguments strictly in favor of historic preservation failed to win public or political support, primarily because they were seen as elitist or irrelevant, and the private property rights argument was strong and vocal. The campaign against Watson Hill therefore underscored the need to build a case for support beyond preservation in its purest form and to tie the issue to real-world concerns, such as increased traffic, higher taxes, overcrowded schools, habitat degeneration, water pollution, and/or loss of quality of life. Positioning a campaign in this way helped to bring constituencies into the fray who may have never before allied with pres-

GEORGE W. MCDANIEL

ervationists. For example, by tallying the number of vehicles on the Ashley River Road that Watson Hill would generate, we showed that traffic gridlock would result, a situation no one could support. We posted signs along the road so drivers could see the future if approval were given.

Another constituency was the "hook and bullet" group, that is, fishermen and hunters, who are often members of hunting or fishing clubs and who are often politically conservative, opposed to governmental regulations, and deeply committed to an individual's private property rights. To gain their support, we showed that if they wanted to continue their recreational fishing and hunting in the region, the habitat must be preserved, and that meant managing growth. As one of their members, Coy Johnston, himself an avid hunter, declared in a public hearing, "Asphalt is the last crop!" Due to these and other strategies, plus a measure of good luck, we stopped Watson Hill, and the land has been protected.

In addition to mega-developments, intrusions into the context of historic sites can take different guises. For example, preservationists Estevan Rael-Gálvez and Cindi Malinick have argued that the "sonic landscape" of sites offers important opportunities to connect the past and present. Historic sites should "seize the boundless opportunities harmonic sounds offer," whether they be of music, conversations, work, or play.[27]

How then to respond when that sonic landscape is threatened by irritating intrusions? Again, Drayton Hall serves as a case in point. The site had witnessed a dramatic increase in speedboat traffic on the Ashley River in the 1970s and 1980s, causing both noise pollution and severe erosion from the boat wakes cutting into our soft riverbank and threatening our remarkable riverside archaeological sites. Noise from skiers and jet skis racing up and down the river carried across the water and directly into the main house while tours were being given, fracturing the sonic landscape and the connections between museum interpreter and visitors. Working with the South Carolina Department of Natural Resources (SCDNR) and key state legislators took a lot of time and effort and required that we build a strong case, not just on preservation but also on education, tourism, and jobs.

We invited public officials and legislators to walk the riverbank, played videos of speedboats, and connected to local pride by linking the threatened site of an eighteenth-century garden house to Thomas Jefferson and comparing it today's agricultural experimental stations.

By combining these approaches, Drayton Hall finally secured "no boat wake" zones along its riverfront as well as those of the three other sites along the Ashley on the National Register of Historic Places: Magnolia Plantation and Gardens, Middleton Place, and Colonial Dorchester State Park. This was the first time in the state that the SCDNR had approved no boat wake zones to protect historic sites. As a result, archaeological sites along the riverbanks of these nationally significant sites are now protected, and visitors and museum interpreters do not have to contend with the screams of jet skis and the roar of speedboats racing in front of their sites.[28]

Whole place preservation is essentially about shaping a community ethos—a hard task but a critical one because politics count. Despite your side being "right," if you do not have the votes on the decision-making council, you lose. Winning political support requires long-term political engagement and education campaigns to inform different constituencies about positive alternatives to suburban sprawl and the costs of unmanaged growth. Being strategic and proactive in such directions is much more effective than being reactive. Especially in my early years, Drayton Hall and our allies lost in our public campaigns, but we learned. With this in mind, I thought it might be helpful to focus in-depth on one project because it calls to the forefront a number of issues. First, it begins with the fact that Drayton Hall alone could not sustain efforts by itself to protect the Ashley River. The Middleton Place Foundation, the Historic Charleston Foundation, the South Carolina Coastal Conservation League, the Southern Regional Office and the legal and historic sites departments of the National Trust, and other organizations had all played key roles, but they too had their own work to support. None of us had the staff or finances to fight one battle after another, so we sought designation of the Ashley to the State Scenic River program of the SCDNR, because it called for the formation of an Ashley Scenic River Advisory Council (ASRAC) consisting of a range of stakeholders, including riparian landowners, preservation/conservation organizations, and community leaders who could focus on the Ashley and be its voice, winning broader appeal and impact than any of us alone. In 1999, the Ashley won that designation.[29]

The designation called for a scenic river management plan, which ASRAC produced in 2003, using the occasion to gain wider community input. One of its most popular recommendations was for a park to be located along the upper Ashley River at Bacon's Bridge Road. This seventy-acre tract offered a beautiful mix of upland, wetland, and riverine habitat, along with important archaeological sites related to both the British and Americans during the Revolutionary War. For generations, it had been popular for its swimming holes and fishing spots. In 2004, this tract was offered for sale to the local county council. Although its acquisition had been recommended by ASRAC's scenic river management plan, the council voted not to buy it. There had been no public notice. Fortunately, the council's refusal was reported in the newspaper the next day. When I read about it, I notified key members of ASRAC and the Summerville Preservation Society, and we appeared before the next county council meeting, urging them to change their decision. We were told it was too late. The tract was to be sold and in all likelihood developed for condominiums.

However, we were advised we might have a chance at their next meeting in two weeks. Inspired, we mounted a campaign, contacting diverse constituencies such as those we had worked with against Watson Hill, and over two hundred people, white and black, packed the county council chambers. I knew we were going to win when a fireman, still in his standard blue uniform, rose to speak, holding his four-year-old daughter's hand, and explained that he wanted the park so he could take his daughter fishing just as his father had taken him. How could the council refuse? The only thing missing was a puppy. Coy Johnston, a leading conservationist in the region, arrived to announce that he had secured funds from the South Carolina Conservation Bank to be given to the Lowcountry Open Land Trust to buy the land. The county council supported the offer and agreed to lease the land from the Open Land Trust as a county-operated park, the first ever. The trust in turn passed ownership to a new nonprofit organization, the Dorchester Trust Foundation, which oversees the park today and leases it to the county to operate at minimal cost.[30]

The creation of the new park, named Rosebrock Park after a well-respected, conservation-minded county councilman, marked a significant change in the county's mindset toward conservation and has led to more engagement. Volunteers from Boy Scout troops and nearby schools developed nature trails and boardwalks, the county built shelters and exhibit panels, and the public's enthusiastic response caught the notice of elected leaders. Their change was illustrated by the fate of an eighty-acre tract diagonally across the river from Rosebrock. Consisting of uplands and wetlands, it had been zoned and permitted for commercial development with a restaurant by the river and residential development to the interior. Nature trails and boardwalks had been built along the half-mile or more of unspoiled river frontage. Thanks to the recession of 2008, the land had been repossessed by the bank. Using Rosebrock Park as a precedent, Coy Johnston and I along with others persuaded the county council to buy this land at a heavily discounted price, using money from the county's first-ever bond for parks and conservation, which ASRAC had pushed for.[31]

Looking to the future, the town of Summerville has recently produced its first-ever master plan, which ASRAC promoted to our constituencies. It calls for managing growth in the region, identifies the Ashley as a key asset for the future that warrants conservation, and incorporates recommendations from ASRAC's Ashley River Scenic River Management Plan.[32]

Seen in this light, that small victory of Rosebrock Park, which was built on earlier foundations, led to more conservation successes and helped change the community ethos toward whole place preservation. A master plan has recently been produced for the county's new Ashley River Park to become a passive rather than an active park, with a launch restricted to kayaks and canoes at Bacon's Bridge.

Efforts are underway to designate the Ashley a Blue Trail, a program of the American Rivers organization. The goal is to create a series of linear parks and stations along the river for canoes, kayaks, and hand-carried boats. By providing such access and amenities, we have further enhanced a community ethos for whole place preservation.[33]

Whole Place Preservation: Changing Perceptions and Shaping Our Future

I hope that by providing these examples of preservation in action, I have been able to show both what one site can do by itself and what more it can do in partnership with others. In the early 1990s, when my allies and I were first proposing preservation measures along the Ashley River and road, we were characterized at public hearings as "communists," "big government liberals," "fascists," or "rich elites," and all too often went down in defeat. Today, after engaging in these campaigns, forging diverse alliances, and finding language that connects, we have seen a significant improvement. I hope that all these examples, whether from the Ashley River region, Monticello, Olana, Petroglyph National Monument, or Mount Vernon, demonstrate the range of constituencies that a site can reach in order to change a community ethos from one that is suspicious of or even downright hostile to preservation to one that is much more supportive. Threats will continue to sites across the nation, so we must continue to be proactive in seeking to preserve the cultural landscape of the site's historical residents.[34]

While whole place preservation can be a drain on a nonprofit's budget, it can also bring benefits by way of new supporters and donors who appreciate the broader preservation efforts. It can result in a change in public perception. By stepping out beyond their property lines, sites can become recognized as leaders in the community. Such bold actions can change the common misconception that historic sites and house museums offer only tours and programs for the elite and that preservationists focus solely on the past and architecture. Instead, the public can see sites as active agents in helping to negotiate key decisions for the community on the region's future, and the site may receive support from constituencies previously regarded as outside of the purview of a house museum. According to Stephanie Meeks, president of the National Trust for Historic Preservation, a greater number of stakeholders now view historic sites within the larger context of their communities and regions, not separate and apart from them, and she applauds the fact that many historic sites are changing the public's perception of them.

Campaigns for whole place preservation also teach us that environmental conservation interests and historic preservation interests are not mutually exclusive; in fact, in many cases they converge. With many historic sites around the country struggling to remain relevant, whole place preservation can help forge a new path forward. This question of community relevance is critical as sites struggle in the face of declining admissions, federal budget cuts, and hard-pressed economies. Win or lose, whole place preservation can generate new thinking and discussion among historic sites and within the preservation and environmental conservation communities.[35]

The good news is that for historic sites, as demonstrated by the examples in this essay, whole place preservation has become more and more mainstream. People have realized that preservation is about which future they want. It is about both buildings and places. More and more sites across the country are now engaging with communities and negotiating their futures as never before. Context-sensitive preservation is becoming a fundamental part of the mainstream preservation movement as we negotiate the role of historic sites in the twenty-first century. Looking ahead, historic sites will to be sure remain locally, nationally, and even internationally significant, but equally important is that they, regardless of their stature, not become islands of history. Rather, they need to use their history, resources, courage, and vision to engage people in the campaign for the future by way of whole place preservation. Both within and beyond their property lines, historic sites can and do make a difference. As Stephanie Meeks has declared in regard to historic sites in general, "We can shrink from these challenges, or rise to them. We

GEORGE W. MCDANIEL

have more than enough innovation, creativity, and passion to succeed. So, let's be bold and forge ahead with a zest for what's possible."[36]

Notes

1. Esther C. White, director of Historic Preservation, George Washington's Mount Vernon, personal correspondence, July 22, 2014.

2. Luke J. Pecoraro, "'We Have Done Very Little Investigation There; There Is a Great Deal Yet to Do,'" this volume.

3. Tom Mayes, "Why Do Old Places Matter? An Introduction," Preservation Leadership Forum Blog, November 13, 2013, http://blog.preservationleadershipforum.org/2013/11/13/old-places-introduction/.

4. Quoted in Tom Mayes, "Why Do Old Places Matter? Continuity," Preservation Leadership Forum Blog, November 21, 2013, http://preservationleadershipforum.org/2013/11/21/old-places-continuity.

5. Paul Goldberger, "Preservation Is Not Just about the Past, Salt Lake City, April 26, 2007," quoted in Mayes, "Why Do Old Places Matter? Continuity."

6. Estevan Rael-Gálvez and Cindi Malinick, "Reflections on the Senses of Place," *Forum Journal* 28, no. 4 (Summer 2014): 6–18.

7. Kat Imhoff, personal correspondence, June 18, 2014. Imhoff, now president of the James Madison Foundation, served as vice president of the Thomas Jefferson Foundation during these earlier preservation campaigns.

8. Ibid.

9. Ibid.; Leslie Greene Bowman, personal correspondence, June 11, 17, 18, 2014; Leah Starns, personal correspondence, June 12, 2014.

10. Bowman, personal correspondence, June 18, 2014; Emily C. Pack, "Whole Place Preservation: The Ashley River Region and the Watson Hill Campaign," *Forum Journal* 25, no. 1 (Fall 2010): 33–41.

11. John K. Howat, *Frederic Church* (New Haven, CT: Yale University Press, 2005), 183.

12. Mark Prezorski, personal correspondence, June 17, 18, 2014. Prezorski is the curator of landscape for Olana. Lisa W. Foderaro, "Fight over a Communications Tower Unsettles the Hudson Valley," *New York Times,* September 5, 2013; John Mason Columbia, "Arguments on Blue Hill Tower due Friday," *Register-Star* (Hudson, NY), June 2, 2014.

13. Prezorski, personal correspondence, June 17, 18, 2014.

14. Ibid.

15. "Petroglyph National Monument New Mexico," National Park Service, http://www.nps .gov/petr/index.htm; Pack, "Whole Place Preservation," 38; Diane Souder, personal correspondence, June 30, July 13, 14, August 12, 13, 14, 2014.

16. Souder, personal correspondence, June 30, July 13, 14, August 12, 13, 14, 2014.

17. Ibid.

18. Ibid.

19. Ibid.

20. Esther White, personal correspondence, July 22, 2014.

21. Ibid.

22. Pack, "Whole Place Preservation," 33; "Nomination of the Ashley River Historic District to the National Register of Historic Places," 1994, South Carolina Department of History and Archives, State Historic Preservation Office, Columbia; "Designation of the Ashley River Road to the National Scenic Byway Program," 2000, U.S. Department of Transportation, Federal Highway Administration, Washington, DC; Scott E. Casper, "Saving Mount Vernon, in Black and White," this volume.

23. Robert Goo, "Integrating Watershed Planning and Transportation Planning," presentation to the National Association of Regional Councils, February 8, 2005, http://narc.org /uploads/File/Workshops/Workshop9/Robert_Goo.COGPresentationGOO-2-8-05final .pdf; Nancy Vinson, presentation to the Atlantic Coastal Fish Habitat Partnership, November 2010, www.atlanticfishhabitat.org/Documents/CCL_Vinson.pdf; "Growth Options in the Berkeley-Charleston-Dorchester Region," Building on Prosperity, September 20, 2005, http:// www.bcdcog.com/pdf/BCDCOG_growth_forum_pres.pdf.

24. "The View from Drayton Hall," *Post and Courier* (Charleston, SC), December 25, 1994, A26; "Half of Drayton Hall's Unspoiled View of the Ashley River Is Saved," *Interiors* 13, no. 4 (Winter 1994–95): 1, 6.

25. Jan Cigliano, "Stopping Sprawl, Saving Communities," *Forum News* 1, no. 3 (March–April 1995), http://forum.savingplaces.org/viewdocument/stopping-sprawl-saving-communities; Laura Kusisto, "The Cost of Sprawl: More Than $1 Trillion per Year, New Report Says," *Wall Street Journal,* March 19, 2015, https://blogs.wsj.com/developments/2015/03/19/the-cost-of -sprawl-more-than-1-trillion-per-year-new-report-says/.

26. Pack, "Whole Place Preservation," 37–39.

27. Rael-Gálvez and Malinick, "Reflections on the Senses of Place," 9–10.

28. George Neil, "No Wake Legislation for Upper Ashley River Passed by General Assembly," *Friends of Drayton Hall Interiors,* Spring 1992, 3; South Carolina General Assembly, Journal

of the House of Representatives, 109th Session, 1991–92, January 24, 1992, http://www
.scstatehouse.gov/sess109_1991–1992/hj92/19920124.htm.

29. Bill Marshall, ed., *Ashley Scenic River Management Plan* (Columbia: South Carolina
Department of Natural Resources, 2003), 2–14.

30. Michael Truslow, "Park It, Proposed Purchase Shot Down," *Summerville* (SC) *Journal
Scene,* July 30, 2004, cover; George W. McDaniel, "Ashley River Park Hanging in the Balance,"
Summerville Journal Scene, September 3, 2004, A2; Howard Bridgman, "Celebrate Bacons
Bridge Park," *Post and Courier,* February 17, 2008, A10.

31. Jim Tatum and Leslie Cantu, "County Poised to Buy Property for Park," *Summerville Journal Scene,* February 3, 2012, http://www.journalscene.com/article/20120203/SJ01/302039990.

32. Bob Jackson, "Summerville Creates a Development Master Plan," *Summerville Journal
Scene,* October 15, 2013, http://www.journalscene.com/article/20131015/SJ22/131019809;
Town of Summerville, "Summerville's Vision Plan," 2014.

33. Bo Petersen, "Lowcountry Group Seeks to Organize Emerging Paddlesport 'Blue Trails,'"
Post and Courier, June 1, 2014; Howard Bridgman, "A Southeastern Gem: The Ashley River
Blue Trail," American Rivers, Blue Trails, April 2, 2014, http://www.americanrivers.org/blog
/southeastern-gem-ashley-river-blue-trail/; Eric Davis, "The Ashley River Blue Trail: A Recreational Oasis," American Rivers, Blue Trails, September 11, 2015, www.americanrivers.org/2015
/09/ashley-river-blue-trail-a-recreational-oasis/.

34. "Nomination of the Ashley River Historic District to the National Register of Historic
Places"; "Designation of the Ashley River Road to the National Scenic Byway Program."

35. Pack, "Whole Place Preservation," 40–41; Stephanie K. Meeks, "Introduction," *Forum
Journal* 25, no. 1 (Fall 2010): 5–6; Stephanie K. Meeks, "Stepping Into the Future of Historic
Sites," *Forum Journal* 28, no. 4 (Summer 2014): 3–5.

36. Meeks, "Introduction," 5–6; Wendy Nicholas, "Collaborating to Save Whole Places,"
Forum Journal 25, no. 1 (Fall 2010): 7–10; Mary Pope M. Hutson, "Our Moment to Build a
Cultural Conservation Legacy," *Forum Journal* 25, no. 1 (Fall 2010): 18–23; Thompson M. Mayes
and Ross M. Bradford, "Combining Preservation and Conservation Values: Six Illustrative
Examples," *Forum Journal* 25, no. 1 (Fall 2010): 24–26; Andy Laurenzi, "Land Conservation and
Historic Preservation: A Natural Partnership in the Southwest," *Forum Journal* 25, no. 1 (Fall
2010): 27–32; Roberta Lane, "Make No Little Plans: Community Planning for Whole Places,"
Forum Journal 25, no. 1 (Fall 2010): 42–48; Meeks, "Stepping Into the Future of Historic
Sites," 5.

The Dangers of Preserving while Popular

The Mount Vernon Ladies' Association's Image of
Mount Vernon versus Contemporary Architecture

LYDIA MATTICE BRANDT

Historic preservationists need audiences. Curators, architectural historians, conservationists, and amateur enthusiasts count on consumers to believe (or at least find value) in the material worlds they recreate, reconstruct, or restore. Since purchasing George Washington's plantation house and immediate grounds in the late 1850s, the Mount Vernon Ladies' Association (MVLA) has offered a carefully considered interpretation of the much-beloved "American Mecca."[1] At the same time that the MVLA began to restore Mount Vernon to the home Washington had known, it also tried to control the ways in which Americans consumed the place beyond the estate's boundaries.

By the early twentieth century, the MVLA had discovered that its attempts to regulate Mount Vernon in popular culture were futile. What the public did with the house's image was entirely out of the organization's power. As a lawyer reminded the association's board of vice regents in 1932: "[Mount Vernon] is like the Parthenon, or old St. Peter's or Westminster Abbey or the Liberty Bell:

the design, the method of construction, the dimensions, all are in the public domain."[2]

In preserving Mount Vernon, the MVLA unleashed an enthusiasm for the building that the organization could never have anticipated; Americans copied and commercialized the house's architecture from coast to coast. As the MVLA developed an appealing and believable expression of Washington's material world during the end of the nineteenth and beginning of the twentieth centuries, Americans adapted it to contemporary life as they pleased. Convincing tableaux of furniture and objects inspired spreads in home decorating magazines, while accurate, measured drawings informed line-by-line copies at five different world's fairs. The house's piazza, Chinese Chippendale balustrade, and five-part plan appeared on countless private homes, motels, and other commercial structures. The same consumers who expected accuracy when they visited Mount Vernon happily played with the house's architecture elsewhere.

Such "replicas" proved that the MVLA's aims of keeping George Washington and Mount Vernon at the forefront of Americans' mind were successful, but obviously not in the ways the association had intended. Rather than fruitlessly oppose what it saw as the unfortunate commodification of a sacred patriotic image, the MVLA focused on restoring and emphasizing Mount Vernon's historic fabric. By the 1930s, the MVLA recognized that its ultimate responsibility and expertise rested in preserving Washington's house, objects, and landscapes. If Americans found Mount Vernon so compelling that they copied its iconic architectural features, then the MVLA would ensure that the house's restored architecture and interiors continued to keep its audiences interested.

Preserved historic buildings and popular architecture often have a close but contradictory relationship. Restored and reconstructed sites allow for better understandings of the past as well as for the inspiration of popular taste. As a historical place important to the nation's past, a site accessible for the better part of its history, and the most reproduced building in American architecture, Mount Vernon is the premier example of this uneasy correlation between historic preservation and popular architecture. It demonstrates that when a historic place is preserved, new ways emerge for the public to access and interpret it—ways that are not always intended by the preservationist.

Mount Vernon and Nineteenth-Century Photography

In September 1865, the MVLA's secretary, Sarah Tracy, wrote to the organization's founder, Ann Pamela Cunningham, "The [members of the board] for some time have wanted Photographs taken of the place. . . . I have been tormented by different artists who wanted to make their percentage. . . . This I knew you had said you would never consent."[3] Despite widespread interest in the emerging photographic medium and in the newly public Mount Vernon in the years surrounding the Civil War, only a handful of images of the house were then available to the public.[4] Within weeks of Tracy's letter, the association had hired a pair of local amateur photographers and begun forming a policy that prohibited the production or distribution of photographs of Mount Vernon without the MVLA's permission.[5]

In its earliest efforts to establish Washington's home as a tourist destination, the association understood the power of images; their sale could generate income for the hard-strapped operation and their distribution could drum up enthusiasm for the newly opened historic site.[6] More importantly, the MVLA hoped that exclusive relationships with commercial photographers could offer the "best possible representations of the place."[7] Photographic documentation could prove that the MVLA was actively preserving Mount Vernon, long lamented for its "desolation by utter abandonment to the elements," with an authoritative veracity.[8]

In 1866, the MVLA hired its first official commercial photographer, Alexander Gardner, who had most recently captured images of Civil War battlefields.[9] Sold at Mount Vernon and at his Washington, DC, studio, Gardner's stereographs and cabinet cards were the earliest set of widely available photographs of the site.[10] In a novel form, his thirty stereographs confirmed what visitors' accounts and engravings had long-identified as the place's most significant features.[11] Consisting of two nearly identical photographs of the same subject glued to a card side by side, stereographs were an inexpensive and terrifically popular pastime of the period. When viewed through an optical device, the two photographs converged to create an illusion of a single three-dimensional image.[12] Seen in order, Gardner's stereographic tour began at the Potomac River wharf where tourists disembarked from steamboats, wound past the Washington family tombs and around the exterior of the mansion, peeked into the principal interiors (including the west parlor, New Room, and Washington and Lafayette bedchambers), and finished in the upper garden. The images were sold individually or as a set; their backs featured a complete list of the views in the "Home of Washington Illustrated."[13] Before the introduction of the affordable personal camera and the widespread use of picture postcards, stereographs allowed visitors to relive their pilgrimages after they had returned home and gave those who could not travel an opportunity to discover the site from the comfort of their parlors. These images made it possible for Americans to see and experience Washington's home with a sense of reality impossible in earlier depictions.

While the stereographs did prove successful in making money for the association, the MVLA's restrictions on photography had mixed outcomes. Gardner and his successors returned to Mount Vernon multiple times, adding additional views and replacing others with versions that better represented the MVLA's ongoing preservation and furnishing efforts.[14] They did not, however, always keep up their promises to return their negatives to the association, leaving the images available for others to print long after the actual site changed.[15] In 1876, the MVLA successfully sued a group of local photographers who snuck onto the estate without the organization's permission.[16] These men later sold their photographs, cutting into the MVLA's profits and further saturating the market with unauthorized images.[17]

The MVLA's attempts to control Mount Vernon's likeness were rendered impossible due to improvements in technology for the production and reproduction of photographic images. The Eastman Company's Kodak camera was in use by the end of the 1880s, for example, and allowed amateurs to take snapshots without having to worry about the technicalities of loading or developing film. Further improvements in printing and photographic technology (including in halftone photoengraving, film, lenses, and flash) facilitated the production, publication, and reprinting of clear photographic images.[18]

By 1895, the MVLA finally abandoned its policy against unsanctioned photography. Images by both professionals and amateurs immediately began appearing in a growing number of popular illustrated magazines.[19] That same year, an article in the *American Historical Register* featured photographs of Washington's bedchamber, the east facade, and a mirror alongside a laudatory description that must have thrilled the vice regents, hesitant to lift their restrictive ban: "The place is lovely. There are the trees planted by the hand of the father of our country. . . . And there, too, from time to time, comes the devoted band of American women, whose ever-watchful care preserves to us this hallowed spot in freshness and beauty."[20]

The proliferation of photographic representations of Mount Vernon fed a new way for Americans to express their interest in the building without the consent of the MVLA—replication. Photographs offered rich content for the emerging trend of referencing historic early American architecture in contemporary design, and Americans translated photographs of Mount Vernon into three-dimensional space.[21] A Long Island mansion, the Orchard (1898–1907), for example, featured a Mount Vernon–inspired piazza, five-part composition, Venetian window, and balustrade. Designed by the period's top New York architecture firm, McKim, Mead & White, the Orchard was widely photographed for publications and praised as one of the nation's best country houses in popular magazines like *Architecture* and *Country Life in America*.[22] It encouraged the trend among professional architects such as John Russell Pope and William Adams Delano to copy Mount Vernon in their residential designs for high-profile clients, all of which were photographed and discussed in popular and architectural publications.[23]

While many Americans saw halftone photographs of glamorous Mount Vernon–inspired mansions, millions visited full-scale "replicas" of the house at the 1893

Visitors at Mount
Vernon, May 28, 1889.
(MVLA; photograph by
Luke C. Dillon)

World's Columbian Exposition in Chicago and at the 1915 Panama-Pacific International Exposition in San Francisco.[24] They strolled through period rooms arranged to look just like those in Virginia and marveled at the fidelity of the replicas' architecture, copied at Chicago down to windows with "small panes and sashes fastened with wooden buttons."[25]

"We Are It Seems Powerless to Prevent Reproductions of Mt. Vernon"

Within a few short decades of the MVLA's first attempts to control the distribution of its image, Mount Vernon's architecture—or at least representations of it—was everywhere.[26] By the 1920s, with the bicentennial of Washington's birth looming, the affection for Washington's house blossomed into a full-fledged obsession as Americans duplicated the house's features on everything from hotels to campus buildings to more world's fair pavilions.[27] The MVLA worried that this "indiscriminate erection of copies" detracted "from the sacredness and dignity of the Home of Washington."[28] The vice regents were especially concerned about "those who wish[ed] to exploit commercially the historical significance of Mount Vernon."[29]

A flurry of replicas built as exhibition pavilions prompted particular concern. Mount Vernon copies appeared at the 1931 Paris Colonial and Overseas Exposition, in Brooklyn for New York City's celebration of Washington's bicentennial, and in Chicago for the 1934 Century of Progress Exposition.[30] For the most part, these followed the mansion's dimensions and included furnishings and decorative arts to suggest the MVLA's interpreted interiors.[31] A Houston newspaper impossibly proclaimed that the 1931 version would "excel even the original in its fidelity to Washington and times and manners and fashions."[32] The vice regents found the Chicago version, the centerpiece of a concession called the "Colonial Village," "a more flagrant infringement of our rights than has hitherto occurred."[33] Alongside a copy of Benjamin Franklin's long-lost print shop, a "grog shop," and a "witch's house" that playfully evoked seventeenth-century Salem, Mount Vernon was more of a backdrop for visitors to play with early American history than it was a serious historical exhibit.[34]

The MVLA was appalled that such exhibition replicas—in some cases little more than commercial attractions—could claim any "fidelity" to the Mount Vernon it so carefully preserved. With a mission to "perpetuate the sacred memory of The Father of His Country and, with loving hands to guard and protect the hallowed spot where rest his mortal remains," the vice regents believed they had a duty to halt what they saw as inappropriate uses of the house's architecture.[35] The board had long proclaimed a "rigid rule" forbidding "giving dimensions or allow[ing] interior photographing for the purpose of aiding reproductions of anything."[36] Mount Vernon's popularity had guaranteed, however, that architectural drawings of the house (some authorized by the MLVA for preservation purposes) had long

"Colonial Village" at the Century of Progress, 1934. (Photograph courtesy of Chicago History Museum, ICHi-092815; photograph by D. Ward Pease)

escaped the group's control. They were widely available in a variety of publications as early as 1900.[37]

Unable to control the proliferation of look-alikes, the vice regents recommitted themselves to the highest standards of preservation in the 1930s. Like many organizations operating historic sites in the period, the MVLA grew increasingly professional and academic in the ways it applied preservation methodologies.[38] The undesirable replicas helped to motivate the MVLA toward a new wave of restoration based firmly in historical research and with employees and consultants who had professional preservation training. In just a few years, the MVLA made some of the most dramatic decisions for the mansion's preservation to date and masterfully publicized the changes. If they could not stem the ever-increasing number of replicas that might "commonize" or "cheapen" Washington's sacred home, then the vice regents would reclaim their rightful monopoly on Mount Vernon's authenticity.[39]

At the same time as it decried replicas seen by millions in Paris, Chicago, and Brooklyn, the MVLA removed both a porch on the building's south side and the Chinese Chippendale balustrade atop the iconic piazza. Research confirmed that both had been additions by Bushrod Washington (George Washington's nephew and the first owner after Washington's death), postdating the MVLA's late eighteenth-century date for the restoration of the mansion.[40] The association had reconstructed the porch in the mid-1870s. The vice regents did not discuss whether or not it was of the Washington era so early in their preservation efforts; they most likely assumed it was original.[41] Backed with far more scholarly preservation methodologies fifty years later, the MVLA was finally prepared to return the house's exterior to its eighteenth-century appearance. With little fanfare, employees removed the porch in 1931 and replaced it with windows of the "original height and size" and a cellar door like that on the north side.[42] The elimination of the Chinese Chippendale balustrade in 1936 was a more difficult decision. Attached to the iconic piazza, it was a much more noticeable part of the mansion than the small porch. Despite the "great feeling" many vice regents had for the railing, they ultimately decided not to "let sentiment alone govern [them] in so serious a matter."[43] After appearing in more than six decades of photographs of the east elevation, the balustrade finally went into storage.[44]

To publicize the ongoing restoration and to reaffirm its claims of authority on Mount Vernon, the association (and especially its new regent, Harriet Towner) encouraged a series of "imposing articles" in popular and academic journals in 1937–38.[45] Led by landscape architect and preservationist Morley Jeffers Williams, the head of the MVLA's newly established Office of Research and Restoration, the effort attempted to ensure that the public remained as familiar with the real

Mount Vernon as with willy-nilly copies.[46] In the *New York Times, Landscape Architecture,* the *Magazine Antiques* and elsewhere, the articles took "great care to be sure that every little statement had proper support from original sources."[47] These pieces laid out the historical development of Mount Vernon's architecture and landscape and explained the MVLA's methodologies for their preservation and interpretation.

The most extraordinary publication in this "burst" of publicity was a richly illustrated article in the magazine *American Architect and Architecture* in 1938.[48] Using technical vocabulary to describe details and building materials, the text focused squarely on the development of the house without the usual attention to Washington's biography. It reserved special comment for the oft-replicated piazza, emphasizing its unique design: "Since nothing like it is known to have appeared on contemporary or earlier buildings in that part of the country, it would appear to be Washington's much-copied contribution to American architecture."[49] The article also featured two two-page spreads of recent measured drawings, completed to the standards of the new Historic American Buildings Survey (HABS), the first systematic attempt to document American architecture by the federal government.[50] After fighting the replication of Mount Vernon's architecture for years, the MVLA clearly resolved to make available the most accurate and up-to-date information on the house's architecture.

Even more surprising about the *American Architect and Architecture* article, however, was its photographs by Frances Benjamin Johnston.[51] The leading architectural photographer in the country at the time, Johnston and her "straight" photographs of American vernacular buildings helped to determine documentation standards for HABS.[52] Besides recording the MVLA's preservation efforts (especially the piazza newly stripped of its balustrade), her photographs of the exterior elevations, dependencies, details, and interiors allowed the architecture to speak for itself; for the first time, the vice regents permitted their carefully curated interiors to be emptied almost completely of textiles, decorative arts, and furniture. The photographs focused entirely on the house's architecture and provided documentation that was in itself a preservation effort. Millions might see replicas of Washington's home at world's fairs or in design magazines, but only the mansion in Virginia had the moldings and mantels chosen and touched by the hero himself.

At the same time that the MVLA was reasserting its authority over the authentic Mount Vernon, the craze for its replication heightened. Most "replicas" of the 1930s and 1940s did not copy Mount Vernon as faithfully or as publicly as the exhibition pavilions. Designs for private houses most often simply referenced the mansion with a tall piazza with square columns and a balustrade. As the leading producer and retailer of prefabricated buildings in America, Sears, Roebuck, and Company led the trend that expanded the reproduction of Mount Vernon's piazza from the massive mansions of McKim, Mead & White to the modest homes of the middle class.[53] After successfully building the public exhibition pavilions in Paris and Brooklyn, Sears offered the "Jefferson" in its 1932 *Homes of Today* catalogue.[54] The house was only superficially "along the same lines as historic Mt. Vernon"; the white, symmetrical, side-gabled building featured dormers, shutters, two prominent chimneys, and a wide, square-columned piazza with a chinoiserie railing.[55] Available for purchase as a kit that included everything from lumber to nails, appliances, and fixtures, the Jefferson could be constructed on any site. Many developers simply adapted its plans, sourcing their own materials and further spreading the reach of the design.

A growing number of similar home catalogues offered Mount Vernon–inspired residences within the next fifteen years, reducing the house's iconic architectural features to a "colonial type" that was increasingly detached from its model. Aladdin Readi-Cut Homes; Hollands, the Magazine of the South; the L. F. Garlinghouse Company; the Gordon–Van Tine Company; and the *Ladies' Home Journal* promoted plans similar to Sears's for a range of budgets, and Americans built Mount Vernon from coast to coast.[56] The piazzas on these nearly identical houses denied the originality of Washington's design so carefully preserved by the MVLA and erroneously gave the impression that such a feature was common in

Plan 2032-C. *Holland's: The Magazine of the South, Distinctive Southern Homes,* 1946. (Courtesy of Southeastern Architecture Archives, Special Collections Division, Tulane University Libraries)

2032-C

Complete plans and specifications, $25

Pleasing Dignity and Charm

BOTH dignity and charm have been achieved in the design of this house by the application of the refinement and delicacy of the Colonial style. The close relationship between the house and terrace is more intimate than extensive, as in the usual formal gardens of this period. Special attention has been given to the interior to make it a fitting background for beautifully designed modern or period furniture.

Note how the large rooms separately have some attractive feature— a fireplace, bay windows or with an interesting view to the garden area to the rear. The first floor bedroom has all the conveniences necessary for comfort to special friends and overnight guests. The stairway is placed so as to be more private for family use in going from the living area to the family bedrooms and baths on the second floor. Each of these bedrooms is large and well ventilated and provided with good sized closets for clothes, linen and storage.

This entire plan is the type so many people want some day to have as their own lovely home.

eighteenth-century America. While some catalogues, such as Sears's, recognized the debt to Mount Vernon, others regarded it more generally as "southern," "colonial," or even "typical." A 1915 book titled *Inexpensive Homes of Individuality* featured a Mount Vernon lookalike with the caption "A modern home . . . showing a return to the stately high-columned Colonial porch that was common in early Southern work."[57] Decades later, *Holland's* 1947 *Distinctive Southern Homes* catalogue offered complete plans of a Mount Vernon–inspired dwelling for twenty-five dollars. With a piazza and a garage attached to the house via an arched colonnade, the design supposedly represented "the type so many people want some day to have as their own lovely home."[58] Anything but typical in its own day, Washington's highly idiosyncratic plantation house was simplified and widely available for a range of budgets by midcentury.

"Mount Vernon in Virginia" . . . and along the Roadside

Americans did not just want to live in a version of Washington's home by the 1950s; they also wanted to see it for themselves. The MVLA broke its attendance records in 1952, when over one million people visited Mount Vernon.[59] By now, well aware that it had no way to control the use of Mount Vernon's image, the MVLA focused its attention on clarifying the public's understanding of the site's significance to Washington's biography and the nation's founding.[60] Using new technology and advertising techniques, the vice regents reminded their audiences that only at the restored Mount Vernon could Americans truly connect to Washington. Copies, meanwhile, departed even further from their model. Replicas now copied replicas, with the most recognizable features denoting a general air of timeless American history rather than specific references to Washington's plantation house. The deepening divide between the MVLA's emphasis on Mount Vernon's authenticity and the increasingly liberal interpretation of the replicas indicated two different ways of thinking about the house's place in contemporary life; while it was always a place in flux for the association, Mount Vernon could be a static image in popular architecture.

In 1950, the MVLA commissioned its first film, *Mount Vernon in Virginia,* to introduce the house to a broader audience. The board hoped that the twenty-two-minute, sixteen-millimeter film would, "supplement the experience of the average visitor, who by reason of crowded conditions . . . may carry away only a superficial impression of the place."[61] With an original score, "beautiful photography, smooth camera movement, and an intimate and sensitive story," the film had the potential to articulate Mount Vernon's significance better than any other medium.[62] The MVLA regarded the film as "the most important thing in the line of publicity that the Association has ever undertaken." [63] It was certainly the most expensive publicity effort in the organization's history to date; the association spent $27,311 producing, publicizing, and distributing it to schools, libraries, and patriotic organizations nationwide.[64] The film was translated into forty foreign languages and aired on television stations from Buffalo to Los Angeles within a year of its release.[65]

Even more dramatically than Frances Benjamin Johnston's photographs of the house's details, the film reminded viewers that what made Mount Vernon special was the authenticity of its physical fabric. Organized like a "conducted tour," the film presented "the land of the estate, its buildings, and the most significant objects inside them so as to reveal what [Washington's] character means for us."[66] The camera moved through the house, hovering over individual objects and scenes of furniture and decorative arts to humanize the people who had used them two centuries before. When introducing George Washington's step-granddaughter Eleanor (Nelly) Parke Custis, for example, tinkling music played as the camera rested on the keys of her harpsichord before sweeping up to her portrait above the mantle. The narrator conjured an impression of the young woman that surely resonated with many midcentury children: "Sometimes Nelly grew weary of her music lessons, for life could be such fun on a planation like Mount Vernon." The combination of the script, the shots of the instrument, and the portrait created not only a relatable (and likable) Nelly but also a paternalistic side to Washington, noting "how she could make the general laugh by mimicking some of his most important visitors."[67]

The film's conclusion articulated Mount Vernon's unique ability to tell stories about American history: "And when we pay tribute at [Washington's] grave, we are also able to admire the harvest of his life. We can feel the force of the spirit that was caught by the great sculptor Houdon over 150 years ago. It is evident in every part of the shrine we can visit today."[68] Comparing a restored Mount Vernon to the most accurate life portrait of Washington, the film claimed that the site was the best way to get close to the long-dead hero. The final moments featured tourists of all ages exploring the estate's buildings, providing a visual representation of the audience and driving home Mount Vernon's accessibility. The board laid out the value it saw in *Mount Vernon in Virginia* in its annual report of 1950; it hoped "that the picture will fulfill its primary purpose of making the home of George and Martha Washington more meaningful for the visitor, and that the inspiration of the living memory of George Washington, which is strongest at Mount Vernon, will also reach thousands who may never come to Virginia."[69]

As the vice regents focused on reinforcing the building's historical importance and authenticity, replicas grew more abstract in how they interpreted the house's architecture. Made iconic through decades of now-outdated photographs, for example, the balustrade continued to appear in contemporary architecture despite its decades-long absence from the mansion. It persisted in decorating colonial revival residences similar to Sears's version of the 1930s but also in more modern-style houses. Running along the low-slung, side-gabled roof of a ranch house in Pease Homes's 1954 catalogue, for example, a simplified version of Mount Vernon's balustrade supposedly conveyed the "excellent taste and individuality of its owner" along with "inviting hospitality and a lifetime investment."[70] Even though it was no longer referencing Mount Vernon in particular, the railing connoted tradition and elegance.

The balustrade and the piazza also began appearing on a new building type at midcentury—the roadside motel. Motels developed after World War II to service the growing numbers of Americans traveling greater distances in private automobiles.[71] Usually oriented to the roadside, modest motels often used "highly emotional architecture" to "compete for the eye of the motorist."[72] With its long-replicated piazza and reputation as a historically hospitable destination, Mount Vernon was an obvious source of inspiration for the motel. Using recognizable architectural features (even if the audience did not attribute them directly to Mount Vernon) also provided a sense of familiarity to what was still a very new industry.

Some motels copied Mount Vernon relatively faithfully. The Mount Vernon Motel in Albany, New York, featured a two-story central lobby with a cupola and "Mount Vernon" in giant letters in place of the balustrade on the tall piazza. Long rows of rooms stretched out on either side like the colonnade and dependencies, this time facing a parking lot rather than a bowling green. Far simpler versions used

Dale's Mt. Vernon Motel, Canandaigua, New York, postcard, c. 1957. (MVLA)

only the balustrade; it was an even cheaper and easier way to reference something familiar. The Colony Motor Lodge in Strongsville, Ohio, consisted of only a long, flat-roofed row of eighteen individual units with a lobby on one end in the 1940s. A simplified, more geometric version of the Mount Vernon balustrade topped the shallow, shed-roofed portico that wound around the brick exterior. A late 1950s postcard for Dale's Mt. Vernon Motel in Canandaigua, New York, boasted of its "Colonial setting," which consisted of inoperable shutters, a small cupola (identical to those on top of many contemporary suburban homes), and—of course—a geometric railing. Even today, Mount Vernon–inspired railings continue to appear on commercial and residential buildings as both a specific holdover to an earlier memory of the house and as a general nod to the colonial period.

The enthusiasm for Mount Vernon's image in popular architecture proved correct; the MVLA's 1950 film concluded, "Mount Vernon is not an empty house of memories that are dead."[73] The house was—and still is—relevant to contemporary

American life. The MVLA's experience with Washington's home suggests that the stories historic preservationists tell with historic objects can take on a life of their own in popular culture. And that is okay. The replication of Mount Vernon is in many ways evidence of the MVLA's great success; its carefully preserved artifact has proven so compelling that Americans endlessly reproduce it. Along roadsides and in neighborhoods across the country, Americans create their own versions of Mount Vernon, reinforcing the importance of and reverence for the house in Virginia.

Notes

This essay is based in part on research also published in Lydia Mattice Brandt, *First in the Homes of His Countrymen: George Washington's Mount Vernon in the American Imagination* (Charlottesville: University of Virginia Press, 2016). The author would like to thank Philip Mills Herrington, assistant professor of history at James Madison University; Dawn Bonner, manager of visual resources at Mount Vernon; Lauren Greenwald, assistant professor of photography at the University of South Carolina; and Adam Erby, associate curator at Mount Vernon, for their help with this essay.

1. For a selection of publications using some version of this phrase, see H. F. H., "Washington's House," *Ladies' Companion*, January 1840, 103; "Mount Vernon," *Columbian Lady's and Gentleman's Magazine*, February 1849, 87; Robert Criswell, *Godey's Lady's Book*, October 1849, 247; C. H. Brainard, "A Visit to Mount Vernon," *Prisoner's Friend: A Monthly Magazine Devoted to Criminal Reform, Philosophy, Science, Literature, and Art*, August 1, 1849, 538; "The Home of Washington," *Maine Farmer*, August 3, 1865, 4; and MVLA, Minutes, 1876, 4.

2. George Wharton Pepper to Alice Richards, February 29, 1932, folder "Mt. Vernon, Replicas of," AMVLA, NLSGW.

3. Sarah Tracy to Ann Pamela Cunningham, September 9, 1865, Early Records of the MVLA, AMVLA, NLSGW.

4. Researchers at Mount Vernon have identified a few examples: William and Frederick Langenheim made talbotypes of the house and tomb in 1850 for their "Views of North America" and stereotypes in 1856. Talbotypes (or calotypes) are made using paper coated with silver iodide. Israel and Biddle made a salted paper print of the mansion "as it appear on May 14th 1859" for Baltimore bookseller H. E. Hoyt. People also took unique daguerreotypes (also at

Washington's tomb) for private consumption. Dawn Bonner, manager of visual resources at Mount Vernon, personal correspondence, August 11, 2016. See also "19th-Century Photography at Mount Vernon," Mount Vernon, http://www.mountvernon.org/preservation/historic -preservation/19th-century-photography-at-mount-vernon/.

5. Sarah Tracy to Margaret Comegys, September 26, 1865, Early Records of the MVLA, AM-VLA, NLSGW. On amateur photographers in the period, see Robert Taft, *Photography and the American Scene: A Social History, 1839–1889* (New York: Dover, 1964), 204–22.

6. Abby Wheaton Chase to Sarah Tracy, November 1, 1865; Sarah Tracy to Ann Pamela Cunningham, September 9, 1865, Early Records of the MVLA, AMVLA, NLSGW.

7. MVLA AR, 1880, 7.

8. "Washington's Home Going to Ruin," *New York Observer and Chronicle,* January 28, 1869, 30. See also Alan Trachtenberg, "The Emergence of a Keyword," in *Photography in Nineteenth-Century America,* ed. Martha A. Sandweiss (New York: Harry N. Abrams, 1991), 16–47.

9. Eleanor Jones Harvey, *The Civil War in American Art* (New Haven, CT: Yale University Press, 2012), 73–111 ("The Art of Wartime Photography").

10. The MVLA worked with Gardner from 1866 until 1878. See Alexander Gardner to Sarah Tracy, August 21, 1866, and Alexander Gardner to Nancy Halsted, July 16, 1878, Early Records of the MVLA, AMVLA, NLSGW.

11. On early views of Mount Vernon, see Lydia Mattice Brandt, "Picturing Mount Vernon," *Imprint* 38, no. 1 (Spring 2013): 2–19.

12. See Laura Schiavo, "'A Collection of Endless Extent and Beauty': Stereographs, Vision, Taste and the American Middle Class, 1850–1880" (Ph.D. diss., George Washington University, 2003), ProQuest (3075205), and Pauline Stakelon, "Travel through the Stereoscope: Movement and Narrative in Topological Stereoview Collections of Europe," *Media History* 16, no. 4 (2010): 407–22. For a period account of the experience, see Oliver Wendell Holmes, "The Stereoscope and the Stereograph," *The Atlantic,* June 1859, 738–48.

13. On captions and sets of photographic landscape views, see Martha A. Sandweiss, "Undecisive Moments: The Narrative Tradition in Western Photography," in Sandweiss, ed., *Photography in Nineteenth-Century America,* 98–129.

14. Over the next twenty years, the MVLA had at least two other official photographers who made and sold photographs (including stereoviews) of Mount Vernon: N. G. Johnson and Luke C. Dillon. Most of the stereoviews (including Gardner's) were marked as being "official" or "authorized." See MVLA, Minutes, 1879, 9, 16; 1882, 22, 25; 1883, 11; 1884, 20–21.

15. Nancy Halsted to Alexander Gardner, July 23, 1878; Colonel J. McHenry Hollingsworth to Margaret Sweat, July 25, 1878; Margaret Sweat to Susan Hudson Johnson, August 14, 1878,

Early Records of the MVLA, AMVLA, NLSGW; "19th-Century Photography at Mount Vernon."

16. MVLA AR, 1880, 7; Scott E. Casper, *Sarah Johnson's Mount Vernon: The Forgotten History of an American Shrine* (New York: Hill and Wang, 2008), 137–38; MVLA, Minutes, 1877, 16.

17. MVLA, Minutes, 1877, 16–17.

18. See William Welling, *Photography in America: The Formative Years, 1839–1900* (New York: Thomas Y. Crowell, 1978), 321–401; Estelle Jussim, *Visual Communication and the Graphic Arts: Photographic Technologies in the Nineteenth Century* (New York: R. R. Bowker, 1983), 45–76; and Beaumont Newhall, *The History of Photography from 1839 to the Present Day,* 4th ed. (New York: Museum of Modern Art, 1978), 175–90.

19. King Laughlin, "Mount Vernon and Photography," October 1992, NLSGW; MVLA, Minutes, 1895, 32–33. See also Amanda Hinnant and Kerley Hudson, "The Magazine Revolution, 1880–1920," in *The Oxford History of Popular Print Culture,* ed. Christine Bold, 9 vols. (Oxford: Oxford University Press, 2011–12), 6:113–31.

20. Mrs. Roger A. Pryor, "The Mount Vernon Association," *American Historical Register,* January 1895.

21. This impulse characterized the colonial revival. See Vincent Scully, *The Shingle Style* (New Haven, CT: Yale University Press, 1955); William B. Rhoads, *The Colonial Revival* (New York: Garland, 1977); and Richard Guy Wilson, *The Colonial Revival House* (New York: Abrams, 2004), 34–87.

22. "Architectural Criticism," *Architecture,* January 15, 1912, 1, 3, plates 5–7; Henry H. Saylor, "The Best Twelve Country Houses in America: The Home of James L. Breese," *Country Life in America,* March 1915, 46–49. The Orchard was also included in the firm's significant monograph (McKim, Mead & White, *A Monograph of the Work of McKim, Mead & White* [New York: Architectural Book Publishing, 1915], 3:plate 270).

23. "House, Robert J. Collier, Wickatunk, N. J.," *Architecture,* July 1, 1917, plates 114–20; "The Georgian House," *American Architect,* January 7, 1920, 4–6; Samuel Howe, *American Country Houses of To-day* (New York: Architectural Book Publishing, 1915), 240–46.

24. The Commonwealth of Virginia constructed buildings at each of these fairs.

25. Rossiter Johnson, ed., *A History of the World's Columbian Exposition* (New York: D. Appleton, 1897), 485. Whereas the version in Chicago replicated Mount Vernon's architecture inside and out, the San Francisco building only faithfully copied the exterior.

26. Regent Alice Richards wrote the despondent quote in the heading above in a letter to Harriet Carpenter in April 1934: Alice Richards to Harriet Carpenter, April 14, 1934, folder "Fair—Chicago," AMVLA, NLSGW.

27. For examples, see the dining hall at the Jackson's Mill 4-H Camp, West Virginia (1926); the Lowell Inn in Stillwater, Minnesota (1927); Wesleyan College in Macon, Georgia (1926–29); and the Metropolitan Philadelphia branch of the Young Women's Christian Association's "Mount Vernon House" at the Sesquicentennial Exposition in Philadelphia (1926).

28. George Wharton Pepper to Alice Richards, February 29, 1932; Alice Richards to Nathan Straus, Jr., March 6, 1932, folder "Mt. Vernon, Replicas of," AMVLA, NLSGW.

29. Charles Cecil Wall to Doctor C. J. Goebel, February 14, 1935, folder "Policy—Misc.," AMVLA, NLSGW.

30. Both the 1931 and 1932 versions were built by Sears, Roebuck and designed by Charles Kirkpatrick Bryant. Thomas Eddy Tallmadge designed the 1934 replica.

31. The Chicago version was built at 8/9 scale and had colonial revival interiors. Unlike the exhibition pavilion replicas that came before it, this model regularized the house's fenestration.

32. "Historic Mount Vernon Goes to Paris," *Houston Chronicle,* February 22, 1931.

33. Harriet Carpenter to Alice Richards, April 13, 1934, folder "Fair—Chicago," AMVLA, NLSGW.

34. See Thomas E. Tallmadge, *The Colonial Village: A Reproduction of Early American Life in the 13 Colonies, A Guide to the Buildings of Historical Interest* (Chicago: Century of Progress, 1934), and *Colonial Village* (Chicago: Unk Ebenezer and 100 Nabers, 1934).

35. Alice Richards to Nathan Straus, Jr., March 6, 1932, folder "Mt. Vernon, Replicas of," AMVLA, NLSGW.

36. Charles Cecil Wall to Honorable Robert Ramspeck, March 25, 1933, folder "Rep. of Bldgs," AMVLA, NLSGW; George Wharton Pepper to Alice Richards, February 29, 1932; Jason Young to Guy Sears, November 23, 1925, folder "Mt. Vernon, Replicas of," AMVLA, NLSGW; MVLA, Minutes, 1914, 32.

37. Accurate drawings were available in J. C. Haden et al., *The Georgian Period, Being Measured Drawings of Colonial Work,* 12 vols. (Boston: American Architect and Building News, 1898–1902), 6:46, plates 33–35; Paul Wilstach, *Mount Vernon: Washington's Home and the Nation's Shrine* (New York: Doubleday, Page, 1916), 129; Glenn Brown, "The Message of Mount Vernon," *Garden and Home Builder,* March–August 1927, 464; and *Great Georgian Houses of America,* 2 vols. (New York: Kalkhoff Press, 1933–37), 1. The first measured drawings were commissioned by the MVLA and published in a British magazine ("Our Lithographic Illustrations," *Building News,* September 21, 1877, 278 and plate).

38. See James M. Lindgren, "'A New Departure in Historic, Patriotic Work,'" *Public Historian* 18, no. 2 (Spring 1996): 41–60; Daniel Bluestone, "Academics in Tennis Shoes: Historic Preservation and the Academy," *Journal of the Society of Architectural Historians* 58, no. 3 (September

1999): 300–307; and Charles B. Hosmer, Jr., *Presence of the Past: A History of the Preservation Movement in the United States before Williamsburg* (New York: Putnam's Sons, 1965), 153–259.

39. Harrison H. Dodge to P. A. Manker, June 29, 1932, folder "Rep. of Bldgs," AMVLA, NLSGW.

40. "Mt. Vernon Mansion Restored; Looks Now as It Did in 1776," *New York Times,* July 25, 1931, 16; Library of Congress to Harrison H. Dodge, memo, November 14, 1934, box 3, folder "Piazza," Restoration Files, NLSGW; MVLA, Minutes, 1936, 34; Charles Cecil Wall to John Owen, July 19, 1937, folder "Policy—Publicity," AMVLA, NLSGW.

41. Nancy Halsted to Benson L. Lossing, August 5, 1873, September 7, 1874, box 1, Benson Lossing Papers, NLSGW; MVLA, Minutes, 1876, 3. Sarah Tracy and Upton Herbert, Mount Vernon's custodians during the Civil War, did seem to know that the features were not original. John H. Rhodehamel to the director, memo, December 9, 1980, box 6, folder "Summerhouse," Restoration Files, NLSGW.

42. MVLA, Minutes, 1932, 69, 71.

43. MVLA, Minutes, 1936, 34; Morley Jeffers Williams to Elizabeth Hitz, October 20, 1938, folder "Williams, Morley J. Corres. Sent to Vice-Regents, 1931, 1935–1939," Morley Jeffers Williams Collection, NLSGW.

44. Morley Jeffers Williams to Elizabeth Hitz, October 20, 1938, folder "Williams, Morley J. Corres. Sent to Vice-Regents, 1931, 1935–1939," Morley Jeffers Williams Collection, NLSGW.

45. Morley Jeffers Williams to Lillian Wheeler, October 29, 1937, folder "Williams, Morley J. Corres. Sent to Vice-Regents, 1931, 1935–1939," Morley Jeffers Williams Collection, NLSGW.

46. The MVLA hired Williams, a Harvard-trained landscape architect who had also worked under Arthur Shurcliff at Colonial Williamsburg, in 1936. Alice Richards to Morley Jeffers Williams, February 6, 1936, folder "Williams, Morley J. Misc. Papers: Office Expenses, Budgets, Reports & Corres.," Morley Jeffers Williams Collection, NLSGW.

47. Morley Jeffers Williams to Annie Burr Jennings, January 10, 1939, folder "Williams, Morley J. Corres. Sent to Vice-Regents, 1931, 1935–1939," Morley Jeffers Williams Collection, NLSGW. See also Morley Jeffers Williams, "Washington's Changes at Mount Vernon Plantation," *Landscape Architecture,* January 1938, 62–73; Henry I. Brock, "Mt. Vernon: Domain of a 'Planned Economy,'" *New York Times,* February 20, 1938; and *Magazine Antiques,* February 1938, 94, 96.

48. Morley Jeffers Williams to Caroline Brown, February 11, 1938, folder "Williams, Morley J. Corres. Sent to Vice-Regents, 1931, 1935–1939," Morley Jeffers Williams Collection, NLSGW; "The Portfolio: The Mansion House, Mount Vernon, Virginia, Seat of General George Washington," *American Architect and Architecture,* February 1938, 41–52.

49. "The Portfolio," 45.

50. See Hunter Hollins et al., *American Place: The Historic American Buildings Survey at Seventy-Five Years* (Washington, DC: National Park Service, 2008).

51. Johnston photographed Mount Vernon in May and June 1937. Williams also used her pictures of the gardens, service lanes, and the house's west elevation in his 1938 *Landscape Architecture* article.

52. Maria Elizabeth Ausherman, *The Photographic Legacy of Frances Benjamin Johnston* (Gainesville: University Press of Florida, 2009), 124–48, 206–14.

53. Boris Emmet and John E. Jeuck, *Catalogues and Counters: A History of Sears, Roebuck and Company* (Chicago: University of Chicago Press, 1950), 108, 226–28. On Sears, Roebuck, see also Amanda Cooke and Avi Friedman, "Ahead of Their Time: The Sears Catalogue Prefabricated Houses," *Journal of Design History* 14, no. 1 (2001): 53–70, and Katherine Cole Stevenson and H. Ward Jandl, *Houses by Mail: A Guide to Houses from Sears, Roebuck and Company* (Washington, DC: Preservation Press, 1986).

54. The design was probably named after Thomas Jefferson because Sears had already used "Mount Vernon" for an existing plan. Jefferson was a popular historical figure at the time, an early president, and was also identified with Virginia plantations of the eighteenth century.

55. Sears, Roebuck, and Company, "The Jefferson," in *Homes of Today* (Chicago: Sears, Roebuck, and Company, 1932), 30.

56. Mount Vernon–inspired plans appeared in Aladdin in 1941, Hollands in 1947, Garlinghouse in 1940, and *Ladies' Home Journal* in 1937.

57. Henry A. Saylor, ed., *Inexpensive Homes of Individuality* (New York: McBride, Nast, 1915), 16.

58. *Distinctive Southern Homes* catalogue (Dallas: Holland's, the Magazine of the South, 1947), 50.

59. MVLA AR, 1952, 10.

60. Alice Richards to Harriet Carpenter, April 14, 1934, folder "Fair—Chicago," AMVLA, NLSGW.

61. MVLA AR, 1950, 27.

62. "Mount Vernon in Virginia," flyer by McGraw-Hill Text-Films, folder "Public Information—Film, 'MV in VA,' Agreements, Sales. McGraw Hill. 1960–69," AMVLA, NLSGW.

63. MVLA, Minutes, 1950, 76.

64. Public Information Committee, report, October 1951, folder "Public Information: 1948–1951," AMVLA, NLSGW; MVLA, Minutes, 1950, 30–32.

65. MVLA AR, 1952, 14; Public Information Committee, report, October 1951, folder "Public Information: 1948–1951," AMVLA, NLSGW.

66. "Mount Vernon in Virginia," flyer; Charles Cecil Wall to Kenneth Edwards, November 30, 1948, folder "Public Information: 1948–1951," AMVLA, NLSGW; "Memorandum on the Theme and Treatment of the Film, 20 March 1950," folder "Public Information—Film, 'MV in VA,' Production, Affiliated Film. 1950–67, C. C. W.," AMVLA, NLSGW.

67. *Mount Vernon in Virginia* (Affiliated Films, 1950), https://vimeo.com/107067777.

68. Ibid.

69. MVLA AR, 1950, 27.

70. *The Book of Pease Homes for 1954* (Hamilton, Ohio: Pease Woodwork Company, 1954), 35.

71. On the history of the motel, see John A. Jakle, Keith A. Schulle, and Jefferson S. Rogers, *The Motel in America* (Baltimore: Johns Hopkins University Press, 1996).

72. Geoffrey Baker and Bruno Funaro, *Motels* (New York: Reinhold, 1955), 140–41.

73. *Mount Vernon in Virginia.*

Saving Mount Vernon, in Black and White

Toward an Alternative History of Historic Preservation

SCOTT E. CASPER

At Mount Vernon today, African Americans are an important part of the narrative that visitors see and hear. The names of enslaved men and women appear on the interpretive placards around the estate and in the script told by docents within the mansion. The recent addition of a slave cabin in the Pioneer Farm area of the estate, as well as the restoration and reinterpretation of the slave quarters near the mansion, testify to the Mount Vernon Ladies' Association's (MVLA) present-day recognition of the work that enslaved men, women, and children performed there in the eighteenth century. That work cushioned the Washingtons' existence, making possible both their style of living and George Washington's long absences from Mount Vernon to serve as commander in chief of the Continental Army and first president of the United States.

Another history is less visible, indeed well-nigh invisible at today's Mount Vernon: not a story of African Americans' significance in George and Martha Washington's lifetime but rather a story of black people's centrality to the preservation of Mount Vernon in the century after Washington died. Although we are increasingly familiar with eighteenth-century Mount Vernon, George Washington's Mount Vernon, in black and white, the history of its nineteenth-century preservation tends still to be told entirely in white, as the narrative of the Washington heirs and the MVLA. However, throughout the entire nineteenth century, across three generations of Washington family owners and the first two generations of the MVLA, the constant at Mount Vernon was the presence of African Americans. Their story is essential to understanding how this place, its spaces, and its stories came to be preserved for posterity.[1]

At the core of that story lies a key irony; in reinforcing the stories of George Washington and participating in restoring his home and landscape to its eighteenth-century appearance, these African Americans helped ensure that their own stories—the stories of their own lives—would be erased from memory. By

East front of the Mansion House with enslaved men, woman, and children on the piazza, 1858. (MVLA)

SCOTT E. CASPER

helping to place the eighteenth century at the forefront of Mount Vernon's historical memory, they contributed to the historical forgetting of the nineteenth-century Mount Vernon where they themselves lived and worked.

A pencil sketch, probably drawn in the 1880s or 1890s, offers a first window into their story. This image of Edmund Parker is likely the handiwork of Harrison Howell Dodge, superintendent of Mount Vernon from 1885 to 1937. Cropping notes around the side indicate that it likely served as a proof picture for Dodge's 1932 memoir, *Mount Vernon: Its Owner and Its Story*. The sketch depicts an African American man in uniform with a badge seated on a small stool or folding chair, his hands clasped in his lap. His hat lies on the ground beside the chair. Under the picture appears a caption in Dodge's handwriting, which became the caption for this illustration in Dodge's book: "'Uncle Edmund' Parker,—for 34 years the Guard at Washington's tomb."[2]

What was Edmund Parker's story? We might answer that question in two ways. First, what was the story that Parker told visitors, six days a week, from the 1870s until 1898? Second, what was the story of Parker's own life? These were very different stories.

Parker's story for visitors went something like the following, as we know from numerous visitors' accounts:

You are standing on sacred ground. Here you see the sarcophagi of the old General and Mrs. Washington. Some 40 members of the Washington and Custis families are interred here. The general was originally interred in the old tomb, near the river. In 1831 this tomb was erected on a site selected by General Washington himself. He and Mrs. Washington and the other Washingtons were moved to this new tomb. The two shafts outside the tomb were erected to the memory of Mr. Bushrod Washington and Mr. John Augustine Washington II, the successors of General Washington who inherited the property. Bushrod Washington, a nephew of General Washington, was a justice of the Supreme Court and an executor of the General's will. John Augustine Washington II was the nephew of Bushrod Washington, and the father of John A. Washington III, the last owner of the estate, until 1858, when the Ladies' Association which now own it purchased it from him. I came here in 1841, aged 14, as the slave of John A. Washington II. I helped place Mrs. Jane Charlotte Washington into the tomb back in 1855. After she was interred, I watched her sons lock the vault and throw the key into the Potomac River. I have seen dignitaries from across the globe make pilgrimages to this tomb: presidents and first ladies, retired generals, the princess of Spain. The elm tree you see over there was planted by Emperor Dom Pedro of Brazil in 1876. That oak was planted by request of the Prince of Wales, to replace a tree he planted when he was here in 1860, which died. Every one of these trees has a story. Please, ma'am, don't take a cutting from those vines. Please don't take the pebbles around the tomb as mementoes.[3]

When a newspaper reporter for the *Evening Star* of Washington, DC, came to Mount Vernon in 1891 to write about the MVLA's annual meeting, Edmund Parker told him that John A. Washington III had been "a pretty good massa, as they went in dose days," just enough to hint that slavery days had not been happy but not enough to alienate white visitors who harbored fantasies of the Old South. Indeed, visitors who returned to Mount Vernon frequently across the years saw a picture of continuity: the same old buildings overlooking the Potomac, the same ancient trees and paths, and (in one visitor's words) "the same old Virginia darky" keeping watch over the hallowed tomb. The 1891 *Evening Star* article implied as much: "The servants are a very interesting part of Mount Vernon. Edward [*sic*] Parker, the faithful guardian of the tomb, has been on the place, man and boy, just fifty years." For this reporter and probably for hundreds of other visitors, Parker affected a quaintness right down to his description of tourists' Kodak cameras: "Nowadays somebody makes a picture out of me ebery day. Dat is, dey say so; I never sees any of dem. Dey all carries dem little boxes with a hole in one end." After Parker died in 1898, newspapers from Georgia to Nevada ran his obituary because

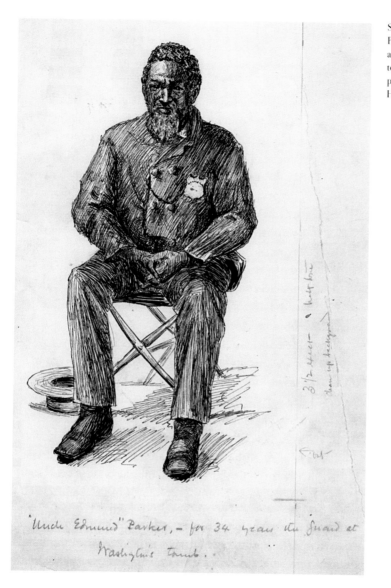

"Uncle Edmund" Parker, – for 34 years the guard at Washington's tomb.

Sketch of "Uncle Edmund" Parker (182?–98), who served as a guard at George Washington's tomb for thirty-four years, possibly drawn by Superintendent Harrison Howell Dodge. (MVLA)

his position had bestowed on him a minor degree of celebrity: "Born a slave," they all said, he had lived to see freedom, but "such changes had few charms for him. He preferred to spend his days as they had begun, within the beautiful and historic enclosure of Mount Vernon."[4]

Visitors heard and obituaries reported only the barest glimpse of Edmund Parker's life story, the part that had brought him to Washington's tomb and the scenes he had witnessed at that spot. But it is possible to reconstruct more of his life, thanks to demographic records (U.S. censuses, the wills of Washington family members who owned him and his family as slaves), documents written by Mount Vernon's white proprietors (John A. Washington III's farm diaries, letters by Dodge and members of the MVLA), and an interview that Parker gave to a *Washington Post* writer in 1898, not at Mount Vernon but at his daughter's home in Washington, where he was dying of stomach cancer. That interview is remarkable as the closest extant document to an oral history of a nineteenth-century African American employee at Mount Vernon, relatively (though by no means entirely) unmediated by a white person's preconception or by the careful calibration of Parker's daily speech at Washington's tomb.[5]

Edmund Parker first came to Mount Vernon neither as an employee of the MVLA nor to stand watch at Washington's tomb. As he said, he arrived many years earlier, as the fourteen-year-old legal property of Jane Charlotte Washington. He had spent his earlier years at Blakeley, the Jefferson County (now West Virginia) plantation where Jane Charlotte spent much of the year. Parker's parents, Milly and Harry Parker, lived there and belonged to Jane Charlotte (and previously to her late husband, John Augustine II); they had at least eleven children. In 1841, Washington made her twenty-one-year-old son, John A. Washington III, the proprietor of Mount Vernon and leased him twenty-one slaves to run the place, including Edmund and his fifteen-year-old sister, Hannah. Along with grown men and other teenagers, Edmund hoed crops, drove plows, and toiled at other farm chores. In the mid-1850s, he married a woman named Susan, whom John A. Washington III had purchased in 1852. According to the *Post* interview, a white parson

SCOTT E. CASPER

married them in the library of the Mount Vernon Mansion. They had nineteen children over the next two decades, including several pairs of twins. Mostly, Parker recalled, slavery meant "mighty hard work. Had more put onto me than I could perform, 'cept as I took care of myself. There was mighty heavy timber on that Mount Vernon farm, and we slave folks was pulled and hauled. Altogether, as far as kindness was concerned, I reckon they meant well enough, although life is a burden to a slave person; indeed it is—left without eddication and the mind terrified all the time." After the Civil War broke out, Parker escaped from Mount Vernon. He worked for the U.S. Army, cooking for Union troops—first the Zouaves in Alexandria and later in the Capitol Prison and at Fort Washington across the Potomac from Mount Vernon.

When he told Mount Vernon's stories to visitors in the 1870s, 1880s, and 1890s, Edmund Parker did not report any of this. It would have seemed entirely at odds with the image he cultivated as the keeper of George Washington's memory: after all, it revealed that Mount Vernon might be someplace a person might wish to escape from, and that the keeper of Washington's tomb had sided with the Union against the army that sought to preserve Old Virginia. Nor did he mention to visitors that he did not really live at Mount Vernon. His family resided in Alexandria; with a load of groceries, Parker took the steamboat to the historic estate every two weeks and bunked in the old laundry building. In short, visitors who imagined him solely "within the beautiful and historic enclosure of Mount Vernon" had no conception that Parker's world was not so enclosed.[6]

At Mount Vernon, Parker became a folk character, old "Uncle Edmund," aging into the part as his hair whitened. Even the term "Uncle," which Harrison Dodge used in his caption, suggested the role. It was the term white people employed to describe African American men of a certain age or appearance: think of "Uncle Tom" or (a more apt parallel in the 1890s) "Uncle Remus," the elderly black man telling stories to white people in the fiction of Joel Chandler Harris. Men of similar age and experience played comparable parts at Andrew Jackson's Hermitage, newly preserved as a historic site, and at other southern plantations that opened to tourists during these years.[7] At home, however, Parker was a husband, father, provider, and eventually a grandfather. His children forged new lives in Washington, DC, distinct from the old plantation: two daughters were a seamstress and a cleaning woman; his sons included a private watchman and a janitor in the halls of Congress. Parker's story was the story of America in the nineteenth century, with enslaved people being worked to the bone while seeking freedom and autonomy, building families in slavery and in freedom—and telling their life stories selectively to white people who might not want to hear everything. Meanwhile, in his work at Mount Vernon, Parker was preserving another set of stories, the eighteenth-century legacies of George Washington.

Parker's stories, both the ones he told visitors and the ones he lived apart from their view, were microcosms of a larger narrative—the essential role of African Americans in American historic preservation. Just as the story of historic preservation in the United States begins at Mount Vernon, so too does the history of black people's part in it. At Mount Vernon, African Americans' work fostered preservation in three significant ways: first, telling stories; second, performing physical labor and commercial work; and third, contributing behind the scenes to recreating the eighteenth-century place.

Parker's storytelling role had a long history. Throughout the nineteenth century and beyond, black people narrated Mount Vernon's stories to visitors from across the country and around the world. From the early 1800s, older black men guided visitors in the mansion and around the grounds and stood watch at the tomb, telling stories of bygone days. Their earliest model was William (Billy) Lee, Washington's Revolutionary War body servant, who was freed by the terms of Washington's will and lived on the grounds until his death in the 1820s. The garrulous Lee told stories of the old general to those who came to listen. A series of African American men inherited stories from Lee or from other black people who had been there earlier. Oliver Smith, whose family had been the property of the first John Augustine Washington, George Washington's brother and Bushrod Washington's father, arrived at Mount Vernon after Bushrod inherited the man-

SCOTT E. CASPER

sion and surrounding grounds in 1802. In his most compelling story, tears in his eyes, Smith told of watching George Washington take his dying breaths. Of course he had not been there; he got his knowledge from Christopher Sheels or one of the other slaves who had. It does not seem to have mattered to most visitors, because Smith gave them exactly what they craved—ostensibly firsthand reminiscences of America's greatest founding father. Like Edmund Parker, Smith had a more complicated personal history, which eventually included Bushrod Washington and his heirs selling most of his children, another slice of nineteenth-century life mostly erased from memory at Mount Vernon (though briefly captured in the newspapers in 1821).[8]

After Oliver Smith came his son Phil (1790–1846), who became the keeper of Mount Vernon's horticulture in the 1830s and 1840s and continued to tell the stories of George Washington's Mount Vernon. Because his post was in the old greenhouse, he added Washington dirtying his hands in the garden, a narrative inherited not just from Smith's father but also from Washington's German gardener Johann Ehlers. Phil Smith gave or sold (at Jane Charlotte Washington's instigation) small souvenirs from the gardens—bouquets of roses or other flowers but never leaves from "the Ginnerl's" exotic lemon tree.[9] Next came the carpenter West Ford (c. 1784–1863), freed by the terms of Bushrod Washington's mother's will, who had worked at Mount Vernon since Bushrod's day. Ford sometimes escorted visitors around the grounds, such as a father and daughters from Norfolk in 1850. He volunteered to tell them everything he knew about George Washington and also how he cared for Washington's grave, unlocking the iron railing every morning, brushing off the flowers and leaves that visitors had thrown onto the sarcophagi as offerings of reverence. Like Oliver and Phil Smith before him and Edmund Parker after, Ford said little about the rest of his own life—for example, the fact that he kept Mount Vernon's accounts when John Augustine Washington III was away or that he owned 214 acres of his own nearby, making him a significant African American landholder in Fairfax County.[10]

Starting with Edmund Parker in the 1870s, the MVLA made the informal practice of black men telling Mount Vernon's stories into a formal position that endured for almost a century. To the ladies and the superintendents of Mount Vernon, this role required just the right sort of man. After Parker died, his son Esau—who had worked at Mount Vernon for several years—applied for the job, but Dodge wanted someone taller and older, a successor "as typical of 'ye olden time'" as Edmund Parker had been, to maintain "as long as we can the time-honored spirit of the place." Thomas Bushrod, the sexton at nearby Pohick Church, looked the part: in his seventies, "especially deferential," and "black with white wool and beard, an

Thomas Bushrod (d. 1902), former sexton at Pohick Church, chosen due to his "character and type" to succeed Edmund Parker as guard at George Washington's tomb. (MVLA)

182

SCOTT E. CASPER

William (Will) Holland served as tomb guard in the 1940s and 1950s. (MVLA)

attractive combination." It helped that he had once been the slave of two fine Virginia families and that his ancestors may have belonged to Bushrod Washington's maternal grandfather. The *Washington Post* described him as "a regular old down-South plantation darky" with just the right appearance, voice, and demeanor for the role. A series of aged African American men succeeded Thomas Bushrod, ending with William (Will) Holland in the 1940s and 1950s. Interviewed for *Ebony* magazine in 1955, Holland attributed his role to destiny and a fascination with George Washington that, he said, went back to his childhood. Raised nearby, he had been a teenaged waiter at the restaurant outside the grounds and then a mansion guard; his father-in-law was his immediate predecessor at the tomb. Probably unlike his nineteenth-century predecessors, Holland read extensively about Washington and consulted with historians. According to *Ebony,* he designed the sentry booth near the tomb, a version of which remains today.[11]

When Holland retired in 1965, the MVLA did not replace him. No documentation reveals why not, but the national context may have played a part. During the civil rights movement, in the year of the Voting Rights Act and at a time of significant unrest, the longtime role may have seemed (as it surely was) a vestige of the Jim Crow South, uncomfortable to local African Americans and perhaps increasingly to the MVLA or its resident director, Charles Cecil Wall. In the 1970s and 1980s, local African Americans—notably Gladys Quander Tancil, the descendant of an enslaved family freed by the terms of Washington's will—would pioneer another sort of storytelling at Mount Vernon: the stories of its enslaved community in Washington's day, stories largely untold by the generations of narrators from Billy Lee to Will Holland. These new stories were the foundations of the "Slave Life" tour that continues at Mount Vernon today (now titled "Enslaved People of Mount Vernon"), specifically examining enslaved lives in the late eighteenth century.

African Americans' physical and commercial work also fostered historic preservation in the decades following the Civil War. Imagine a day in the life of Mount Vernon, circa 1875. If you were a visitor, you would most likely board the steamboat in Alexandria or Washington around 10:30 in the morning, arrive at Mount Vernon around 11:30, enjoy a stroll around the grounds, tour the mansion, and eat a lunch that you prepared. Around 2:00 p.m. you might think about returning to the boat—and at 2:15 the steamboat's whistle would summon the last straggling visitors for the 2:30 departure. If you were a black employee at Mount Vernon, your workday would have begun many hours before 10:30 a.m., when you donned working clothes appropriate to your duties. Tom Mitchell and Warner May (Edmund Parker's brother-in-law) did farm work; Mount Vernon in these years produced hay for the horses and cows, small amounts of other grains, fruit in the orchards, and a few vegetables and herbs. Young West Ford, likely the grandson of the antebellum carpenter-storyteller, worked in the garden under the supervision of a white gardener. This work continued until a little before 11:00 a.m., when the laborers changed into uniforms similar to the one in Dodge's sketch of Edmund Parker. In uniform, they interacted with visitors—Mitchell driving the "ambulance" that transported visitors uphill from the wharf for ten cents if they preferred not to walk and Ford selling bouquets of flowers. After the visitors left at 2:30 p.m., the workers returned to laboring clothes and duties, perhaps until sundown.[12]

African American women were an essential part of this work. The most significant of them, Sarah Johnson, could legitimately call Edmund Parker "Uncle Edmund" because she was his sister Hannah's daughter. A few months after the Civil War ended, a northern abolitionist toured the defeated South to write a travel book for northern readers. At Mount Vernon on September 4, 1865, he met a young African American woman "industriously scrubbing over a tub." He described her as twenty years old and "intelligent and cheerful," with a husband who also worked there and a four-year-old son. And he recorded her words—an extraordinary find in the scores of the travelers' accounts of Mount Vernon. She told him about being one of John Augustine Washington III's slaves and said that Washington had "kept me hired out" because he could make more money off her that way. She told him about how the MVLA had brought her back after the Civil War. She now made seven dollars a month—"a heap better 'n no wages at all!" She put it like this, not unlike her uncle Edmund Parker's description to the *Washington Post* reporter three decades later: "The sweat I drap into this yer tub is my own; but befo'e, it belonged to John A. Washington. You know, the Bible says every one must live by the sweat of his own eyebrow. But John A. Washington, he lived by the sweat of my eyebrow. I alluz had a will'n mind to work, and I have now; but I don't work as I used to; for then it was work to-day and work to-morrow, and no stop." The abolitionist who wrote these words down had his own agenda, to remind readers that slavery had been wrong and that slave owners had exploited their slaves. He sought to demonstrate that former slaves, like this intelligent young woman, were willing to work hard in freedom, contrary to many white people's preconceptions. At first glance, this narrative reads like many others, a white visitor projecting his own ideas onto the black people he saw at Mount Vernon (in this case, abolitionist ideas rather than notions of so-called happy slaves).[13]

Like most white visitors too he did not record the name of the young woman with whom he spoke. Other research fills in the picture. The 1870 U.S. Census lists among Mount Vernon's residents Sarah Johnson, aged twenty-five (so she would have been twenty in 1865); her husband, Nathan; and a son named Smith, aged nine. Other documentation confirms that this was the same young woman the abolitionist had spoken with back in September 1865. Sarah and Nathan Johnson had returned shortly after the war to work for the MVLA. Working backward in time, John Augustine Washington III's farm journals from the 1840s reveal that she was born there in September 1844. A December 1857 advertisement that Washington placed in the *Alexandria Gazette* to hire out several slaves includes a thirteen-year-old girl "accustomed to house work"; that was Sarah too, the only thirteen-year-old girl Washington owned in 1857. If the abolitionist visitor's spin reflected his perspective, his facts came directly from Sarah's life.[14]

Sarah was among approximately a dozen former enslaved people who returned to Mount Vernon after the Civil War as employees of the MVLA, including Warner May, Tom Mitchell, Edmund Parker, and the younger West Ford. Each of them performed a variety of duties before, during, and after the tourist hours. Each earned a monthly wage, ranging from six dollars for a very old man or a small child to the thirty dollars that Nathan Johnson earned by the 1880s. They also earned small sums for additional work; for example, May took the disgusting job of cleaning the outhouses for a few extra dollars a month. Sarah's seven-dollar wage in 1865 rose over time; it was thirteen dollars a month by 1869, twenty in the 1880s, and ultimately thirty dollars in her last years there in the 1890s. Her position at Mount Vernon became more and more significant over those twenty-seven years. Like the men working on the grounds, she performed different duties when

SCOTT E. CASPER

An MVLA employee serves milk from the well house behind the old kitchen around the turn of the century. (MVLA: photograph by Luke C. Dillon)

the visitors were there and when they were not. While most of the men prepared the grounds, she and Nathan readied the mansion for visitors, sweeping, dusting, and placing screens in front of the doors to keep relic-hunting tourists at bay. For the years from about 1874 to 1884 when the MVLA ran a lunchroom in the old kitchen, the Johnsons were its proprietors. Sarah prepared plates of sandwiches, fruit, and ice cream; made coffee; and poured milk. She and Nathan accepted visitors' money, and their son Smith and a rotating cast of other young black men were the waiters.[15]

At the same time these African Americans performed the labor necessary to operate a historic site, they contributed to its eighteenth-century image by effacing the fact that they did their jobs for a monthly wage. Visitors with visions of eighteenth-century hospitality imagined these employees' endeavors as acts of devotion to a hallowed place and the father of his country. The Johnsons, Mays, and Fords knew it was work. They asserted its monetary value in negotiations with their employers, at least once going briefly on strike and later hastening the departure of a superintendent who had run afoul of them and behind on their wages. Some visitors imagined the employees' lives as circumscribed within the historic grounds, but these African Americans themselves used their wages to forge lives apart. Sarah Johnson, for example, purchased four acres of land that had once belonged to John A. Washington III. By the 1910s, long after she left the MVLA's employ, she described herself as a "market woman" who sold her farm produce in Alexandria. She had honed her market skills running the Mount Vernon lunchroom and, after it closed, selling guidebooks and postcards to visitors for a few cents' commission apiece.[16]

In the late nineteenth century, African Americans also became the equivalent of historical consultants in the process of preservation itself, because some of them had known Mount Vernon before the MVLA purchased the mansion, when it remained in the hands of Washington family members. In 1896, with the ceiling in the central hallway of the mansion sagging, Harrison Dodge wondered whether to reinforce it with a straight beam or an arch, depending on historical authenticity. The existing iron girder with round columns installed by his predecessor was obviously a nineteenth-century replacement. Dodge consulted everyone who might remember: the previous superintendent, John A. Washington's son (a small boy when his family moved out in 1858), and Sarah Johnson. "Sarah says she remembers perfectly," he wrote, that it had been a straight timber "when she was a child here," and she reported that an arch had been installed later. For Dodge, memories from a slave childhood were valuable clues to the authentic architectural past. Like many visitors, Dodge and the MVLA sometimes collapsed history and imagined present-day African American employees as relics of a past before their lifetimes: Sarah had been born forty-five years after George Washington died.[17]

SCOTT E. CASPER

A similar episode concerned the younger West Ford, born a few years before Sarah and, like her, employed at Mount Vernon in the decades after the Civil War. By 1909, Ford had been away for almost twenty years, but Dodge sought his memories as well concerning the old slave quarters that had burned down seventy-five years earlier. In the Mount Vernon archives is this affidavit, "signed by West Ford in September 1909":

I am West Ford. I was born at Mount Vernon and belonged to Mr. John A. Washington. I am now 75 years old. My parents & all my grandparents were at Mount Vernon & belonged to Gen'l George Washington. After Mr. John A. Washington sold Mount Vernon to the Mount Vernon Association the Ladies kept me on as Head Gardener. But one day I got to be a minister & had to leave the Ladies & Mount Vernon.

Now, some of the Mount Vernon Ladies want me to tell what I remember about the Quarters that were burned down. I mean the Quarters, nearly N.E. of the Well—opposite the Quarters rebuilt on both sides of the Greenhouse. The place was burned before the Green Houses were burned. My Father lived there in those Quarters. What I remember is, when I was a little boy I played in the ruins & built houses of the old bricks and stones—there were not many left for they were carted away to fill in the low places on the road to the West Lodges, but there was enough for me to play with.

The exact spot I pointed out to Mr. Dodge last year when I was at Mount Vernon. The Quarters were by two old Cherry Trees.[18]

Ford's affidavit is remarkable in several ways. Like Dodge's consultation about the beam in the mansion, it reveals Mount Vernon's white proprietors and stewards seeking the reminiscences of elderly African Americans as evidence for potential reconstruction of the "authentic" Mount Vernon. Further, it illuminates something about African American childhood on the estate in the 1830s and 1840s; it is a source for the nineteenth century, not the eighteenth.

However, like the Works Progress Administration interviews with former slaves conducted in the 1930s, Ford's affidavit was filtered through a half-century of memory and forgetting, storytelling and embellishment. Young Ford's parents and grandparents had never belonged to George Washington; they came later, when Bushrod Washington inherited the mansion. His narrative of religious calling was partly true: when he told this story in 1909, he was indeed a preacher in Stratford, Connecticut. In the late 1880s, when he still worked at Mount Vernon—not as head gardener, but as the assistant to the white head gardener—he had been licensed as a marriage celebrant and begun preaching in Fairfax County and in Maryland, as the Reverend John West Ford. But other factors probably played at least as great a role in his decision to "leave the Ladies & Mount Vernon," including his first wife's illness and his desire to live on the land he owned near his children's school, three miles away.[19] Even at two decades' remove, Ford continued to calibrate his stories for the white people who would hear them. We can see this in every generation, from Oliver Smith describing the Washington deathbed scene he had never witnessed to Edmund Parker pretending not to know what a camera was.

Across the nineteenth century and into the twentieth, African Americans transported visitors vicariously to George Washington's eighteenth-century world through their gracious hospitality, their stories of the past, and their daily work maintaining and reconstructing the appearance of the grounds. In preserving and creating historical memory, they simultaneously helped erase the historical memory of their own lives—their struggles and strivings in slavery and especially in freedom. We might say, of course, that this is always the case at historic sites; visitors do not come to hear the life story of the person giving the tour, serving them lunch, or sweeping the grounds. But at Mount Vernon in the late nineteenth century, there was this difference: visitors imagined they *were* seeing these African Americans' own life story—fixed to the place, "belonging to the family" (in the parlance of the day)—and for the most part, those black people did not contradict that preconception. They knew what it meant to the visitors and to the MVLA.

SCOTT E. CASPER

They knew also that it afforded them a measure of dignity in the visitors' eyes and, not inconsequentially, a monthly wage that compared favorably with the wages earned by African Americans elsewhere in the vicinity.

Over the past several decades, scholars of preservation and interpretation have analyzed the presentation of slavery and the contemporary experience of nonwhite interpreters at historic sites. Sociologists have categorized the different levels at which present-day sites integrate enslaved people's experience into the stories they tell, from neglect to "segregated knowledges" (black history on the grounds and in outbuildings, white history in the big house) to full reinterpretation everywhere on the estate. Historians have unearthed and analyzed past and recent debates from within governmental agencies such as the National Park Service and at specific sites over how to tell the stories of slavery, "the tough stuff of American memory." Anthropologists and scholars of cultural performance have explored the ways African American and Native American interpreters employed at historic sites conjure up an "authentic" past for mostly white tourists, an often-uncomfortable experience for interpreters who are imagined into subordinate positions in the process.[20]

The life stories of Mount Vernon's African American residents and employees in its "post-historic" (that is, after George Washington) period—and by extension the stories of those who have labored and told the stories at historic sites across the 150-year history of American historic preservation—offer a challenge to students of preservation and visitors alike. To the extent that a site presents the stories of those who worked for the owners of the place during the period being interpreted, how can we understand the full humanity of the people who did the storytelling? Can we incorporate the stories of people like Edmund Parker and Sarah Johnson alongside the heroic stories of the pioneering preservationists like the Mount Vernon Ladies' Association into the interpretation at the places that were also the sites of their own history? How can we recount—on their own historic ground—the narratives of their lives and accomplishments, joys and struggles, the stories that they themselves effaced when they recounted the "official" stories of an earlier past? These are the questions and challenges current and future stewards of historic sites like Mount Vernon face.

Notes

1. Their fuller story appears in different form in Scott E. Casper, *Sarah Johnson's Mount Vernon: The Forgotten History of an American Shrine* (New York: Hill and Wang, 2008).

2. Harrison Howell Dodge, *Mount Vernon: Its Owner and Its Story* (Philadelphia: J. B. Lippincott, 1932), illustration following p. 94; original pencil sketch in Visual Resources Collection, NLSGW.

3. For visitors' descriptions of Parker's narration (summarized in this paragraph and the next two), see "Guardian of the Dead: Watchman for Half a Century at the Tomb of Washington," *Washington Post*, November 18, 1894, 17; "The National Capital: Old and New Guard of the Tomb of Washington," *Mansfield* (Ohio) *News*, February 22, 1899, 6; Mrs. O. W. Scott, "Little Folks: Where Washington Lived," *Zion's Herald*, February 13, 1895, 103; J. S. Patterson to John Young, May 9, 1896, J. S. Patterson Letters, Special Collections, University of Arkansas Libraries, Fayetteville; "At Mount Vernon," *Harper's Bazaar*, May 13, 1893, 378; and "Sketches of Mount Vernon as It Is Today," *Chicago Daily Tribune*, February 22, 1900, 14.

4. "In the Old Mansion: The Ladies of the Mount Vernon Association in Session," *Evening Star* (Washington, DC), May 16, 1891, 11; obituaries of Parker include "Guarded Mt. Vernon Tomb: Death of Edward [*sic*] Parker, Watchman There for Half a Century," *Washington Post*, December 31, 1898, 3 ("such changes had few charms"); "A Faithful Guardian of Washington's Tomb," *New York Sun*, January 15, 1899; and "The National Capital."

5. For this and the next paragraph, see "Guardian of the Tomb: Edmund Parker, Watchman of Mount Vernon Dying," *Washington Post*, August 14, 1898, 11.

6. "Guarded Mt. Vernon Tomb."

7. See James M. Lindgren, *Preserving the Old Dominion: Historic Preservation and Virginia Traditionalism* (Charlottesville: University Press of Virginia, 1993), 110, and "Draws Many a Visitor: 'The Hermitage' an Attraction to Strangers in Nashville," *Chicago Daily Tribune*, May 23, 1897, 50.

8. Casper, *Sarah Johnson's Mount Vernon*, 2, 8–9, 52–55, 70–72; *Morning Chronicle and Baltimore Advertiser*, August 24, 1821, 2; "Judge Washington," *Niles' Weekly Register*, September 29, 1821, 70–72; "Judge Washington" and "Notes and Remarks by the Editor," *Genius of Universal Emancipation*, October 1821, 52–55.

9. On Jane Charlotte Washington's role, see Jean B. Lee, "Jane C. Washington, Family, and Nation at Mount Vernon, 1830–1855," in *Women Shaping the South: Creating and Confronting Change,* ed. Angela Boswell and Judith N. McArthur (Columbia: University of Missouri Press, 2006), 30–49.

10. Casper, *Sarah Johnson's Mount Vernon,* 24–30, 58–60.

11. Harrison Howell Dodge to Justine Van Rensselaer Townsend, August 5, 1898, Harrison Howell Dodge Letter Books, Mount Vernon Archives, NLSGW; "Mt. Vernon's Keeper: Thomas Bushrod, of the Fitzhughs and the Lees, Successor of Edmund Parker," *Washington Post,* February 26, 1899, 16; "Tomb Watcher: Negro Guards Famous Vault," *Ebony,* October 1955, 135–38.

12. See Casper, *Sarah Johnson's Mount Vernon,* 132–34, and elsewhere for descriptions of employees' daily work, derived from visitors' descriptions and letters and diaries of the MVLA superintendents.

13. J. T. Trowbridge, "A Visit to Mount Vernon," *Our Young Folks,* February 1866, 91.

14. U. S. Census, 1870, Fairfax County, VA, Mount Vernon District, 34–35, Ancestry.com; John Augustine Washington, Diary, September 30, 1844, Mount Vernon Archives, NLSGW; *Alexandria Gazette,* December 18, 21, 23, 25, 29, 1857.

15. Information about employees' wages is found in ledger books in the Mount Vernon Archives, NLSGW.

16. For Sarah Johnson's self-description as a "market woman," see Deposition of Sarah Robinson, November 7, 1910, in *Wilbert P. Brown v. Florence E. Brown,* chancery case 1910–003, Circuit Court, Fairfax County, VA, Fairfax County Court Historical Records, http://www.lva.virginia.gov/chancery/case_detail.asp?CFN=059-1910-003.

17. Harrison Howell Dodge to Upton Herbert, April 13, 1896, Harrison Howell Dodge Letter Books, Mount Vernon Archives, NLSGW.

18. "Copy of Affidavit Given & Signed by West Ford in September 1909," Restoration Files for the Historic Structures Report, folder "Greenhouse, 1784–1990," NLSGW.

19. U.S. Census, 1910, Stratford, Fairfield County, CT, 25, Ancestry.com. For Ford's history, see Casper, *Sarah Johnson's Mount Vernon,* 168–70, 175–76.

20. On slavery in historic site preservation, see Jennifer L. Eichstedt and Stephen Small, *Representations of Slavery: Race and Ideology in Southern Plantation Museums* (Washington, DC: Smithsonian Books, 2002); James Oliver Horton and Lois E. Horton, eds., *Slavery and Public History: The Tough Stuff of American Memory* (New York: New Press, 2006), especially the essays by Marie Tyler-McGraw and Dwight L. Pitcaithley; and Paul A. Shackel, *Memory in Black and White: Race, Commemoration, and the Post-Bellum Landscape* (Lanham, MD:

AltaMira, 2003). On the challenges faced by nonwhite interpreters, see, for example, Laura Peers, "'Playing Ourselves': First Nations and Native American Interpreters at Living History Sites," *Public Historian* 21 (Fall 1999): 39–59, and Paige Raibmon, *Authentic Indians: Episodes of Encounter from the Late-Nineteenth-Century Northwest Coast* (Durham, NC: Duke University Press, 2005). For one interpreter's perspective, see Karen E. Sutton, "Confronting Slavery Face-to-Face: A Twenty-First Century Interpreter's Perspective on Eighteenth-Century Slavery," *Common-Place* 1 (July 2001), http://www.common-place.org/vol-01/no-04/slavery/sutton .shtml. The February 2014 issue of *Public Historian* (volume 36, no. 1) is devoted to the issue of race and slavery in historical interpretation; see especially Ywone Edwards-Ingram, "Before 1979: African American Coachmen, Visibility, and Representation at Colonial Williamsburg" (9–35), for instructive parallels with the stories of William Holland and other Mount Vernon employees described here, and Amy M. Tyson and Azie Mira Dungey, "'Ask a Slave' and Interpreting Race on Public History's Front Line: Interview with Azie Mira Dungey" (36–60), for the perspective of a recent African American interpreter whose web series about the experience has gained considerable attention.

SCOTT E. CASPER

Mount Vernon and America's Historic House Museums

Old Roles and New Responsibilities in the Preservation of Place

CARTER L. HUDGINS

Let me begin by reporting that historic preservation is alive and well in South Carolina, Ann Pamela Cunningham's home state, where, happily, the news for historic house museums is generally optimistic. It is said that many of the tools the modern historic preservation movement has plied were invented in Charleston in the middle of the twentieth century, but earlier, nearly a century earlier, Miss Cunningham's effort to save Mount Vernon inspired a movement that has enriched each of us and the nation immeasurably. Our stories, Charleston's and Mount Vernon's, are inextricably linked. When the historic preservation movement found its feet in Charleston in the 1920s, it followed the Mount Vernon formula. The Society of the Preservation of Old Buildings, later the Preservation Society of Charleston, acquired venerable houses and opened them to the public.

This essay was first presented as the keynote lecture at the 2013 George Washington Symposium "Unveiling the Past at Mount Vernon: Shining New Light on the Man by Preserving the Place," November 16, 2013.

This is a solution the Charleston Museum, Historic Charleston Foundation, and the Classical American Homes Preservation Trust have plied ever since the first decision to save the city's most important buildings by operating them as museums.[1] We are better for it.

Americans know a great deal about the narrative of our shared national experience because we can visit and learn from the places where history unfolded. It matters, I think, that we can, quite literally, walk in the footsteps of America's founding fathers, that we can tramp through ground hallowed by bravery and sacrifice, and that we can trace the waystations slaves followed north toward freedom. We can, in short, pose questions about the American past and our relationship to it by standing where history was made. That is one reason why falling visitation and the financial uncertainty that bedevil far too many of the nation's and Charleston's historic places is so puzzling. One of the great ironies of living in a state that values its history—and where there is seldom any shyness about using history as a political cudgel when it is convenient—is that state appropriations for state historic sites, state archives, and other venues of public history have declined with roughly the same velocity as state support for higher education.[2]

Public support for history and popular interest in it have followed parallel courses in the last two decades. We know more about the former than we do the latter. The Great Recession from which we are still recovering precipitated many challenges to long-held assumptions. One of them was that the budgets of local, state, and federal governmental agencies would retain the kind of funding that some of us remember fondly. Not too long ago, public monies and the public policies those funds expressed supported our efforts more actively than they do now. We know today that much needed—and for some sites essential—support has ebbed away as debate about the purposes of government have roiled the nation's political discourse. While there may indeed be some aspects of American corporate and banking life that are "too big to fail," we have yet to hear any discussion about whether any historic places are "too important to close."

This essay struggles with the knotty question of whether historic house museums are sustainable. That simple question raises complicated issues, at once both essential and, as I understand them, existential. One of the problems wrapped up in the question of the sustainability of historic house museums concerns the old dynamic relationship of historic houses to historic preservation: Will historic house museums continue to be recruiting grounds for new generations of experts and new converts to historic preservation's cause? I see the future of our profession every day in the students I teach and see in them cause for great optimism. Even so, I sometimes worry that those of us who teach are perhaps preparing our students to meet expectations that no longer hold. Be warned, then, that what follows is part jeremiad, part exegesis, and part pep talk. This is, in short, a cautionary tale that leads toward a set of recommendations that hope to assure the ideological and intellectual integrity and sustainability of historic house museums while bolstering their roles as the training grounds for Ann Pamela Cunningham's twenty-first-century successors, the next leadership generations of America's historic preservation movement.

This is probably a good place to indulge in a little history on how we got here. It is commonly understood that America's first house museums planted the seeds for using historic places to mark American cradles, to commemorate events and persons instrumental (perhaps indispensable) to the beginning of the republic and its success. These places quickly became venues for lessons in American citizenship. Mount Vernon was certainly one of those places, but so were the buildings gathered by William Sumner Appleton and the Society for the Preservation of New England Antiquities (SPNEA) and the stalwart women of the Association for the Preservation of Virginia Antiquities (APVA), who saved Jamestown and soon thereafter the Rising Sun Tavern and Mary Ball Washington's house in Fredericksburg. Stratford Hall, home to the Lee Family and revolutionary fervor, and Monticello, refuge of its resident aesthete, were rescued later as were the barns, sheds, houses, and tools that Henry "history is bunk" Ford gathered up for Greenfield Village. Carefully created and tended tableaux of "colonial" furniture, arranged more for aesthetic effect than historical accuracy, offered lessons about the moral duties of American women and the rewards of tidiness and domesticity. Historical accuracy ceded precedence to being in the presence of the instructive, transformative power of history.[3]

History was for leaders of the founding generation of historic house museums a somewhat malleable construct. While the medium was important, the message mattered more. The result was that in the tension between accuracy and indoctrination, the latter won more than the former. James Branch Cabell, a Richmond writer connected by kinship to early efforts to save Virginia's most historic places by transforming them into museums, expressed attitudes about the role of history that bear recalling. As heroic versions of Virginia's role in the founding of the nation gathered momentum in the first decades of the twentieth century, Cabell remarked, "For in Virginia, I can but repeat, we shape our history with discretion, in the same instant that we decline to stint the higher needs of our patriotism by accepting anything one whit short of the most edifying and pleasing history." He continued, "When outsiders babble that a great deal of this history did not ever happen, they speak beside the mark. The past is done with; but our beliefs as to the past endure. Upon all imaginable counts, it is far better that these beliefs should be agreeable and inspiring and magnanimous; and that they should so prompt us to live in a manner not unworthy of our forefathers."[4] For Cabell and not a few of his contemporaries, historic places and buildings were useful as venues for venerating selected slices of the past and inspiring virtuous civic deportment. That impulse remains with us. Archaeologist Julia A. King's recent study of the cultural landscape of rural St. Mary's County, Maryland, discovered a similar process. King traces the origins of Maryland's powerful founding myths to antiquarian John Pendleton Kennedy, an attorney whose essays created a reality more endurable and more resilient than the truth. Like Cabell's Virginia, Kennedy's eastern Maryland was dotted with sites where America's best virtues, among them tolerance, liberty, opportunity, and fair play, anchored a historical narrative that has proven durable and resistant to correction.[5]

America's historic house museums laid the foundations for what later would

CARTER L. HUDGINS

be called historic preservation. But before that phrase described the process that saved Monticello and Stratford Hall, these houses served as incubators for the professionalization of the movement in the second quarter of the twentieth century. In the 1920s, organizations formerly led by committed women surrendered leadership, philosophy, and policy to credentialed men. As the Great Depression herded technical expertise to the Historic American Buildings Survey (HABS) and other state and federal projects, thinking about historic houses shifted subtly from supposing that historic houses like Monticello were venues for domestic tableaux to considering them as artifacts whose survival depended on more than a spinning wheel or two and a dash of paint.

Securing the future for America's important places depended, it was then argued, on experts, and experts were, by the definition of the time and with few exceptions, men. One of the most active of these new male experts was Fiske Kimball. Elizabeth Hayes, secretary to Reverend W. A. R. Goodwin, rector of Williamsburg's Bruton Parish Church and local leader in the effort to restore Colonial Williamsburg, occupied a privileged position from which she observed the early iterations of preservation philosophy. Hayes recalled that Kimball was "very aggressive and says just what he thinks." She remembered that Kimball was "on the side of the archaeological architects who believe that anything that was known to have been erected at a certain period, whether beautiful or not, should be reproduced truthfully." Other members of the architectural oversight committee disagreed and contended that restored buildings "should be improved and made more pleasing." Friction between the "archaeological" and "pleasing" points of view was not resolved, of course, at Williamsburg and would resurface after World War II.[6]

If preservation-minded experts still argued philosophical perspectives after World War II, then who should fill leadership roles at places saved earlier by women was not. Trends set in motion during the Depression, one of them the pursuit of curatorial excellence, gathered momentum. Historic house museums espoused the creation of historic sets, staged recreations of interiors prized for aesthetic brilliance and for what was then understood as truth and accuracy. This inclination—

history rendered as a snapshot of a single exceptional moment—has had remarkable staying power and still shapes the interpretative protocols of many American historic sites. This mode of presentation, admirable as it is for suggesting human agency in the scenes visitors were invited to view, ruled at the time of the passage of the National Historic Preservation Act (NHPA) of 1966. Proponents of the "time piece" room, however, were, it seems, only vaguely aware that the new social history was already opening a door to a broadening view of history and accordingly the responsibilities of historic places to present a more inclusive and democratic history. As national preservation leaders set in motion the programs prescribed by the NHPA, the celebration of America's bicentennial inspired what one observer has called an "astounding fervor to set aside local homes and turn them into museums." What turned out to be a brief if enthusiastic commemoration would not, however, save Cold War–era historic house vignettes of unperturbed domestic tranquility that implied a world in which genial, uncomplaining laborers, artisans, domestic workers, and slaves were unseen and unheard.[7]

Meanwhile, back in the 1950s, some of the twentieth-century fathers of the modern historic preservation movement, Charles Peterson and James Marston Fitch prominent among them, emerged from HABS to assume professional positions from which they shaped national approaches to historic preservation and how it was taught.[8] The retirement of the Fitch/Peterson cohort and formidable women such as Frances Edmunds in Charleston and Anne St. Clair Wright in Annapolis—who both shaped local historic preservation organizations—marked the passing of a generation and of a broadly shared set of assumptions about the value and purpose of historic preservation and the public role of historic places. This generation had recruited acolytes to the cause who in turn assumed their mentors' places in the 1970s and 1980s in the national apparatus and at historic house museums and historic sites. That generation is now graying. Four decades ago, this generation championed and built new organizations, among them the Vernacular Architecture Forum and the National Council for Preservation Education. Both groups played important roles in the expansion of what the nation considered important. Their meetings have, of late, assumed the look of the church congregations where row on row of graying heads outnumber new converts. Questions about the future of the historic house museum are the insistent companion of this generational shift. As the founding members of these two organized retire, the historical sites and museums they created and led number in the thousands.[9] Some historical house museums have welcomed visitors for more than a century. Most opened to the public more recently. They range in size from the mansions of Newport, Rhode Island, to prairie cabins. Collectively, they provide points of entry into a broader history than did the places open for visitation prior to passage of the NHPA. But just as historic site museums and historic houses assumed a broader set of interpretative responsibilities, they encountered strong financial headwinds, stirred up in part by the Great Recession and in part by changing habits in the consumption of history.[10]

That brings us to these two questions: First, now what? And second, who will follow us? Another way to grapple with these essential, existential questions is asking the question this way: What responsibilities will historic houses museums embrace in recruiting, training, and sustaining the next generations of experts on whose shoulders the future of historic house museums will rest? The answer lies in no small part in the ways that the nation's historic houses will compete, as they have for at least three decades, with a broadening view of not only how American audiences consume history but also how they understand and define it. Historic house museums, once alone, occupy an increasingly crowded marketplace where history, some of it real, some of it faux, and much of it more accessible than the codes conveyed by coves, cornices and cymas, have captured larger and larger shares of the history market.[11]

America's venerable historic houses find themselves in an increasingly competitive and crowded marketplace as the composition and diversity of American audiences expand and embrace wider and wider aspects of the national experience.[12] This essay does not address audience building per se. It would, however, be shortsighted to consider how to recruit and train the next generation of house museum leaders without at least acknowledging the growing gap between Cold War–era models and where we are today.

We all know that we are in the entertainment business. If I needed proof, it hit me more than a decade ago when the Historic Charleston Foundation conducted the first scientific measurement of visitor attitudes toward history and its consumption in Charleston. The foundation already knew that the amount of time Americans allocate annually to leisure was small and growing smaller. The weeklong family vacation for most is an artifact of a bygone era. What leisure remains is occupied largely by shopping, an activity now as much recreation as necessity. In short, most American families, given a choice between a museum and a mall, will choose the mall. Declining visitation at our national parks reflects many contributing factors, among them shorter vacations, less disposable income, and computer games. The large share of American leisure now occupied by recreational retail is a factor we of course have acknowledged by insinuating shopping opportunities into the visitor experience at our own sites.

More troubling, perhaps, is this. Once they are "on the road," that dwindling tribe of American families in search of history find it in places that cause some of us hives. A night or two at the Paris or the Venetian in Las Vegas will be as good as a trip to the real things and, for more than a few visitors, acquire the same historical validity. Robert Venturi and his colleagues were right; we can learn from Las Vegas. We just did not anticipate that the Strip would teach European history and geography.[13] A carriage ride in Charleston with a driver who gladly spins tall tales will be the real history of Charleston for visitors who venture no further into the rich, contested, complex history of the hometown of the Stono Rebellion, Christopher Gadsden and "Don't Tread on Me," the Denmark Vesey insurrection, nullification, secession, Robert Smalls, and Fort Sumter.

We should acknowledge the willingness of many Americans to accept without critical reflection what flies at them from movie screens. The film *Gravity* will, for too many, be the history of American space exploration. Other films such as *The Help* and *The Butler,* social/cultural commentary meant to goad discussion or provoke introspection and dialogue about contemporary issues, will for many be the history of the civil rights movement. No one has as of yet accurately measured how much of Americans' "historical knowledge" comes from films and fiction. We tell ourselves "not too much," but few of us watched even one episode of Henry Louis Gates's documentary *Many Rivers to Cross,* and fewer still will visit civil right museums in Birmingham or Memphis. That more of us experience the past through fictionalized cinematic portrayals is attributable to Hollywood's power. One of the cleverest tag lines I wish I had written said this: "Real History Is Real Close." Regrettably, real history for most Americans is not close enough.

So what is our responsibility in the face of the asserted and much-lamented rise of American ignorance about its past and American indifference toward its history? Do we continue to build audiences as we always have, hoping that some of what we purvey will stick? Does our understanding of our audience change knowing that as many people visited the Stax Records and Sun Records studios in Memphis last year as visited John Adams's house? What messages for us are there in the now equal lines of visitors at Graceland, Elvis Presley's colonial revival–styled house in Memphis, and Thomas Jefferson's Monticello? Or in the attendance reports that indicate that Graceland and Biltmore attracted as many visitors as Colonial Williamsburg, Monticello, and Mount Vernon combined? What lessons might we draw from Historic Jamestowne, where, after a spike in visitation at Jamestown coinciding with the commemoration of the four hundredth anniversary of its founding, the number of tourists who find their way there is declining despite significant marketing efforts and an archaeological program that is predicated on the assumption that the digging will draw higher numbers of visitors?

Many of our colleagues have admitted that the old model of the historic house museum, so successful during the era of world wars and cold wars, is worn out, old, outmoded, drawing declining annual audiences that number far below the numbers we once attracted.[14] There are, of course, exceptions. Mount Vernon is one of them. Graceland is another.

Therein lies at least part of an answer. There is, simply put, more history—more of the past — to embrace and to interpret now than there was when historic preservation's heroic founding generation raised markers at places it agreed were important. The Cold War, the civil rights movement, John F. Kennedy, Martin Luther King, social/cultural upheaval, technological revolutions, and more separate us from what we may soon call the Golden Age of the Historic House Museum. And all of this history is more immediate and more relevant to more Americans than was the case when the historic house museum first appeared as a way to save an important place and tell an important story. The decline of visitation at Colonial Williamsburg and Jamestown and rising visitation at the Spy Museum and the Newseum tell us much about what we need to know. At the very least, the successes of these museums should help us frame the questions we should be asking about where the future is taking us.

Let me suggest that I am confident that as we move forward we will find funding solutions based squarely on audience-building. I suspect, however, that we will embrace more of the tours for differentiated audiences some historic sites have already adopted; behind-the-scenes tours, tours with experts, and after-hours tours all provide greater access, individualized attention, and less waiting. Each will come with challenges, staffing among them, as we think about moving outside our typical 9:00 a.m. to 5:00 p.m. operating hours and scratch our heads about how to monetize our assets.[15]

How we tell our stories and to whom deserves considerable attention. So too should what for many of us is this more interesting, and more important, question: how do we recruit, train, and retain the next generation of museum professionals? I suggest that the answer has six components. Each of these recommendations is grounded on three assertions. First, historic house museums are inherently interesting. Those of us who work at historic sites need no reminder that we find professional and intellectual challenge and fulfillment in what we do. The sites we administer, their surroundings, and their collections and interpretative programs draw visitors because the engagement they provide with the past, both its personalities and processes, is immediate, emotionally satisfying, and intellectually stimulating.

Our houses are, as we know they have been, places of learning. Second, the operation of a historic house museum is challenging. We administer places that were complicated to operate before they became historic. Our modern management tasks are made geometrically more difficult by piling on the challenges of public programming, research, collections, and funding, to name but three modern operational overlays. Third, the continued success of historic house museums matters. I believe that the nation's fundamental sense of itself depends on the continued access to and interpretation of its historic sites and house museums. We are stewards of places that for more than a century have conveyed important chapters of our history to millions. The continued thoughtful preservation of the nation's most important places depends on our organizations and expertise. That is no small challenge.

There is this caveat: What I am about to suggest is possible for some places but perhaps not all. Large institutions have greater capacities and abilities than smaller sites. I appreciate the financial constraints and burdens that historic sites bear and understand the limitations, as well as the responsibilities, that range broadly from small to large institutions. Small or large, all of the thousands of historic houses now in operation across the country have important stories to tell. The six recommendations presented here are intended to spur efforts to build capacities necessary to achieve a sustainable future for them and their progeny, the historic preservation movement.

First, Build Recruitment

All of us who work in the realm of the history museum can recall when the idea of working in historic preservation or historic site museums first struck us. What and where was our epiphany? I recently heard architect Roll McLaughlin, now ninety-three, recall that his moment came during a visit to Colonial Williamsburg while he was stationed at nearby Camp Peary training as a Seabee. Deployed to England and later to France, McLaughlin participated in designing, building, and installing the Mulberry Harbors at Normandy. Roll spent the rest of his professional life engaged with Indiana Landmarks saving his home state's early architecture. This coincidence of person, place, and profession is not unusual. Knowing more than we do currently about the pattern of our decision-making and the shared experiences that inspired us might help with recruitment. Are there, in short, patterns in our conversions narratives that help us understand when the sense of the possible first gripped us?

We have the great advantage of living in a large, populous country where we assume that ad hoc-racy in how we choose our life work will fetch up bright, qualified, committed persons eager to continue the work started a century and a half ago. That system has after all served us well. It may serve us still. I would, however, like to improve the odds and propose that it may be time to survey the profession, or at least a sample of our colleagues, about how and when and why they made their career decisions.

There is a corollary to this recommendation. Some of you will ask, aren't there more than enough capable applicants for the few jobs that open at historic places? The short answer is yes. The longer and more complicated answer takes us to the broadening view of American history and the responsibility we hold to address gender and ethnicity and expertise, a trifecta of backgrounds that very rarely line up. We are better positioned today than we were, but if we are to correlate the history of our sites more effectively with the histories potential visitors are seeking, then we need more assertive, effective recruiting efforts.

There is no easy way to measure the impact of a visit to a historic place. We hear anecdotes, but we really do not have much solid data. What I suggest is that we should stack the odds for success by proactively engaging undergraduate and graduate classes from public history, historic preservation, American studies, and related academic programs populated by students already invested to some degree in our mission. In short, we should move toward a more proactive posture. The field schools in historic architecture and historical archaeology at Old Salem, Sturbridge Village, and Colonial Williamsburg hold great potential. Even so, our succession and sustainability plans must include more purposeful recruiting.

CARTER L. HUDGINS

Second, Build Expectations

Our work is never finished. We know that, but we fail to communicate that clearly. Cutting ribbons, actually or metaphorically, offer important opportunities to thank contributors and patrons. By offering completed projects, from exhibitions to restored rooms, we suggest, even if subliminally, that all is done, that there is nothing left to discover.

We know enough about our audiences to acknowledge that the sense of discovery, of seeing something no one else has seen before or understanding something in a new way, is electric. Perhaps the antidote for anodyne interpretations, what one observer has called "museumification," is to turn the process of discovery, curation, and conservation toward the public. Our work evolves. It changes. What we know changes and so does how we understand the past. Our visitors are capable of understanding that. They find engagement in process far more interesting than exhibit labels that seem to encapsulate for all time the only meaning that can be wrung from an object or room. The cluster of inquisitive visitors who bunch up around the perimeters of archaeological excavations at Jamestown, Mount Vernon, Williamsburg, and everywhere else a pit opens within public view tells us this. Broadcasting that our work is unfinished is perhaps also a good way to share our enthusiasm for what we do and the career opportunities we offer.

Is it time for us to tell our own stories, to interpret the taphonomy of our restoration efforts? Should we tell the story of how we went about doing what we did to secure and stabilize and restore our sites? Should we explain why we did what we did? If the answer is yes, how should we do that? Should we be telling visitors how we saved this place, and in saving it how we shaped the shared memory of it and the historical and cultural narratives that accompany our efforts? We have been busy for 150 years, long enough that it is time to include the history of our engagement and interaction with the houses we interpret and preserve in the story we present to our visitors.

Much as we hate to admit it, we are in the twilight of what John Adams called an epocha, a singular era. Boomers like me will, this year and next and the five years that follow, retire in droves. During the boomer era, objects became an important source of historical questions. Our collections unlocked more about the lives of previously unstudied, unappreciated, unacknowledged residents of early America than previously thought possible. That scholarship did more than simply push back the boundaries of ignorance. It uncovered new knowledge, developed new techniques, and led to new thinking about the past. Much of what was learned will be passed along in admirable publications, but there is much else that will, unless we develop new mechanisms for information transfer, not survive much beyond the retirement receptions that I envision over the next five years.[16] That brings me to my third recommendation.

Third, Build Expertise

America's historic house museum and historic sites have for many decades cultivated site-specific and broad topical expertise. Some of that expertise was gained on site, on the job. Some of it was hired in the form of expert consultants who could solve problems and provide technical advice we could not. From the 1960s on, formal academic training has assumed a significant share of the responsibility for training curators, administrators, and historians. The result is that America's historic house museums are in better-trained hands than ever. Much of that hard-won expertise, and some argue most of what the current generation of experts has learned, will be lost because we are better at training than we are at succession planning and the intergenerational transfer of knowledge. Among the challenges we face in caring for historic buildings and their collections, maintaining the expertise we need may be our most complicated task.

We will, I suspect, always be able to call in expert consultants when we need them. There is, however, other kinds of expertise. The first is expertise of place. What I mean by expertise of place might also be called experts in place, and when I say it that way I think about two colleagues in particular. John Pearce, now retired director of the James Monroe Law Office Museum in Fredericksburg, Virginia, knew intimately the history of his site, President Monroe, and the early republic. John Larson, recently retired from Old Salem, garnered his deep knowledge of German culture in western North Carolina from longtime employment there. All of us know other museum professionals like them. Every place needs at least one John, that person who knows two histories, both the history the museum interprets and the history of the institution itself. We frequently forget that there is value in making sure that we understand the place and its history. We tend to overlook the benefits that come from moving expert to expert into the future, passing along what one generation learned to the next. That seldom happens, and the cost is that we reboot often, sometimes several times a decade. It is time for us to create succession plans that are clear-headed, purposeful processes, included in our master plans, to provide a mechanism to insure that what long-serving experts know is transferred to their successors. We all have friends who will when that proverbial bus hits them take all they know with them. We should not let them go without first passing their expertise along to the next generation.

The second kind of expertise is the kind leading historic sites already produce. The production of new scholarship is certainly one of our most important charges. And it is one of the most important ways that we build expertise for our sites and for others. The production of new scholarship and our active participation in the scholarly and professional organizations that inform what we do is one of our most important obligations. That is also what separates historic sites from historic attractions, education from entertainment. The production of new scholarship requires staff dedicated to the pursuit of questions and projects that matter to us and to our educational programs. This means we must recruit young scholars to do the research. That, in turn, will lead to careers in our field. This has happened serendipitously. I can trace the intellectual genealogies of many of our colleagues through research programs that once flourished at Plimouth Plantation and St. Mary's Cittie. You can probably think of others.

There is a third leg to building expertise. In addition to deep knowledge about place and institution and collection, building expertise suggests to me building relationships with educational programs, formalizing programs that bring nascent curators, administrators, and historians to take on significant projects. And that takes us to sustainability.

Fourth, Build Sustainability

There are ways to make our endeavor more sustainable. Internships have long been both opportunities for cross training and stepping-stones to first jobs and then careers. I suggest that we need to investigate more formal and longer training opportunities, that we look for ways to lengthen internships into apprenticeships. Colonial Williamsburg has, for example, initiated digital imaging fellowships with funding from a generous Mellon Foundation grant. Short-term residencies in Williamsburg provide a venue though which Colonial Williamsburg accomplishes, incrementally, the creation of virtual Williamsburg while it provides training that will energize and inspire parallel efforts at the fellow's home institution. The National Trust for Historic Preservation sponsors an engineering exchange program, an opportunity for a structural engineer to spend six months shadowing and working with the trust's architectural program. Both strike me as the kind of short-term apprenticeship/externships that invest in our future. Both programs bring new expertise to our side while they win support and encourage interaction with co-operating professional disciplines.

Another mechanism that deserves attention is the creation of entry-level appointments—two- to three-year limited term staff appointments that would allow young professionals an opportunity to hone new skills as well as provide a vehicle through which advanced programs transfer skills, information, and technical expertise to the broader field. Some universities have done this for decades. So too have churches. Why not historic house museums? To do this we will need to extend what we might call the benefit horizon, or perhaps point of investment recapture, from weeks or months to years and perhaps decades. We think in longer time scales when we write strategic plans, interpretative plans, and collections policies. It is time we did the same thing with human capital. Embracing this kind of outreach will redefine how we describe our broader obligations. That process will entail transforming the way we see ourselves, from consumers of talents to producers of it. I suggest that one of the measures of our success will be the number of leaders we produce. The Getty Conservation Foundation has made that transition and so too, in part, has Monticello with its Digital Archaeological Archive of Comparative Slavery fellowships.[17]

There is a shorter, compressed (let's call it the "executive") version of this. Consider two-day symposia, offered in the academic off-seasons (early January and mid-May) where students with a professed interest in what we do immerse themselves in the history of a site, the trajectory of its mission, its purpose, and its practices. These short, intense symposia would provide opportunities for young proto-professionals to immerse themselves in the scholarly work underway at places like Mount Vernon and the opportunities that research provides to demonstrate the connections among material culture, archaeology, landscape, and architectural conservation. Fieldwork opportunities to dig, draw, and document would provide further exposure. Some participants will demure, but others will encounter the transformative experience that all of us had somewhere, sometime, at an early point in our graduate work.

Fifth, Build Capacity

America's graduate programs in public history, historic preservation, and allied disciplines, among them archaeology, American studies, landscape architecture, and planning, from which current professional leadership is drawn reflect our current pedagogical strategy. These academic programs provide sound training, but the complexities of museum operation and museum educational programs are now, and have been, daunting. The tasks essential to the administration of a historic house museum ultimately present us with responsibilities and challenges few of us predicted and few of which appeared on any course syllabus. Most of us are thus well but narrowly trained, well siloed with curators here, historians there. As a result, there is tension between the technical professional competencies we admire and celebrate in fields related to the museum's mission and the inclination to cede leadership responsibility to intelligent men and women with track records as managers.

Let me suggest that it is time to institute cross-training for entry-level staff and midcareer professionals. Unless we train our own young experts in managerial skills, we run the risk of imposing a new kind of glass ceiling, a new career barrier above which CEOs and COOs come and go, and below which experts labor in obscurity with little hope of rising to positions of leadership. We tell young professionals that professional accomplishment matters and that they are valued for their technical expertise and scholarship. And they are. If, however, we signal that our young experts will never be quite grown up enough to lead—to hold top jobs—we risk curtailing the flow of capable young professionals on which the success of our profession depends.

Sixth, Build Passion

As the energetic and emotional style of preaching that propelled America's eighteenth-century Great Awakening gathered momentum, critics of rationalist theologians were said to have crowed, "Cold reason cannot convert." We may have reached such a point in our efforts to secure the future of historic house museums. I suggested earlier that historic house museums have never been in better hands. The technical expertise we can bring to bear on the conservation of our collections, the assessment of historic fabric, and the histories of our buildings is more advanced and more sophisticated than it ever has been. Our expertise allows us to know more (and know more precisely) than could any of our predecessors. The generation of museum professionals now on the verge of retiring, and their younger colleagues who will take their places, exude cool professional competence. But are we too coldly technical? Can we convert new professionals, new leaders, and new supporters to our cause by "cold reason," by technical brilliance alone?

Yes, we will in part. We know that the technical challenges posed by architectural riddles, conservation of objects, and discovery of architectural finishes will entice many. The technical riddles we face and the imminent possibility of discovery lies at the heart of why what we do professionally is inherently interesting. Most of the visitors who pass through one of our houses, however, may never encounter our excitement. No matter how skillful, how animated, and how knowledgeable a docent or tour guide may be, unless our interpretative narratives focus on the processes of investigation, analysis, and discovery, our visitors will see only the end result. The process—from question to discovery to installation—will remain unseen and unknowable. Let's pull back the curtains. Let's share what we know and how we know it with our visitors. If the story is too complicated to tell during a standard twenty-minute tour, then we have the electronic capabilities to open the processes of discovery. We will, as a result, have better-informed visitors. And we will build broader support, attract new professionals, and draw new leaders to our cause.

In the second half of the twentieth century, a quiet revolution transformed the historic house museum and its role. Newly professionalized curators continued to pay intense attention to getting historic rooms "right," but many of them expanded their responsibilities. Influenced by broad changes in the specialized academic programs that became the primary venues for professional training, the curators and museum directors who assumed leadership after the bicentennial knew the finer points of connoisseurship. But they also thought in broader terms. They expected to discuss how cultural expressions, from houses to tablewares, changed over time. They assumed they would explain variation and change in fashion and culture. They assumed that they would address social and political movements and other questions essential to understanding the broader context of the historic sites and houses they minded. They assumed that race and gender and ethnicity mattered in writing and revising interpretative narratives. They embraced, in short, a much broader set of responsibilities and faced much higher professional expectations.

The boomer generation of museum professionals has succeeded, I think, on two levels. They have crafted intellectually stimulating interpretative programs. They have applied technically astute methods to the conservation of collections, the restoration of buildings and their interiors, and the reconstruction of lost or ignored buildings and landscapes important to telling the stories of laborers and the enslaved. They have done this while remembering that what they do is inherently interesting.

Not everyone is pleased by the direction America's historic houses have taken since this quiet revolution began to unfold in the 1980s. Indeed, there is a historic site parallel to "take our country back" political posturing.[18] Technical precision and cool professionalism fended off most attacks on the broader, and more democratic, questions posed by boomer curators and museum directors. But the questions posed by critics of wider interpretative initiatives underscore the ongoing need to lay a path toward a sustainable future for historic house museums. We will if we communicate the excitement that attracted us in the first place. And we will if we remember that we are proprietors of the raw material of history, the artifacts, houses, and manuscripts to which the public turns for entertainment and to learn about the nation's past. Their questions change, and so should we.

Notes

1. See Stephanie Yuhl, *A Golden Haze of Memory: The Making of Historic Charleston* (Chapel Hill: University of North Carolina Press, 2005), 21–52, and Robert R. Weyeneth, *Historic Preservation for a Living City: Historic Charleston Foundation, 1947–1997* (Columbia: University of South Carolina Press, 2000), 1–54. See Charles B. Hosmer, Jr., *Preservation Comes of Age: From Williamsburg to the National Trust* (Charlottesville: University Press of Virginia, 1981), 230–27, and William J. Murtagh, *Keeping Time: The History and Theory of Preservation in America* (Pittstown, NJ: Main Street Press, 1988), 103–12, for earlier narrative summaries of Charleston's place in the national historic preservation movement.

2. Robert Behre, "Why SC Preservationists Are Trying to Keep a Key Tax Break," *Post and Courier* (Charleston, SC), November 26, 2017; Cleve O'Quinn, "South Carolina's 46 Counties Home to More Than 1,500 Sites in National Register of Historic Places," *Post and Courier,*

November 26, 2017; Avery Wilks, "SC Students Will Pay Hundreds More in USC Tuition Next Year," *The State* (Columbus, SC), June 23, 2017; Cynthia Helba, Reethy George, and Glynis Jones, *South Carolina National Heritage Corridor Evaluation Findings* (Rockville, MD: Westat, 2012).

3. Patricia West, *Domesticating History: The Political Origins of America's House Museums* (Washington, DC: Smithsonian Institution, 1999).

4. James Branch Cabell, *Let Me Lie: Being in the Main an Ethnological Account of the Remarkable Commonwealth of Virginia and the Making of Its History* (1947; reprint Charlottesville: University Press of Virginia, 2001), 74.

5. Julia A. King, *Archaeology, Narrative, and the Politics of the Past: The View from Southern Maryland* (Knoxville: University of Tennessee Press, 2012).

6. "The Background and Beginning of the Restoration of Colonial Williamsburg, Virginia," typescript, 1933, Elizabeth Hayes Papers, 1924–38, Special Collections Research Center, Swem Library, College of William and Mary. For Kimball's role at Colonial Williamsburg and as one of the new "experts" who transformed historic preservation and historic house museum restorations in the first half of the twentieth-century, see West, *Domesticating History,* 121–27, and Hosmer, *Preservation Comes of Age,* 899–903, 962–65.

7. Gerald George, "Historic House Museum Malaise: A Conference Considers What's Wrong," *History News* 57, no. 4 (2002): 2; Gerald George, "Historic Property Museums: What Are They Preserving?" *Forum Journal* 3, no. 4 (1989): 4. On Colonial Williamsburg's interpretative transition, see Richard Handler and Eric Gable, *The New History in an Old Museum: Creating the Past at Colonial Williamsburg* (Durham, NC: Duke University Press, 1997).

8. For recent analysis of how Fitch and Peterson shaped national policy, see John H. Sprinkle, *Crafting Preservation Criteria: The National Register of Historic Places and American Historic Preservation* (London: Routledge, 2014).

9. Patricia Chambers Walker and Thomas Lanham, *AASLH Directory of Historic House Museums* (Lakewood, CA: AltaMira Press, 1999), 2; Museum Universe Date File, FY 2015 Q3 (Washington, DC: Institute for Museum and Library Services, 2015), https://data.imls.gov /Museum-Universe-Data-File/Museum-Universe-Data-File-FY-2015-Q3/ku5e-zr2b; "Sustainability of Historic Sites in the Twenty-First Century: A Call for a National Conversation" (National Trust for Historic Preservation, report, 2007); Donna Ann Harris, *New Solutions for House Museums: Insuring the Long Term Preservation of America's Historic Houses* (Lanham, MD: AltaMira Press, 2007); Cary Carson, "The End of History Museums: What's Plan B?" *Public Historian* 30, no. 4 (Fall 2008): 9–27.

10. James Oliver Horton and Lois E. Horton, eds., *Slavery and Public History: The Tough Stuff of American Memory* (Chapel Hill: University of North Carolina Press, 2006); Paul Shackel,

Memory in Black and White: Race, Commemoration and the Post-Bellum Landscape (Walnut Creek, CA: AltaMira Press, 2003).

11. Magaly Cabral, "Exhibiting and Communicating History and Society in Historic House Museums," *Museum International* 53, no. 2 (April–June 2001): 41–44; Rosanna Pavoni, "Towards a Definition and Typology of Historic House Museums," *Museum International* 53, no. 2 (April–June 2001): 10–21.

12. Harris, *New Solutions for House Museums.* Harris and other observers have emphasized how tenuous many historic house museums are. It is estimated that slightly more than half receive fewer than five thousand visitors annually, that 65 percent have no full-time staff, and that 80 percent have annual budgets of less than fifty thousand dollars.

13. Robert Venturi, Denise Scott Brown, and Stephen Izenour, *Learning from Las Vegas* (Cambridge, MA: MIT Press, 1972).

14. Carol Stapp and Ken Turino, "Does America Need Another House Museum?" *History News* 59, no. 3 (2004): 7.

15. Robert L. Janiskee, "Historic Houses and Special Events," *Annals of Tourism Research* 23, no. 2 (1996): 398–414; D. Chhabra, *Sustainable Marketing of Cultural and Heritage Tourism* (London: Routledge, 2010).

16. Cary Carson and Carl Lounsbury, eds., *The Chesapeake House: Architectural Investigations by Colonial Williamsburg* (Chapel Hill: University of North Carolina Press for the Colonial Williamsburg Foundation, 2013), summarizes the results of research conducted by Colonial Williamsburg architectural historians over four decades, beginning in the 1980s. This publication is remarkable both for its contributions to historical understanding of early Virginia and Maryland and as a demonstration of how knowledge collected at history museums can be assembled and disseminated.

17. Digital Archaeological Archive of Comparative Slavery, http://www.daacs.org/.

18. Edward T. Linethal and Tom Engelhardt, eds., *History Wars: The Enola Gay and Other Battles for the American Past* (New York: Henry Holt, 1996), and Kirk Savage, *Monument Wars: Washington, D.C., the National Mall, and the Transformation of the Memorial Landscape* (Berkeley, University of California Press, 2005), broadly address shifts in political climate and their effect on the presentation and interpretation of history, as do Horton and Horton, eds., *Slavery and Public History,* and Handler and Gable, *New History in an Old Museum.*

Conclusion

CAROL BORCHERT CADOU AND LUKE J. PECORARO

In the final essay of this volume, Carter L. Hudgins issues a challenge to the American historic preservation community to think critically about historic preservation's trajectory. We concur with Hudgins, appreciate the challenge, and hope that this group of collected essays will inspire dialogue about the field's future. We also hope that it offers a few helpful thoughts for our professional colleagues and supporters. Since it will take years, even decades, to evaluate the long-term effectiveness and sustainability of initiatives described in these collected essays, we submit a couple of Mount Vernon's efforts at best-practice historic preservation for immediate reflection and consideration. The reader will see these efforts echoing MVLA founder Ann Pamela Cunningham's interest to preserve George Washington's estate in its entirety discussed in the introduction, George W. McDaniel's compelling advocacy for whole place preservation, and Carter L. Hudgins's "call to action."

The MVLA's formation of the Department of Historic Preservation and Collections is foremost among the institution's recent efforts. By combining the Department of Restoration with the Department of Collections, the association placed cognate disciplines working toward the goal of preserving Washington's estate in a most collaborative and productive environment. The addition of the agricultural sciences (horticulture and livestock) to the divisions of archaeology, architecture, and collections, and the curatorial department provided Mount Vernon with an integrated historic preservation team. All historic collections, living (i.e., heirloom plants, heritage breed animals) and nonliving (i.e., fine art, archaeological artifacts), are now catalogued, cared for, and preserved as a unified assemblage of cultural resources. This shift toward bringing new and innovative strategies from multiple perspectives is broadening horizons and opening up more potential for research; Thomas A. Reinhart and Susan P. Schoelwer's essay on George Washington's New Room is a fine example of how this combined departmental structure is envisioned to work and bear fruit. Furthermore, this holistic organization of preservation efforts enables Mount Vernon's historic preservation team to build the expertise Hudgins notes is critical to establishing a program that can serve as a stronger leader within the field.

The philosophical shift within Mount Vernon's organizational structure, and the department's focus on developing and retaining staff, is an important factor as we consider the future strength of historic house museums and heritage-driven institutions. As Hudgins suggests, recruitment, the building of expertise, and the transfer of knowledge to a younger generation of scholars are crucial for any organization. Shortly before this publication went to press, a programmatic change within the Colonial Williamsburg Foundation resulted in staff layoffs and retirements, including personnel in the research-driven departments of architecture and archaeology. The scaling back of these two departments realized the loss of the architectural "brain trust" Hudgins describes. It was also a major departure from Williamsburg's Zeus-like status in the pantheon of scholarship on the American colonial period and leaves a void in the ever-shrinking number of institutions where future generations can turn for training in the historic preservation field.

This commentary is not meant to single out Colonial Williamsburg as the only institution to have proceeded down this course, for there is a larger issue at hand. The essays in this volume written by McDaniel, Hudgins, and Carl R. Lounsbury all reference the era of American historic preservation when federal, state, and local entities offered a great deal of financial support to initiatives that have, in recent years, declined significantly or disappeared. As described in the introduction, the MVLA's approach to American historic preservation is quite unusual. It offers a business model focused entirely on private citizens and private funding; the MVLA has never, and presumably never will, accept federal, state, or local government funds. In light of decreasing governmental support for historic sites, perhaps others can utilize this successful business model as a template. And perhaps it is incumbent on all in the American historic preservation field to raise the awareness of our country's men and women—the millennial generation in particular—to the fleeting nature of our historic sites unless they receive sufficient funds and care. Given the growing interest in environmental issues, if we can encourage these individuals to see themselves as able to contribute to the preservation of vistas, views, and lands—not just the "old buildings" and "dusty antiques" of our forefathers—then perhaps we have an opportunity to create relevance as well as the funds necessary to endow our nation's treasured sites for their long-term sustainability.

The challenges of financial sustainability may also mean that we enter a period of stronger collaboration with like institutions in order to bring collective resources to bear when attempting to solve preservation challenges. For instance, Mount Vernon recently added a full-time staff member in the Historic Preservation and Collections Department to manage spatially collected data using geographic information software (GIS). This staff introduction is unique in historic site management, despite the widespread use of GIS across many disciplines, and has occasioned six one-day meetings at Mount Vernon where participants utilizing GIS for historic preservation are invited to share their experiences. These meetings have provided a networking and development opportunity that is not often available at professional conferences. The gatherings have led to the intermingling of those from the academic, cultural resource management, and government sectors. With this venue for easy discussion on preservation challenges, participants have made connections for future collaboration, and the result has proven quite fruitful toward reaching common goals. These shorter meetings aimed at colleagues in the preservation community could be easily adapted to any field of inquiry or study in the preservation field. Sharing challenges and potential or proven remedies also demonstrate to those attending that institutions and individuals are not alone; historic preservation in America started as—and can remain—a group activity. As one colleague aptly notes, "House museum professionals are struggling to find answers—ways to make house museums meaningful and relevant to diverse 21st century audiences. The fallacy of this exercise is that perhaps house museum professionals shouldn't try to do it alone."[1]

Collaboration and inclusiveness may serve well preservation professionals in addition to the next generation of historic site visitors and supporters. It is difficult to project who these groups will be, but looking to the past can perhaps provide some answers. In their essays, Scott E. Casper, and Robert L. Fink, Thomas A. Reinhart, and Alyson Steele offer avenues for bringing meaning to new audiences as they experience history in ways not done before. A recent unpublished survey of Mount Vernon's visitor base suggests that the top reason visitors make the trip to the estate is to see the preserved home of George Washington. These survey results run counter to the notion that visitors no longer want to see homes of singular individuals (especially those of the founding era); instead, perhaps, historic sites need to bring new and different narratives and interpretations to historic house museums in order to fuel future visitation. The story of site preservation in itself is quite compelling and provides fruitful avenues for increasing the audience base either through the deployment of technology (see the essays by Fink, Reinhart, Steele, and Schoelwer), the intersection with landscape preservation (McDaniel's essay), or the presentation of new histories that focus on the power of place (the essays by Casper, Lounsbury, and McDaniel).

CAROL BORCHERT CADOU AND LUKE J. PECORARO

As we contemplate the future of historic preservation in America, maybe the most central message of this volume is that preservation does not happen in a vacuum. It requires the thoughtful work of a range of disciplines, people, and methods focused on a common goal. If we are committed to the long-term sustainability of the field, then we need to take seriously a careful study of the business models, staff organization, funding sources, and visitor surveys that can inform future strategies. This undertaking must be approached collectively and collaboratively by members of the historic preservation field. The MVLA will look forward to once again hosting preservationists to discuss pressing issues and the state of the field on the very spot that inspired America's first historic preservation organization—George Washington's private residence high on the banks of the Potomac River.

Notes

1. Deborah Ryan and Frank Vagnone, "Reorienting Historic House Museums: An Anarchist's Guide," in Beyond Architecture: New Intersections and Connections, Proceedings of the ARCC/EAAE 2014 International Conference on Architectural Research, ed. David Rockwood and Marja Sarvimaki (Honolulu: University of Hawaii at Manoa, 2014), 97–106.

Contributors

Douglas Bradburn is President and CEO of George Washington's Mount Vernon. He previously served as Founding Director of the Fred W. Smith National Library for the Study of George Washington at Mount Vernon. He is the author of two other University of Virginia Press publications: *The Citizenship Revolution: Politics and the Creation of the American Union, 1774–1804* (2009) and *Early Modern Virginia: Reconsidering the Old Dominion,* edited with John C. Coombs (2011). He is a current member of the board of directors for the University of Virginia Press, a board member for the Washington Family Papers Project, and a member of the Alexandria Library Company. Bradburn previously served as a professor of history and director of graduate studies at Binghamton University, State University of New York. Bradburn earned his Ph.D. in history from the University of Chicago and his B.A. in history and economics from the University of Virginia.

Lydia Mattice Brandt is Associate Professor of Art History in the School of Visual Art and Design at the University of South Carolina's Columbia campus.

She is the author of a recent University of Virginia Press publication, *First in the Homes of His Countrymen: George Washington's Mount Vernon in the American Imagination* (2016). Brandt serves as Vice Chair of the South Carolina State Board of Review for the National Register of Historic Places, the Board of Directors for the Southeast Chapter of the Society of Architectural Historians, and the Board of Directors of the Columbia Development Corporation. She holds a Ph.D. in art and architectural history and an M.A. in architectural history from the University of Virginia. She received her B.A. in art history from New York University.

Carol Borchert Cadou is Charles F. Montgomery Director and CEO at the Winterthur Museum. She was previously Senior Vice President for Historic Preservation and Collections at George Washington's Mount Vernon, an institution she served for nineteen years. Cadou also served as Curator of the Maryland Commission on Artistic Property and the Curator of Education and Interpretation at Historic Charleston Foundation. Her articles and books include *The George Washington Collection: Fine and Decorative Arts at Mount Vernon* (2006) and *George and Martha Washington's Mount Vernon: At Home in Virginia, 1759–1799* (forthcoming). Cadou holds an M.A. in early American culture from the Winterthur Program at the University of Delaware and a B.A. from Wellesley College. She serves on the Board of Governors of the Decorative Arts Trust.

Scott E. Casper serves as Dean of the College of Arts, Humanities, and Social Sciences and Professor of History at the University of Maryland, Baltimore County. He is the author of *Sarah Johnson's Mount Vernon: The Forgotten History of an American Shrine* (2008) and *Constructing American Lives: Biography and Culture in Nineteenth-Century America* (1999), and the co-author, editor, or co-editor of seven other books, most recently *The Oxford Encyclopedia of American Cultural and Intellectual History* (2013).

Carter L. Hudgins is Director of the Graduate Program in Historic Preservation jointly sponsored by Clemson University and the College of Charleston. Hudgins was previously a member of the history faculties at the University of Alabama–Birmingham, where he implemented the graduate curriculum in public history, and the University of Mary Washington, where he was Chair of both the Department of History and American Studies (2002–8) and the Department of Historic Preservation (1984–93), a program in which he held appointment as the Hofer Distinguished Professor of Early American Culture and Historic Preservation. Hudgins holds a Ph.D. in early American history from the College of William and Mary, an M.A. from Wake Forest University, and a B.A. from the University of Richmond.

Robert L. Fink is the Design Technology Director at Quinn Evans Architects. Throughout his twenty-two-year architectural career, he has focused on integrating digital technologies into a diverse array of planning, preservation, and adaptive use projects. Since 2001, Fink has been leading QEA's computer-aided design and building information modeling (BIM) efforts. His recent work has focused on the integration of data within BIM systems and improving effectiveness, teamwork, and quality through mobile, cloud-based, and desktop platforms. Fink graduated with a Bachelor of Architecture degree from Roger Williams University.

Carl R. Lounsbury served as Senior Architectural Historian in the Architectural Research Department of the Colonial Williamsburg Foundation, where he was responsible for major research and restoration projects in the historic area from 1982 to 2016. His publications include *Architects and Builders in North Carolina: A History of the Practice of Buildings* (1990); *An Illustrated Glossary of Early Southern Architecture and Landscape* (1994); and *The Courthouses of Early Virginia* (2005), all three of which won the Abbott Lowell Cummings Award from the Vernacular Architecture Forum. Lounsbury was the co-author and a contributor to *The Chesapeake House: Architectural Investigation by Colonial Williamsburg* (2013). He earned his B.A. from the University of North Carolina and M.A. and Ph.D. in American studies from the Smithsonian Program at George Washington University.

George W. McDaniel is President of McDaniel Consulting, LLC, which offers strategic services to both historical and environmental organizations. He earned a B.A. from Sewanee, an M.A.T (history) from Brown University, and his Ph.D. in history from Duke University. The author of *Hearth and Home: Preserving a People's Culture,* he served twenty-five years as Executive Director of Drayton Hall in Charleston, SC, where his work earned awards at the local, state, and national levels in historic preservation, environmental conservation, education, and community outreach. Drawing on this experience, he advises historical and environmental organizations as they face questions about the future, including protecting their environs and bridging racial and cultural divides.

Luke J. Pecoraro, a historical archaeologist, serves as the Director of Archaeology at Mount Vernon. He has worked in cultural resource management archaeology in the mid-Atlantic, the Chesapeake, and New England on a variety of prehistoric and historic sites, and for several years as a staff archaeologist on the Jamestown Rediscovery Project. Pecoraro earned his Ph.D. and M.A. in archaeology from Boston University and his B.A. in history from Virginia Commonwealth University.

Thomas A. Reinhart is Mount Vernon's Director of Architecture. He previously served as Administrator of Architectural Research at the Maryland Historical Trust. Reinhart is a graduate of the College of William and Mary and holds an M.A. in classical archaeology from Florida State University and an M.A. in historic preservation from George Washington University. He led restorations of Mount Vernon's New Room (2014), the mansion's 1758 staircase (2015), the

Chintz Room (2016), and the Blue Room (2017), as well as spearheaded Mount Vernon's Historic Building Information Model.

Susan P. Schoelwer is the Robert H. Smith Senior Curator at Mount Vernon, where she has directed the refurnishing and reinterpretation of the New Room, the reinstallation of the greenhouse slave quarter, and numerous other room furnishing projects and exhibitions. She previously headed the museum collections at the Connecticut Historical Society and has edited and authored volumes on slavery at Mount Vernon, George Washington's landscapes, the Alamo, western American art, Connecticut needlework, furniture, and tavern signs. Schoelwer holds a Ph.D. in American studies from Yale University, an M.A. from the Winterthur Program at the University of Delaware, and a B.A. in history from the University of Notre Dame. She currently serves as President of the Decorative Arts Society, Inc.

Alyson Steele is the Executive Vice President and Chief Design Officer at Quinn Evans Architects, leading its Cultural Practice Area. Her work for cultural institutions and historic sites employs a collaborative analysis, planning, and design process to revitalize these sites' visitor experiences and preserve them for future generations. She plays a pivotal role in master planning efforts for museums and other cultural institutions, most notably the Smithsonian Institution's National Museum of Natural History, the Peabody Institute, and North Carolina's Tryon Palace. Steele holds a B.A. in urban studies from Stanford University and a Master of Architecture from the University of Virginia.

Index

15–16; dendrochronology, 20–21, 38n15, 38n17; funding for, 219; future of, 217–21; historic house museums and, 197, 198–200; MVLA and beginnings of movement, 1–2; new social history and, 22–23, 25; popular culture and, 11, 202–3. *See also* whole place preservation

Historic Sites Act of 1935, xxvi

historic structure report for the Mansion House (1993), 97

history: meaning of, 197–98; popular culture and, 11, 202–3. *See also* new social history

Holland, William (Will), 183–84

Holland's: The Magazine of the South, Distinctive Southern Homes, 160, 161

Hollingsworth, J. McHenry, 97

Holmes, William H., 73

Holtorf, Cornelius, 79–80

home catalogues with Mount Vernon–inspired designs, 160–61

Home of Today catalogue (Sears, Roebuck and Company), 160

"Home of Washington Illustrated" (stereographs), 153

Horton Grove (Durham County, NC), 27, 28, 29

Houdon, Jean Antoine, bust of Washington, xix, xx

House for Families slave quarter, xxxi, 76, 77

Hoyt, H. E., 166n4

Hudgins, Carter L., 11–12, 217, 218, 219

Hudson River, view from Olana, 129

Hudson River School, 61, 129

Humphreys, David, 54–55, 66n35, 67n45

Hunter, William, 73

Illustrated Glossary of Early Southern Architecture and Landscape (Lounsbury), 111

Imhoff, Kat, 127

Independence Hall (Philadelphia), xviii

Indiana Landmarks, 206

Inexpensive Homes of Individuality, 161

internships, at historic house museums, 210

interpretation: changes in at historic house museums, 18; HBIM and, 114–15; at Mount Vernon, 162–64

Israel and Biddle, 166n4

James Monroe Law Office Museum, 208

Jamestown Church, 21

Jamestown, preservation of, 197, 203, 204

Jefferson, Thomas: architectural drawings, 23; view from Monticello and, 126

Jensen, Amelia B., 47–48

John Milner Associates, 97

Johnson, Lyndon, xxix

Johnson, Nathan, 186–87

Johnson, Sarah, 185, 186–87, 188, 191

Johnson, Smith, 186, 187

Johnston, Coy, 141, 143, 144

Johnston, Frances Benjamin, 159–60, 163, 171n51

Jones, Inigo, 43

Jordan, Dan, 128

Keeling House (Virginia Beach, VA), 38n17

Kenmore (Frederickburg, VA), 15, 16, 20

Kennedy, John F., 87

Kennedy, John Pendleton, 198